Holocaust Studies Annual

Volume II

Holocaust Studies Annual

Volume II

The Churches' Response to the Holocaust

edited by

Jack Fischel

and

Sanford Pinsker

The Penkevill Publishing Company
Greenwood, Florida

Editors

Sanford Pinsker
Franklin & Marshall College

Jack Fischel
Millersville University of Pennsylvania

Advisory Board

Sarah Blacher Cohen
State University of New York at Albany

A. Roy Eckardt
Lehigh University

Leslie Fiedler
State University of New York at Buffalo

Ellen Fine
Kingsborough Community College

Henry Friedlander
Brooklyn College, CUNY

Henry Huttenbach
The Historical Data Institute

Lyman H. Legters
*Institute for the Study of
Contemporary Social Problems*

Deborah Lipstadt
University of California, Los Angeles

Franklin H. Littell
Temple University

John Mendelson
Silver Springs, Maryland

Joanne S. Mortimer
Muhlenberg College

Charles J. Wissink
New Brunswick, New Jersey

Holocaust Studies Annual
The Penkevill Publishing Company
Box 212
Greenwood, Florida
32443

Manuscripts concerned with the Holocaust should be sent to Professor Sanford Pinsker, Department of English, Franklin & Marshall College, Lancaster, Pennsylvania, 17604; or to Professor Jack Fischel, Department of History, Millersville University of Pennsylvania, Millersville, Pennsylvania, 17551.

Books for Review, subscriptions, advertising, and business correspondence should be sent to Stephen H. Goode, Managing Editor, Holocaust Studies Annual, The Penkevill Publishing Company, Greenwood, Florida, 32443

*Copyright © 1986 by the Penkevill Publishing Company
Printed in the United States of America*
ISBN 0–913283–12–6
ISSN 0738–0739

CONTENTS

i
Preface

1
*The Relationship of Church and State During the
German Occupation of Norway, 1940-1945*
by Samuel Abrahamsen

28
*From Rivalry to Repression: The German Protestant Leadership,
Anti-Leftism and Anti-Semitism 1933*
by Shelley Baranowski

45
*Lutheran Conscience and the Holocaust:
The German and Norwegian Cases*
by Stephen MacDonald

55
*The German Catholic Bishops and the Jewish Question:
Explanation and Judgment*
by Sister Ethel Mary Tinnemann

87
*Racial Eugenics in the Third Reich:
The Catholic Response*
by Donald Dietrich

127
Perverse Witness to the Holocaust:
Christian Missions and Missionaries
by Robert W. Ross

141
The North American Mennonites' Response
to Hitler's Persecution of the Jews
by Jack R. Fischel

155
The Death's Head and the Watchtower*:*
Jehovah's Witnesses in the Holocaust Kingdom
by Brian R. Dunn

173
A Selected Bibliography
by Christopher Fritsch

CONTRIBUTORS

Samuel Abrahamsen is the author of *Sweden's Foreign Policy* and has published extensively on the Scandinavian Countries. He is Chairman, Advisory Council, Seminar on Scandinavian Studies, Center for European Studies, Graduate School, CUNY.

Shelly Baranowski is Visiting Assistant Professor of Religion at Kenyon College

Donald Dietrich is Professor of History at the University of Wisconsin, Stevens Point, and is the author of the forthcoming *Catholic Citizens in the Third Reich: Psycho-Social Principles and Moral Reasoning*, which will be published by Transaction Publishers of Rutgers University.

Brian Dunn is Chairman of the Department of History at Clarion University of Pennsylvania.

Jack R. Fischel is Chairman of the Department of History at Millersville University of Pennsylvania and Co-Editor of the *Holocaust Studies Annual*.

Stephen MacDonald is the Director of the Central Pennsylvania Consortium — Dickinson, Franklin and Marshall, and Gettysburg Colleges.

Robert W. Ross teaches courses in Jewish Studies at the University of Minnesota and is also a member of its Graduate faculty.

Sister Ethel Mary Tinnemann is Professor of History at Holy Names College, Oakland, California.

Preface

Volume II of the *Holocaust Studies Annual* raises important questions regarding the responses of European Churches and their clergy to the excesses of Nazi Germany. That some clergymen, both inside and outside of Germany, stood up to Hitler's murder of European Jewry and others did not, invites the question as to what factors — religious, political, cultural, played a role in the determination of some churches to help save Jewish lives and others to shut their eyes to the entire process which culminated in the death camps.

In five of the eight essays included in this volume an effort is made to find an answer to this very difficult and elusive question. Samuel Abrahamson informs us that in the case of the Lutheran Church in Norway, factors other than religious considerations brought the Norwegian Church into conflict with the illegitimate regime of Quisling. The efforts of the Lutheran Church in Norway to protect its Jewish population was part of an overall confrontation, which the church joined, against a government that was imposed on the Norwegian people by a foreign power. In contrast, Shelly Baranowski shows that in Germany, the Lutheran Church from the beginning accepted the Nazi argument that the Jews dominated German society and should be restricted. Many Protestant ministers accepted the view that National Socialism represented a national renewal in Germany in which the churches would play a significant role. Be they Lutheran or members of the Confessional Church, all seemed uninterested in the laws that were passed in the early years of Nazi Germany which delegitimized the status of the Jews. The ire of the Protestant churches appeared to be aroused only when the Nazi racial laws were applied to Christians with Jewish ancestry.

Both Abrahamsen's and Baranowski's essays were presented at Millersville University's Fourth Annual Holocaust Conference and at that time Stephen MacDonald commented on both papers. The essay included in this volume is an expanded version of his comments. MacDonald notes the important place of Martin Luther's ideas in the concept of the Christian's duty to the state. MacDonald shows us that different interpretations of Lutheran theology helps us to understand the different responses to National Socialism in Germany and in Norway.

Lest the reader conclude that it was the Protestant churches alone that failed to unite in a common front against Hitler in Germany, one must also consider that the Catholic Church faced many of the same problems and, with notable exception, also failed to reach unity with regard to Hitler's persecution of the Jews. Ethel Mary Tinnemann and Donald Dietrich call our attention to the indifference of most of the Catholic Church hierarchy to the plight of the Jews in Germany. Tinnemann shows that the anti-Semitism of many of the German Catholic bishops prevented any action from taking place in behalf of their Jewish countrymen. That a Catholic Church determined to confront Hitler on the question of the Jews might have brought results is the implication drawn from Dietrich's essay which shows us that when the Catholic Church in Germany refused to countenance the Euthanasia program, it was able to mobilize public opinion and force the government to back down. Had the Catholic Church been of one mind with regard to the persecution of the Jews, could a similar result have been accomplished? The answer to that tantalizing question must forever be left for historical speculation.

Although the seeming indifference of the Christian Churches towards the destruction of the Jews dominates the literature of that relationship, it is often overlooked that some Christian denominations saw in the trials and tribulations of the Jews an opportunity to bring the Jews to Christ. The historiography of this aspect of the Holocaust is scant but it is nevertheless true that missionaries both in Europe and the United States saw the salvation for Jews in becoming Christians. At the same time, as Robert Ross shows in his essay, missionaries in Europe were witnesses to the tragic dimensions of the unfolding Holocaust. In fact, it was in the missionary press that one finds some of the earliest reports with regard to the Nazi policy toward the Jews. Jack Fischel's essay also touches on this theme in his study of the response of American Mennonites. Although divided on how to interpret the persecution of the Jews, some Mennonites urged conversion and others, most notably in the Mennonite Central committee which

Preface

did relief work in Poland, showed an almost total indifference to the plight of the Jews.

Jews were unique in the history of World War II because they were marked out, as a people, for extinction. We often overlook the fact that although the organized churches did little to prevent the destruction of Jews, they sometimes did as little in protesting the treatment of fellow Christian sects. Brian Dunn's essay deals with the Nazi treatment of the Jehovah's Witnesses. It would appear, from his essay, that like the Jews, the Witnesses stood alone as the Nazis attempted to break their religious spirit. They suffered horribly in the concentration camps and certainly their reaction, as Christians, to the excesses of National Socialism merit comparison with the responses of the larger institutional churches in Germany.

The second volume of the *Holocuast Studies Annual* owes a great debt to the Annual Holocaust Conference held at Millersville University. The editors of the *Annual* are indebted to many people for their contributions in making this volume possible. Specifically, the Department of History at Millersville University was both supportive and helpful. In particular the editors would like to thank Millersville University President Joseph Caputo for his support of the Conference, Reynold Koppel for his editorial assistance, Dan Martin and Joy Allen for the Index, and Betsie Lesher for her patience and understanding. Franklin and Marshall College also provided a generous research grant. We hope Volume II warrants the good wishes and the efforts of so many people.

Jack Fischel

Sanford Pinsker

*The Relationship of Church and State
during the German Occupation of Norway, 1940–1945*

Samuel Abrahamsen

It is a common observation to compare Western Civilization to a river whose original source was Greece and enlarged successively by two contributories, one from Rome and the other from the Holy Land.[1] Regarding the Norwegian Lutheran Church, however, there was a third contributory – from Germany. Lutheranism had been introduced to Norway as the official state religion on September 2, 1537 through a Latin Church Ordinance authored by Martin Luther's friend, Johann Bugenhagen (1488-1558), one of the leading Protestant Reformers.[2] At that time, Norway was united with Denmark. The "Treaty of Kiel," between Denmark and Sweden, of January 14, 1814, which Norway repudiated, ceded Norway to Sweden.[3] To show their oppoisition to the Kiel Treaty, the Norwegians decided to call together a Constituent Assembly at Eidsvold, where the delegates, on May 17, 1814, adopted a Constitution known as *Norges Grunnlov* or *Norway's Fundamental Acts*. Article 2 stated that:

> The Evangelical-Lutheran Religion shall be maintained and constitutes the established Church of the Kingdom. The inhabitants who profess the same religion are obligated to educate their children in the same. Jesuits and Monastic orders shall not be tolerated. Jews are still excluded from admission to the Kingdom.[4]

In this presentation, only the first two sentences of Article 2 of the Norwegian Constitution will be considered, where the religious principles became crucial in the fight of the Norwegian Lutheran Church against Nazism.

One major consideration is to regard the conflicts as a national fight for human rights and for spiritual liberty against the invaders who were bent on destroying the judicial system, the schools and the church, and on propagating an ideology, which was alien to the moral and religious traditions of the Norwegian people. The aim of the German occupation forces was to nazify consistently the Norwegian way of life. Therefore, the Norwegian people did not only have a military front, but also cultural and religious fronts to fight on.

One of the most important issues was that of non-violent resistance or "holdningskamp" to oppose nazification.[5] During the occupation, the fight of the Norwegian Church concentrated mainly on moral values: justice, humanity and freedom of conscience. The church became a focal organization in guiding the Norwegian Resistance Movement. The role of the church became crucial; it was to protect the Christian values which the Nazis aimed at destroying. The Nazis had proved experts at transforming their own society and made a determined effort to do the same in Norway. They knew exactly what their aim was and how to achieve it: by controlling all institutions through terrorism and by nazifying the population through schools, youth and trade organizations, and the churches.

Little did they realize that leading clergymen insisted on speaking their own minds. Time and again we find that the clergy expressed opinions which were completely contrary to Nazi edicts. The differences were instantaneously approved by the majority of the Norwegian population. Throughout the occupation, it was the pulpit that became the most commonly utilized means of communication through consistent opposition to Nazism. On some occasions, the churches were the main institution protesting against brutalities, such as the deportation of the Norwegian Jews in the fall of 1942.[6] Another courageous example was the church's protest against the German mobilization of Norwegian youth to join the German war effort. In these instances, the church spoke on behalf of the nation. The fight of the Norwegian Church became identical to the fight for the national concept of freedom, and it waged this fight, not on the periphery, but in the middle of the battles to be fought.

For the purpose of waging such a fight, the churches were theoretically well prepared. They provided an ideal basis of resistance because the congregations were spread all over the large country of Norway. In addition, the church, which represented all social classes, had access to the intellectual elite as well as to the working class. It had the popular support for organizing an effective opposition.[7]

Another way of evaluating the Norwegian Church is to regard it, not from a national standpoint only, but from the point of view of Christian beliefs and values. It can, in retrospect, be seen as a fight against the non-Christian Nazi totalitarian efforts to prevent Christian survival. In this respect, the Norwegian Church showed a determined course of action prior to being challenged and attacked by the Nazis. This attitude was in sharp contrast, for instance, to the German Evangelical Churches which did not act until their own churches were being attacked, and then it was too late; or, as Pastor Martin Niemøller, the German theologican, said:

> First the Nazis went after the Jews, but I was not a Jew,
>   so I did not object.
> Then they went after the Catholics, but I was not a Catholic,
>   so I did not object.
> Then they went after the Trade-Unionists, but I was not a
>   trade-unionist, so I did not object.
> Then they came after me, and there was no one left to
>   object.

The Norwegian Lutheran Church did not make that mistake. With Hitler's rise to power in 1933, the German churches faced one severe crisis after another. The Norwegian public opinion had been critical of the Nazi takeover. The development of the German Lutheran Church was, of course, followed with great interest in the "Motherland of Protestantism." Except fot the Norwegian Nazi party (Nasjonal Samoing) established in 1933 by Vidkin Quisling, there was little sympathy for the "New Germany." On the contrary, the population was shocked to read about concentration camps, torture, suppression of free speech, book burning and persecution of "all enemies of the Third Reich." The Labor Party movement which formed the new government in 1935 reacted strongly against the rise of Nazism in Germany.

The reactions of the German Lutheran Church was, of course, followed with great interest in the "Motherland of Protestantism." It was disturbing for Norwegian clergy to notice that supporters of Nazism within the German Protestant Church also supported anti-Jewish legislation. What was noticed with satisfaction was Niemøller's dissident *Bekenntniskirche*[8] which defended the rights of Christians of Jewish origin within the Church. Its memorandum to Adolf Hitler in 1936 was also duly noted. Here it was stated that "when, in the framework of the National-Socialist idology antisemitism is forced on the Christian, obliging him to hate Jews, he has nonetheless the divine commandment to love his neighbor."[9] But the Confessing Church was not capable of uniting the Evangelical Church in Germany in their opposition to Nazism.

The person who took up the fight against the Nazi ideology at an early stage in Norway was Bishop Eivind Josef Berggrav (1884-1959), who played a prominent role in the Norwegian Resistance Movement.[10] He followed very closely the events in Germany, being completely fluent in the German language, but opposed to the Nazi ideology and mentality.[11] In 1933, Berggrav refused an invitation to participate in the inauguration of the Nazi Bishop, Müller, in Germany; nor did the other Scandinavian Bishops participate in these festivities.

Even before the German invasion of Norway in 1940, Bishop Berggrav had reached the conclusion that close cooperation between the various idologies within Lutheranism must be established in anticipation of a conflict between church and state. He made a proposal for a common council for all Lutheran Churches at a meeting in 1930, but the idea was not accepted. With the outbreak of World War II, a joint proposal was published on September 6, 1939.

There had, for centuries, been serious confrontations between the Norwegian Lutheran State Church and the many Lutheran lay churches, which opposed the State Church.[12] A conflict had also occurred between the "liberal" and "conservative" representatives within the church when Bishop Berggrav was appointed to the Oslo Bishopric in 1937. The conservatives threatened to have nothing to do with the newly-appointed Bishop until he had broken with his liberal points of view. The joint proposal in 1939, however, presaged Bishop Berggrav's preeminence and intellectual leadership in the years to come under German occupation.[13]

The Church-State relations during the occupation constituted a unique era in the history of Norway. Extraordinary happenings brought about unusual situations where cooperation with the Quisling government became intolerable to the population in general and especially to a Christian Evangelical Church.

The opposition to Nazism did not start on the day of the invasion, April 9, 1940, but grew gradually through the first few months until the differences became crystallized.[14] The Church had benefitted from a period of Nazi non-interference following Reichskommisar Josef Terboven's speech of September 25, 1940, holding out promises to respect the Hague Convention "regarding full religious freedom in the occupied regions."[15] In fact, Terboven's speech became the signal to increase the Norwegian resistance movements when it became clear that the price for peace was to support the Quisling regime through his Nazi party, *Nasjonal Samling*,[16] which had never been able to elect a single representative to the *Storting* (Parliament). The Quisling party reached a peak membership of 43,000 in 1943.[17] Terboven's speech of September 25, 1940, had clarified the Nazi policy of total nazification of the Norwegian people, which meant a challenge of the very foundations of Norwegian culture. The church was ready to do battle with Bishop Berggrav as the leading spokesman.[18]

At a meeting on October 28, 1940, in Carlmeyergatens Misjonhus (Mission House), the first major consolidation of the Church opposition to the Nazi regime took place with the establishment of an organization, "Kristent Samrad for den norske kirke" (Christian Joint Council for the Norwegian Church). Now, in the hour of danger, the Norwegian Church was united into a single front where important events were discussed in detail and decisions made. Divisions were set aside to face the common enemy. A proclamation, signed by eighteen of the leading churchmen including the seven Bishops, stated that the Joint Council would follow "the inspired words of God according to the Lutheran Confession of our Church."[19]

On December 12, 1940, the members of Norway's Supreme Court resigned in protest against Terboven's terror-regime in disregarding the 1907 Hague Convention wherein it was stated that the occupying power must "respect the valid laws in the country unless there are absolute hinderances for this."[20] The Norwegian Supreme Court insisted that an independent court, i.e., the Nowegian Supreme Court, must judge whether the occupying power actually adhered to the law. Terboven's reply was that the occupying power itself must have that right. The Supreme Court answered that it could not continue to function under these lawless circumstances, and the judges relinquished their offices.

The resignation of the Supreme Court was the most dramatic and effective action so far to mobilize the Norwegian people against establishing a Nazi lawless society.

It was now the role of the Norwegian Church to defend the foundation of the society built on justice and freedom of conscience. The Supreme Court had shown the road as to the principles of justice, and by resigning, it had given the direction which the Home Front was to follow.[21] The unity, reached within the Joint Council, had proven to be of inestimable importance for the resistance movement, which had suffered the mob rule by the young men in the *Hird,* which was established by Quisling as his bodyguard to maintain law and order. The "Hirdmen" had been very aggressive and brutal. This reign of terror produced feelings of lawlessness in the streets and interference with church duties.

On January 15, 1941, the Norwegian Bishops addressed a document to petition the Acting Head of the Department of Church and Education, Ragnar Skancke. This pastoral letter changed the relationship between state and church. The Bishops called attention to the fact that the foundation of the Norwegian Church was based on a definite constitutional relationship to the state and on the assumption that the duty of the state was to uphold justice and righeousness in accordance with the word of God.

Now the lines were clearly drawn. The church challenged the state on the basis of the Norwegian Constitution which stated that the Lutheran religion shall be the official religion of Norway and emphasized the importance of the state accepting and honoring the legal and moral obligations contained in the Articles of Faith and in the Bible. Bishop Berggrav had consulted widely with other resistance leaders and they were now prepared to fight the lawlessness which the Nazi Quisling government had introduced.

Specifically, three instances were mentioned in the document; namely, the systematic rule of terror by the Norwegian Nazi stormtroopers (Hird); secondly, the resignation of the Supreme Court of Norway; and thirdly, the interference of the state with the minsters' Oath of Silence. These three items were thoroughly documented. The main emphasis, however, was on the last point, whereby a minister could not pledge complete silence to a confessor as long as the state was empowered to force him to break his oath.

The Bishops quoted *Article 16* of the *Augustana Confession of Faith of the Church,* which clearly defined the legitimate relationship between Church and State, especially as to the duty and right of church officials to speak up on topics vital to the church. The Bishops stated that one of the most vital concerns was the order given to the Police Department, whereby the Oath of Silence could be abolished by the police.[22] It was pointed out that professional secrecy is not only guaranteed by law, but had always been a fundamental requirement for the performance of pastoral duties. The letter concluded by saying that it was of utmost importance for the population to have full and unqualified confidence in the pastoral Oath of Silence: *"To abolish this Magna Carta of Consience is an attack upon the very heart of the church. It is an attack which takes on an especially serious character by the fact that Article 5 empowers police to imprison an offending pastor and force him to talk without having been taken before a court of law."*[23]

The letter ended with a demand for a reply to clarify the issues, but no reply arrived. Then the three bishops, Berggrav, Støren and Maroni, went in person to see the Minister of Church and Education,[24] and presented him with an additional letter expressing in even sharper terms the role of the church in a lawless society.[25] Three days later, an unsatisfactory reply was received from Minster Ragnar Skancke. At this time the Bishops decided to "go public" by sending the correspondence as a pastoral letter to be read in the churches all over the country. The following excerpt is especially pertinent:[26]

When those in authority in the society tolerate violence and injustice and oppress the souls of men, then the Church is the guardian of men's conscience. . . . On that account, the bishops of the Church had laid before the Minister some of the facts and official announcements concerning the administration of our society which the Church finds to be in conflict with the law of God.

This episcopal letter was not only read from the pulpits in the Norwegian churches; it found its way to London from where it was broadcast throughout the world.[27]

The wide distribution and the reading from the pulpits of the episcopal letter in February, 1941, led to open disagreement between state and church in occupied Norway. But further actions were being planned by Quisling to completely nazify the Church. The dramatic high point of this struggle too place on February 1, 1942. The background for this incident was as follows:

On Sunday, February 1, 1942, the Nazi Reichkommissar Terboven appointed Quisling as "Minister President" with a solemn "Act of State" at the old fortress of Akershus in Oslo. In this connection, a high mass was scheduled on that day to be conducted at 11:00 A.M. by a Nazi minister, the Reverend Blessing Dahle, in the main National Cathedral, Nidarosdomen, in the City of Trondheim. The Bishops had protested this usurpation of power, since the regular minister, Dean (later, Bishop) Arne Fjellbu, was still in office. He could not be prevented legally from eonducting a High Mass, which was to take place at 2:00 P.M.[28] The police, however, reacted by forbidding this Divine Service to take place and actually closed the doors after a few hundred persons had entered the church. Several thousand of the congregants had assembled in the cold weather outside to support their church. An eye witness, Pastor Bang-Hanssen, said: "We froze so that our teeth chattered, but we could not part from each other. From the most easterly part of the place, I suddenly heard a voice starting Luther's old hymn. All of us took off our hats and joined in the singing of 'A mighty fortress is our God, a trusty shield and weapon.' While we were standing there with uniformed and armed policemen in front of us, the old song carried by thousands of voices sounded prouder and mightier than I have ever heard. Then came Blix's 'National Hymn' and after that Norway's National Anthem. Nothing else was sung, nothing else spoken. I was standing almost in front of the crowd beside some girls fifteen to twenty years old. When I looked at them, I saw that they were crying convulsively. And all of us had difficulty in restraining our tears."[29]

Using force, the police pushed the masses back and informed everyone that the Divine Service had been called off. People were ordered to go home quietly, since they would be waiting in vain. The masses, however, did not disburse. That is what took place outside the Nidaros Cathedral.

What took place inside is told by Dean Fjellbu in his book, *Minner fra krigsarene (Memoirs from the War Years)*:[30]

> I hid in the Cathedral early Sunday morning so that no one should find me. I found this very sensible. Upon pre-arrangement with the architect, Mr. Thiis, I hid in his office in the cathedral yard. From there a secret stairway extends through the workshops to the cathedral and from the workshops I could, unnoticed, come in to the west front of the cathedral. From my hiding place I had a good view of the open space before the cathedral and the main door to the church. There I sat and studied my sermon and watched the stormtroopers marching in for the Nazi Minister, Blessing Dahle's, service. I had two stenographers in the cathedral and my son and his friends acted as lookouts. When Blessing Dahle's service was over, they came up and reported. My wife brought food. People began to stream in for my service which was to begin at 2:00, but at 1:15 I saw that disturbances were beginning at the entrance. There were police in front of the door and at 1:25 I was informed that the police had closed the church. It had been my intention to proceed at once to the pulpit, but my wife advised me to go before the altar; if I were to be arrested it ought to occur at the most sacred spot. I found this entirely right. I went directly

from the altar to the pulpit and gave my sermon without intimating that anything extraordinary had happened.

There were serious consequences of this courageous protest. On February 19, 1942, Dean Fjellbu was dismissed and on February 24th, the seven Bishops of Norway decided unanimously to "cease administrative cooperation with a State which practices violence against the Church," although they maintained the right to exercise the spiritual vocation given them by ordination at the Lord's altar.[30] There was thus no *single* act by the state that caused the resignations, but the Norwegian clergy had been subject to police hearings, arrests, confiscation of property, threats of deportation and even the death penalty. Nonetheless, the Church could not be frightened and continued to protest Quisling's efforts at encroachment, stressing that its aim was not of a political but of a spiritual nature. Indeed, it was stated that the Lutheran Chruch was not interested in destroying the State Church, but was fighting for its mission to preach the word of God and to be able to perform their duties in ministering to the needs of the congregations. Therefore, in spite of the resignation, the clergy continued to serve in their capacities as churchmen, regardless of the changed situation of the state.

The clergy also insisted that the councils of the congregation would have to continue regardless of whether the clergy was dismissed by the state.

The issuance, on April 5, 1942, of a declaration known as "The Foundation of the Church," (Kirkens Grunn) constituted a definite break with the Nazi state. This document is of lasting value in drawing the lines between the obedience due to the state and the cases where protest and opposition must be used in terms of non-violent resistance. This declaration was read from the pulpits and emphasized the sovereignty of God above all ideologies. Having read this document from the pulpits, the ministers resigned from their positions as civil servants, but continued to do their work as clergymen. Out of a total of 699 ministers, 645 resigned and only 54 chose to remain in their positions. This protest showed that the Norwegian Lutheran Church was almost unanimous in this opposition to the Nazi Government. Those who remained in their positions became isolated, both from their colleagues and from their congregations. The Church had taken the motto: "Fear not those who destroy the body, but are not able to destroy the soul, but rather fear him who is able to destroy the body and the soul." It was like an echo from Worms when Luther spoke the definitive words: "Here I stand. I cannot do otherwise. So help me God. Amen."

The complete title of the declaration was "The Foundation of the Church. A Confession and a Declaration." It was divided into six parts:

1. Regarding the Freedom of God's Word and our obligation to the Word.
2. Regarding the Church and the Ordination.
3. Regarding the Sacred Solidarity of the Church.
4. Regarding parents and their rights and obligations as to children's education.
5. Regarding the correct attitude of Christians and the Church to the state authorities.
6. Regarding the state church.

One of the main points in this document was the insistence on the independence of the Church over the State in spiritual matters, and of the Word of God as sovereign over all ideologies.[32] Eight prominent Nazi clergymen, however, issued a statement published in the controlled press on June 30, 1942.[33] Here they maintained that those who opposed state authority also opposed the sovereignty of God. They based these assertions on "The Epistle of Paul to the Romans," Chapter 13:2: "Whosoever therefore resisteth the power, resisteth the ordinance of God; and they that resist shall receive to themselves damnation."[34] Needless to say, the "Berggrav Church," as his opponents called it, disagreed sharply with this interpretation. The state was to be considered a divine creation only if it did not force one to act against God's commandments. Only a state based on justice could demand obedience. This was a new interpretation of the Lutheran concept of State.[35]

The "Foundation of the Church," formulated to protect endangered Christianity in Norway under Nazi rule, concluded with:[36]

> We ordained men ... declare that we herewith, for reasons of conscience, lay down our offices, but intend to continue to do all the work and services in our flock which can be done by a non-official, in keeping with the Holy Scriptures, the Church's Confession, and the Service Book of the Norwegian Church.

During Easter, 1942, the leaders of the Church were arrested: Bishop Berggrav and the three ministers, Indrebø, Carlsen, and Wisløff.

Quisling, appointed by Terboven as Minister President on February 1, 1942, had usurped power as "Norway's Supreme Bishop." He now boasted that he had taken over the earlier functions of the King, the Parliament, the Church and the Government. According to the Constitution, the King is Norway's Supreme Bishop. Thus, Quisling had become a sort of "Fürher-bishop." He reacted violently to the resignation of the clergy, characterizing it as an "Act of insurrection directed against Norway's liberty and independence." The law stipulated many years of imprisonment or even death for an individual found guilty of insurrection. The threats were serious, especially against Bishop Berggrav who was told that he had committed treason three times and, according to Quisling, warranted triple execution. Despite these threats from Quisling who, with great justification regarded Bishop Berggrav as the arch-enemy of his party, the Bishop received only a short stay in prison and was kept under "house arrest" in his own home in Asker for the next three years.

Much speculation has been offered to explain this leniency afforded Bishop Berggrav. One plausible explanation has been suggested by Professor Arvid Brodersen in his book, *Between the Fronts*.[37] He traced the relationship between Norwegian and German resistance groups through such leaders as Theodore Steltzer, Helmuth James von Motke and Carl Freidrisch Goerdler. Major Steltzer was with the *Oberkommando der Wehrmacht* in Oslo under General Falkenhorst. There was no love lost between him and Terboven, who received orders, probably from Himmler through Borman, to go easy on the Norwegian Church, and especially not to harm Bishop Berggrav. The reasoning offered was that the "Wehrmacht" did not want additional difficulties among the Norwegian population since that might prevent the German troops from being stationed where they were more urgently needed.

The Norwegian clergy had now severed all relations with the Nazi Quisling state from whom they could expect no further economic help. It was up to the local congregations to support their churches and church leaders. The reaction of the Norwegian people to these arrests was one of extreme indignation. The population responded with generous financial support and made it possible for the ministers to continue holding Divine Services. The issues were now very clear. The Norwegian Church was no longer a state church, but had separated itself from a state with which it could not cooperate.

After Easter, 1942, there were really two churches in Norway, namely the State Church of the Department of Church and Education, which had appointed Nazi Beshops and Ministers, and then the free church. The two churches constituted a chasm which separated the population. Very few attended the services conducted by the Nazis. They preached to empty seats. The other churches were filled to capacity. During this period there was a spiritual revival, led by the resisting Norwegian clergymen who enjoyed great respect and veneration throughout the occupation.[38]

Since the church leaders had to go underground, a separate organization was created on July 26, 1942, called "The Temporary Church Leadership" (D.M.K., Den Midlertidige Kirkeledelsen). This now functioned as the highest church leadership council; i.e., a leadership refusing to accept control by the Quisling government. The latter had declared the Temporary Church Leadership unconstitutional and illegal, to be dissolved as of August 7, 1942. The leadership, however, replied in a letter on August 15th that they could not dissolve themselves and that they intended to continue their active opposition "come what may."

It did not take long before the next outrageous event took place. That was the persecution of the Jews, a process which had started in

1940 but now came to a sudden climax in the fall of 1942. The murder of half of Norway's Jewry constitutes the biggest crime committed there during the German occupation. These murders differed from all the other forms of terrorism inasmuch as they were directed towards an innocent religious group which was being exterminated, not for any criminal acts, but for having been born Jews. As one Norwegian author put it: "Other Norwegians did not have to feel they were threateneed."[39] This fanatical racism took its own murderous path, "no matter how big the cost, no matter how small the yield, the Germans had to strike."[40]

Ever since the invasion on April 9, 1940, the Nazis had managed to make life extremely difficult for the Jews. Their radios were confiscated in May, 1940, and the display windows of Jewish stores were painted over with anti-Semitic slogans: "Jews are not tolerated in Norway."[41] On March 29, 1941, Vidkun Quisling gave an anti-Jewish speech at the Institute for the Exploration of the Jewish Question in Frankfurt am Main. After the German invasion of the USSR in June, 1941 Jews in Northern Norway were arrested. In November, Jewish property was registered, Jewish firms confiscated and Jews arrested. Jews were barred from professional and civil services.

On January 10, 1942, Jonas Lie, Minster of Police, issued an order to have a "J" for *Jøde* (Jew) stamped into identification cards and passports of Jews by the Norwegian police. On March 12, 1942, the 1814 Constitutional prohibition of admission of Jews to Norway was reintroduced. Marriage laws were changed so that a non-Jewish spouse, through a Jewish marriage, became a Jew.[42] The persecutions increased dramatically with the arrival of Hauptsturmführer Wilhelm Artur Konstantin Wagner to take charge of the Gestapo Headquarters in Oslo. A wholesale arrest of male Jews took place on October 26, 1942, the arrest of women and children took place on November 26. The men were transported to concentration camps to await deportation aboard the troop transport *S/S Donau*; the women and children were boarded directly on the same ship, which left the same day "towards an unknown destination." We know, today, this destination was Auschwitz.[43]

Sympathy mingled with courage as the Norwegians protested these acts, undertaking rescue of Norway's Jews to Sweden. Organizations and individuals spontaneously brough Jews and half-Jews out of the country. Many risked their lives to do this. Some of the most active in the rescue efforts had to escape to Sweden across borders guarded by the German police; others committed suicide. It was something of a miracle that a stream of Jewish refugees, about 750, could be brought safely to Sweden during 1942 and 1943. The Norwegians did have some warning of the Nazi plans through secret contacts with the Wehrmacht through Helmuth James von Moltke who had mentioned in September, 1942, during a visit to Oslo, that actions against the Jews in Norway were being contemplated, but he could give neither the exact plans nor the times for arrest and deportation.[44]

If any evidence was needed to prove that the Church's opposition to Nazism was not weakening during the occupation, it came in November, 1942. The Temporary Church Leadership, supported by many other religious groups of other denominations, sent directly to Minister President Quisling a sharp protest against the Jewish persecution that was then being carried out by the Nazis. It was the voice of the Norwegian Church speaking out forcefully. It should be noted, however, that prior to this protest, little had been done by the Church to stem the tide of rising anti-Semitism in Norway. When the Quisling National Union Party accused the Jews in March, 1942, of "poisoning the soul of the Norwegian people," the Church remained silent.[45] But public opinion had been aroused by the brutal treatment, arrests, and deportation of Jews, and this sense of agony was articulated by the Norwegian Lutheran Church.

In their letter of November 10, 1942, the seven dismissed Bishops stated that Jews had had a legal right for 91 years to reside and to earn a livelihood in Norway, but that they had now been deprived of their properties without warning.[46] Furthermore, they were being punished as the worst criminals, wholly and solely because they were Jews. The Bishops pointed out that Quisling had, on various occasions, emphasized that his party would protect the basic Christian values, and one of them was now being endangered: the Christian commandment to "love thy neighbor," the most elementary right for any human being. They stated: "When we now appeal to you, Mr. Minister President, it is not to defend whatever wrongs the Jews may have committed. If they have committed crimes, they shall be tried, judged and punished according to Norwegian law, just as all other citizens. But those who have committed no crime shall enjoy the protection of our country's justice." The letter went on to say that the protest was caused by the deepest dictates of conscience, because silence in view of this legalized injustice against Jews would make the Church co-guilty in this injustice.

> The Church has God's call and full authority to proclaim God's law and God's Gospel. Therefore, it cannot remain silent when God's commandments are being trampled underfoot. And now it is one of Christianity's basic values which is being violated; the commandment of God which is fundamental to all society, namely law and injustice. . . . Stop the persecution of the Jews and stop the race hatred which, through the press, is being spread in our land.

The Bishops emphasized in closing that this appeal had nothing to do with politics. Before worldly authorities the Church maintained that obedience in temporal matters must follow God's word. This protest was supported by theology scholars, nineteen church organizations and six non-state-church religious societies. A total of over sixty signatures from all sections of Norway's Protestant community endorsed the protest.

The Catholic Church, however, did not participate in this protest. Bishop Jacob Mangers, who was in charge of the Catholic Church during the occupation, had sent a letter to the Department of Church and Education on November 10, the same day the Protestant Church sent its protest. The Bishop, however, had written, not to protest the Jewish persecutions, but to secure the release of five baptized Jewish families.[47] The Bishop thought it would be inappropriate to send another letter before he had received a reply to the first one.[48] A letter dated November 10, 1942 from Bishop Mangers to Ole Hallesby, a leader of the Protestant protest and Chairman of the Temporary Church Leadership, stated that "another letter on my part will undoubtedly lead to no consideration for the first one, and thus harm Christians of Jewish descent."[49]

While the protests and prayers of the Norwegian Lutheran Church did not stop the deportation of the Jews, the vigorous protest made a deep impression in Norway and abroad. Additional protests were made by the Swedish Bishops, the British Broadcasting Corporation, and by many countries throughout the free world. The fight of the Lutheran Church to resist nazification had become identical with the fight for national freedom in Norway. The Church struggled, not on the periphery, but in the center of the field of battle. The majority of the population realized, as Ferdinand Schjelderup expressed it, that resistance would pay off "cost what it may — to the bitter end!"[50]

The Germans tried to minimize the effectiveness of the protest. For example, in the daily reports of December, 1942, it was mentioned that the Norwegian churches had pleaded for the Norwegian Jews, but "the radical solution of the Jewish question will be forgotten by the egoistic Norwegians."[51]

The contest between Church and State in Norway was reflected in the protest: "The State cannot enact any law or decree which is in conflict with the Christian faith or the Church's Confession." According to Johan M. Snoek, the reference to Luther is important. The attitude of the Lutheran Churches in Germany had been explained by recalling Luther's conception of the two dominions through which God rules this world: the spiritual one, or the Church, and the secular one, or the "wordly authorities." The people, according to Luther, do not have the right to resist the authorities; only princes have.[52] The Lutheran Church of Norway did not accept his interpretation, but quoted the Confession (Augustana) and Luther in order to stress that it was "the Church's God-given duty as the conscience of the State to object" to the anti-Semitic measures.

The letter of protest won response throughout the country. It was read in the churches on the 6th and 13th of November, at which time prayers were also said for the persecuted Jews. The fight of the Norwegian Church against Nazism became a subject of great interest to the world press. This was not surprising since the activities and opposition of the Church took place in the open, while much of the other activities by the Home Front had to be carried out in great secrecy.

The reaction in Sweden to the deportation of Norway's Jews was strong. The Swedish Bishops quoted the protest of Norway's Bishops and referred to it in pastoral letters. The noted theologian, Nataniel Beskow, stated on the occasion of a large protest meeting in Stockholm:[53]

> A ship that left Oslo harbour had a freight of anguish on board. We can not imagine how much these human beings, men, women and children, are suffering.... We can not call them back. They go to their death or to slavery.... If we can do nothing else we can try to be the voice of the condemned ... and through us call forth their anguish and accusations....

Domprost Olle Nystedt stated on Sunday, November 22, 1942, at the Gothenburg Cathedral that "the churces in Sweden can not remain silent when such things happen on our borders. If we are silent the stones will cry out. We are shaken to our innermost thinking by the suffering of the unfortunates. This is a break of God's law and a violation of the basic values of our civilization."[54]

The Swedish press was almost unanimous in condemning the brutal treatment of Norway's Jews and quoted the protest in full. Ture Newman, editor of *Trots Allt* (*In Spite of Everything*), wrote that "the beastialities which Nazism commits in Norway is nothing new, but it is shocking that it is happening so close by. We protest against the treatment of Norway's Jews."[55] In addition, the Swedish women's organizations published a protest expressing their anger at the persecutions of Jews in Norway: "Persecutions of people belonging to another race is against the Nordic concept of justice and has, until now, been unknown in Nordic countries."[56]

There was a protest within Quisling's party as well. Quisling's party journal, *N. S. Manedshefte* (*National Union Monthly Journal*), stated on December 15, 1942, that:[57]

> ...we must not forget that this (Jewish) problem is not only a racial one, but also a national and, above all, a human one. The Norwegian people have never regarded Jews as countrymen ... since the people is too healthy for that, but they have always been regarded as human beings and, at that, as miserable human beings ... We have to guard ourselves against transgression of feelings of justice within ourselves. It does not help to win the whole world if one harms one's own soul.

Bishop Lars Frøyland, a Bishop of Oslo appointed by Quisling, wrote in 1943 that there was something that shamed the Norwegian people:[58]

> ... our behavior towards a people of another race and another belief within our own borders. I feel bound by my conscience to say this. And I do this even if it shall cost me ever so much. Is it correct to judge everyone the same way, and to punish the guilty with the innocent? We are, after all, Norwegians! We are, after all, Christians!

The leader of the Nazi Party, however, defended the deportation. In a speech in Trondheim on December 6, 1942, Vidkun Quisling commented:[59]

> I want to make one point quite clear to you while touching on the subject of the Jews.... The Jew is no Norwegian; he is an oriental and does not belong to Europe. He has nothing to do in Norway. He is an international element of destruction.

The end of open warfare between the Norwegian State and Church occurred in May, 1943. During the spring, the fortunes of war had turned against Germany. The U.S.S.R. was on the offensive, throwing back the German armed forces from Stalingrad. This offered the Nazis another opportunity to propagandize against the spread of

Bolshevism and Germany represented as the solid bulwark defending Western Civilization. In this battle against "international Judaism," all Aryan nations were told to supply additional labor forces.

On February 22, 1943, Quisling announced the Labor Conscription Act; i.e., a general mobilization of the civilian population. Men, ages 18 to 55 and women ages 21 to 40, were forced to register under threat of losing their ration cards. Those who did not report willingly were rounded up by police. To start with, thirty-five thousand men were to be used for road and railroad building and for the "Organization Todt" which had charge of military installations in Norway.[60]

Again, the Church was the only Norwegian institution to speak up publicly against this breach of the Hague Convention of 1907. On May 8, 1943, the Temporary Church Leadership (DMK) condemned this act in a letter to the Minister President as a purely military undertaking whereby Norwegians were forced against their conscience to participate in the building of military fortifications under German command and in German uniforms. The letter stated:[61]

> As Christians we look upon our land as a gift from God entrusted to our people by God. He has called upon the church to be the guardian of conscience when force threatens the soul. Therefore we must ask the Minister President to withhold the registration of Norwegians contrary to people's conscience and sense of right. Against such violation of conscience, the church cannot remain silent.

The consequences of this attack on Quisling and the German adminstration was only to be expected. Those who had signed the letter, Hallesby and Hope, were arrested on May 13, 1943, and interned at Grini Concentration Camp. Hope was released in August, 1944, but Hallesby had to wait until the end of the occupation to be set free.[62]

The Church did not speak again publicly during the rest of the occupation. The Church went underground as all the other anti-Nazi organizations had had to do. But the terror was not over. Hundreds of ministers were deported from their homes to other parts of the country or to German concentration camps. At the end of the war, 35 Norwegian ministers and one Bishop were in jail or in concentration camps. Two ministers died there.[63]

The Church could, however, be proud that the losses both in human life and material had not been in vain. The Lutheran Church had been victorious. It did not lose its soul during these tragic years. Neither did the various dissenting sects in Norway refrain from protesting Jewish persecutions. At the risk of arrest, they joined in the various protests against the Nazi regime and lent their support against the ruthless treatment of teachers, the persecution of Jews and the other injustices suffered during the occupation.[64] The Norwegian Protestant Churches had created a strong moral front against the inhuman treatment of human beings.

Conclusions

The Second World War, with five years of Nazi-German occupation of Norway (1940-1945), had a profound impact on all aspects of life in Norway, including the religious area. The Church of Norway was a bastion of resistance, under the leadership of Bishop Eivind Berggrav, who established the leadership of the "Joint Christian Council" (Kristent Samrad). The courage and high purpose of the leaders of the Norwegian Church would have been of little avail in the fight against Nazism had they failed to retain the support of the people of Norway. The majority of the population showed repeatedly, by word and act, their complete and uncompromising opposition to Hitler and Quisling in their attempts to establish a Nazi-Norwegian Church.

There were basically five major issues in the conflict between the Norwegian Lutheran Church and the Quisling-Nazi State during the occupation:

1. The protest on January 15, 1941, against lawlessness under Nazism and the Quisling regime.
2. The protest on February 1, 1941, at the Nidaros Cathedral in Trondheim.

3. The issuance of the *Foundation of the Church* (*Kirkens Grunn*) on April 5, 1942, constituting the definitive break with the government.
4. The protest against the Jewish persecutions of November, 1942.
5. The protest against the Labor Conscription Act of February 22, 1943, after which time the Church had to go underground.

Crisis after crisis found the people's loyalty to the Church and its leaders unshaken, just as their loyalty to King Haakon never wavered. The people remained loyal to their Church which, for the first time in Norwegian history, became a self-administering free church without any connection with the state. This break of relations, however, was not a break with the principle of a state-church, as such. Indeed, it was not a struggle for or against any particular form of church organization: it merely marked the end of relations with a lawless government. This took its toll: two pastors died in concentration camps, many more were jailed, and fifty-five were banished to an island. At the end of the war, all bishops and ministers were restored to office in the State Church, following liberation of the country in 1945. In a document, "The Church's Foundation," (Kirkens Grunn), which contained plain, fundamental statements of principle concerning the connection between state and church, the Norwegian Lutheran Church broke with the Nazi state: "The word of God is sovereign over all ideologies." The people made the Church's fight their fight; and the Nazis learned that in attacking the Church, or any of its representatives, they in fact attacked the people of Norway.

The record of te European Lutheran Churches in their opposition to Nazism is uneven and puts the credibility of Christianity in doubt in many countries. But not in Norway. Many Christians in other countries failed to resist the ideas and ideologies of Nazism, but there were church leaders who rendered a clear witness to the reality of the Christian faith in their outspoken anti-Nazi attitudes.[65] Among them were the majority of the clergy of the Lutheran Churches in Norway.

NOTES

[The preparation of this publication has been supported, in part, by grants from the National Endowment for the Humanities and the Royal Norwegian Ministry of Foreign Affairs.]

1. Marc Boegner, *Western Civilization and Christianity* (The Burge Memorial, London: SCM Press, 1948), p. 9.
2. Karen Larsen, *A History of Norway* (New York: The American-Scandinavian Foundation, 1950), p. 245.
3. Amos J. Peaslee, *Constitutions of Nation* (Concord: The Rumford Press, 1950), II, 673.
4. *Kongeriget Norges Grundlov Given I Rigsforsamlingen paa Eidsvold den 17 de mai 1814* (Oslo: H. Aschehoug & Co., 1964), p. 1: "Den evangelisk-lutterske Religion forbliver Statens offentlige Religion. De Indvaanere, der bekjende sig til den, ere forpligtede til at opdrage sine Børn i samme. Jesuiter og Munkeordener maae ikke taales. Jøder ere fremdeles udelukkede fra Adgang til Riget." This edition contains a facsimile in Norwegian of the May 17, 1814, Constitution, but the translations of Article 2 into English (p. 33) and French (p. 49) are of the *amended* versions and therefore do not contain the last two sentences; i.e., "Jesuits and Monastic orders shall not be tolerated. Jews are still excluded from admission to the Kingdom."
5. Gerd Stray Gordon, *The Norwegian Resistance During the German Occupation, 1940-1945: Repression, Terror and Resistance. The West Country of Norway.* (Ann Arbor: University Microfilms International, 1978), p. vi: "a struggle for a right attitude focused against Nazification; a policy of shunning and use of paroles or directives to guide the people's resistance actions."
6. Einar Molland, "Kirkens Kamp," in Sverre Steen (ed.), *Norges Krig, 1940-1945,* (Oslo: Gyldendal Norsk Forlag, 1950), II, 36.
7. Helen Fein, *Accounting for Genocide* (New York: The Free Press, 1979), p. 71
8. Carl Fr. Wisløff, *Norsk Kirkehistorie* (Oslo: Lutherstiftelsen, 1971), III, 415.
9. Guenter Lewy and John M. Snoek, "The Christian Churches," in *Holocaust* (Jerusalem: Keter Publishing, 1974), p. 139.
10. Rolf Kluge, *Hjemmefrontledelsen tar form — Kretsen dannes sommeren 1941* (Oslo: Universiteteforlaget, 1970), pp. 78-79.
11. Ingvald B. Carlsen, *Kirkens kamp i Norge* (København: P. Haase & Søns Forlag, 1946), p. 24.
12. Carl C. Rasmussen, *What About Scandinavia?* (Philadelphia: The Muhlenberg Press, 1948), p. 102-104.
13. Einar Molland, *Fra Hans Nielsen Hauge til Eivind Berggrav* (Oslo: Gyldendal, 1972, p. 87.

14. Eivind Berggrav, *Da kampen kom. Noen blad fra startaret* (Oslo: Land Og kirke, 1945), pp. 80-81.

15. Bjarne Høye and Trygve Ager, *The Fight of the Norwegian Church Against Nazism* (New York: The Macmillan Company, 1943), pp. 5-6. The complete speech by Terboven is found in *Deutsche Monatshefte in Norwegen,* September, 1941, pp, 5-8; see also *Nyordningen i Norge* (Oslo: J. M. Stenersen, 1940).

16. Sverre Kjellstadli, *Hjemmestyrkene. Hovedtrekk av den militore motstanden under okkupasjonen* (Oslo: H. Aschehough & Co., 1959), pp. 25-26: "25.september er blitt kalt den merkedag, hvorfra praktisk talt hele det norske folk ble forenet i motstand mot Quisling og besettelsesmakten."

17. Tore Gjelsvik, *Norwegian Resistance 1940-1945* (Lond: C. Hurst & Co., 1979), p. 14n: "At the last pre-war election in 1936, Quisling's Party of 'National Union' had polled only 26,576 votes (1.84%), rather less than in 1933, the year of its foundation, and by 1939 it was disintegrating for want of unity and money."

18. Torleiv Austad, *Kirkens Grunn. Analyse av en kirkelig bekjennelse fra okkupasjonstiden 1940-45* (Oslo: Luther Forlag, 1974), p. 63 (The Foundation of the Church. An Analysis of a Clerical Confession from the Period of Occupation, 1940-45).

19. Carlsen *op. cit.,* p. 22: "Kristent Samrad vil uten omsvøp følge var gemle prøvede, reformatoriske og haugianski linje pa det inspirerte Guds ords grunn etter var kirkes lutherske bekjennelse. Vi kjenner i denne veldige og kristiske tid som aldri før, at det er det gamle, uavkortede evangelium som alene kan redde vort folk."

20. Edvard Bull, "Motstand. Rettsikkerhet mot terror," in Knut Mykland, *Norges Historie* (Oslo: J. W. Cappelens Forlag, n.d.), 13, 387-388.

21. Chr. R. Christensen, "Hjemmefronten," in *Vare Falne 1939-1945* ["The Home Front," in *Our Fallen, 1939-1945*], (Oslo: 1948), III, 16.

22. Berggrav, *op. cit.,* p. 132.

23. Høye and Ager, *op. cit.,* pp. 156-158.

24. Ture Nerman, *Norsk Front* (Stockholm: Federativs, 1941, p. 115.

25. Berggrav, *op. cit.,* pp. 134-136.

26. *Ibid.,* p. 8.

27. Gjelsvik, *op. cit.,* p. 35.

28. Chr. R. Christensen, *Vart folks historie (The History of Our People),* (Oslo: Ascheboug, 1961), IX, p. 303.

29. Arne Fjellbu, *Memoirs from the War Years* (Minneapolis: Augsburg Publishing House, 1947), p. 141.

30. *Ibid.,* pp. 138-140.

31. John M. Snoek, *The Grey Book* (Assen, The Netherlands: Van Gorcum & Co., 1969), p. 116.

32. Molland, *op. cit.*, p. 54. The English translation of "The Foundation of the Church" is found in Høye and Ager, *op. cit.*, pp. 172-180.
33. The Nazi clergymen were G. Chr. Falck-Hansen, Lars Frøyland, H. O. Hagen, O. J. B. Kvasnes, Einar Lothe, J. E. Sivertsen, L. Daae Zwilgemeyer and Dagfinn Zwilgemeyer, as cited in Arne Hasiing, "The 'Nazi Church' in Occupied Norway, unpublished manuscript.
34. *The New Testament,* American Bible Society, p. 166.
35. Austad, *op. cit.*, p. 176: "Bare rettsstaten har krav pa lydighet."
36. Høye and Ager, *op. cit.*, p. 180.
37. Arvid Brodersen, *Mellom Frontene* (Oslo: Cappelen, 1979), pp. 88ff
38. Frederick Hale, "An Embattled Church," *Scandinavian Review,* 69, 1 (1981), 55.
39. Edvard Bull, *op. cit.*, p. 398.
40. Raul Hilberg, *The Destruction of the European Jews* (Chicago: Quadrangle Books, 1961), p. 355.
41. Chr. A. R. Christensen, *op. cit.*, p. 348.
42. Ludvig Schübeler, *Kirkekampen slik jeg sa den* (Oslo: Lutherstiftelsens Forlag, 1946) p. 211: ". . .ekteskapslovgivningen var endret for a motvirke blanded ekteskaper. En jødes ektefelle ble i kraft av sitt ekteskap selv jøde."
43. Samuel Abrahamsen, "The Holocuast in Norway," in *Contemporary Views on The Holocaust,* ed. Randolph L. Braham (Boston—The Hague: Kluwer-Nijhoff Publishing Co.), pp. 109-142.
44. Brodersen, *op. cit.*, pp. 67-68.
45. Torleiv Austad, "Fra Statskirke til selvadministrert folkekirke. Den norske kirken under krigen." (From State Church to Self-administered Folk Church. The Norwegian Church During the War), in Stein Ugelvik Larsen and Igun Montgomery, eds., *Kirken, Krisen og Krigen (The Church, the Crisis and the War),* (Oslo—Bergen-Tromsø: Universitetsfolaget, 1982), p. 346.
46. "Kirken Protesterer mot Jødeforfølgelsene," (The Church Protests Against the Jewish persecutions), *Norsk Tidend,* London, November 28, 1942, as reprinted in Johan M. Snoek, *op. cit.*, pp. 116-118.
47. The Baptized Jews were Dr. Erenst Adler, Samuel B. Jaffe, Hans Huszar, the families Neubauer and Adolf Neumann.
48. Personal communication to author from Pastor John J. Duin of Hamar Bishopric, dated February 22, 1982.
49. Letter of November 10, 1942, from Bishop Mangers to Professor Hallesby, Archives, Hamar Bishopric, Norway: ". . .jeg finner etter nøyere overveielse ikke a kunne sende noen ny henstilling før det er kommet svar pa den første. En ny henstilling fra min side vilde uten tvil bevirke at den første ikke blir tatt hensyn til og slik bli til skade de kristne av jødisk herkomst." See also, Gottlied W. Rieber-Mohn, "Vi var med. Glimt av den katloske kirke i Norge under Okkupasjonen," (We participated. Glimpses from the Catholic Church

during the occupation), *St. Olav*, No. 57, 1945, p. 94.

50. Ferdinand Schjelderup, *Pa Bred Front* (*On a Wide Front*) (Oslo: Grondahl & Søns, Forlag, 1947), p. 301.

51. *Anlage 120 zum Tatigkeitbericht December 1942 Abt Ic Niederschrift uber die Ic-Besprechung beim AOK Norwegen in der Zeit vom 8.-11.12 1942:* 1. Tag 8.12.1942: "3. *Einzelnes.* Die Gesamtkirche Norwegens hat für die Juden Interpelliert, als bekannt wird, dass die Juden zum Osten transportiert wurden. Die radikale Løsung der Judenfrage wird jedoch der egoistiche Norweger vergessen."

52. Snoek, *op. cit.*, p. 119.

53. Protest Meeting, Stockholm, December 2, 1942, *Yad Vashem Archives*, 0/54/38: "Ett skepp löpte ut fran Oslo hamn med en last av kval ombord. Jag tror knappast nagon av oss riktight kan satta sig in i vad de har lidit och lider ock kommer at lida, dessa mätta sig in i vad de har lidit och lider ock kommer at lida, dessa män, kvinnor, barn och aldringar. . . . Vi kan inte kalla dem tillbaka. De gar till döden eller till slaveriet. . . . Kan vi inte göra nagot annat, sa kan vi forsöka att vära röst at de dömda . . . lata dem genom oss ropa ut sin angest och sin anklagelse."

54. *Nordiska Röster mot Judefvföljelse och Vald. Dokument och Kommentar* (Stockhom: *Judisk Tiddskrift*, 1943), p. 14. *Vad Vashem Archives*, 85.2952.

55. Ture Nerman, in *Trots Allt*, December 4, 1942.

56. *Norsk Tidend*, December 9, 1942: "Forfølgelsen av folk tilhørende en annen rase er i˜strid med den nordiske rettsoppfatning og har hittil vaert ukjent i nordiske land."

57. As quoted by John Scharffenberg, *Morgenbladet* (*Morning Journal*), Oslo, September 15, 1952: "Protester mot Quislings jødeforfølgelse," (Protests against Quisling's Jewish persecutions): "Vart land løser idag et av tidens største problemer, jødespørsmalet. Matte vi da ikke glemme, at dette problem ikke bare er et raseproblem, men ogsa et nasjonalt, og fremfor alt et menneskelig. Det norske folk har aldri betraktet jødene som landsmenn, dertil er folket for sunt. Men det har alltid betraktet dem som mennesker, og som ulykkelige mennesker. Var bevegelse ma sta til ansvar for det norske folk for den mate det løser problemet pa . . . fremfor alt ma vi vaere pa vakt mot a ødelegge rettferdighetsfølelsen i oss selv. Det hjelper lite a vinne hele verden hvis man tar skade pa sin sjel."

58. Lars Frøyland, *I Kiosets Tegn* (*By the Sign of the Cross*) (Oslo: Viking Forlag, 1943), pp. 43-44: "Til slutt lyt eg nemna ting som eg tykkjer er syrgjeleg og som skjemmer folket vart: Framferdi var mot folk av ei onnor rase og ei onner tru, innom vare eigne grenser. Eg kjenner meg bunden av samvitet mitt til a segje dette. Og eg gjer det um det so skal kosta meg aldri sc mykje. Er det rett a skjere alle yver ein kam og straffa dei uskuldige med dei skuldiga? Me er da nordmenn! me er da kristne!"

59. *Fritt Folk,* December 7, 1942, as quoted from Memorandum (Dispatch No. 1408), February 11, 1943, the American Legation, Stockholm, National Archives, Washington, D.C., NND 730032.
60. Gjelsvik, *op. cit.,* p. 94.
61. *News of Norway,* July 23, 1943. The Norwegian text is found in Ingval B. Carlsen, *Kirkens Kamp i Norge,* p. 137: "Som kristne ma vi se pa vart land som en Herrens gave som er betrodd vart folk av Gud. . . . Gud har kalt kirken til a vaere samvittighetens vokter overalt hvor det øves tvang mot sjelene. Ut fra dette vart kall ber vi Ministerpresidenten om a avsta fra a utskrive norske borgere til en tjeneste som strider imot deres samvittighet og rettsfølelse. . . . Overfor denne samvittighetsnød kan kirken ikke tie."
62. Francis Bull, *Minner om mennesker (Remembrances About People)* (Oslo: Gyldendal Norsk Forlag, 1962), pp. 148ff.
63. Carlsen, *op. cit.,* p. 185.
64. Amanda Johnson, *Norway, Her Invasion and Occupation* (Decatur, Georgia: Bowen Press, 1948), p. 258.
65. W. A. Visser't Hooft, *The Ecumenical Movement and the Radical Problem* (Paris, 1954), p. 40, as quoted in Snoek, *op. cit.,* p. 289.

From Rivalry to Repression:
The German Protestant Leadership,
Anti-Leftism and Anti-Semitism, 1933

Shelley Baranowski

The Final Solution presents two seemingly intractable problems. Despite the unprecedented bureaucratic, technocratic and radically racist savagery of the extermination of the Jews during the Second World War, anti-Semitism was not a major component of the Nazi electoral appeal before 1933, regardless of its deep significance for loyal Party elites.[1] Furthermore, while anti-Semitism was, without question, common in Germany, a fact which partially explains the widespread public tolerance of the Nazi government's legal restrictions upon the political, professional, and economic position of the Jews, radical Nazi assaults upon Jewish property and lives during the 1930s met with open disapproval. Most Germans, as one recent account puts it, "apparently wanted to restrict Jewish rights substantially, but not to annihilate Jews."[2]

Thus, anti Semitism by itself cannot answer the crucial questions: How was the extent of the Nazi terror possible? What, if any, social supports existed for it? The answers lie in the recognition that anti-leftism, more than any other single issue, emerged as the principal justification for the repressive measures which accompanied the Nazi assumption of power in 1933. Anti-leftism, in turn, incorporated the conviction that the Jews enjoyed a "disproportionate" influence in German politics and culture; one that contributed to the toleration, and even encouragement of, the regime's "legal" persecution. The consequences of anti-leftism, the expansion of the Nazi regime's police power, enabled the terror to mushroom even after the left had been defeated.

The suppression of organized labor, which the Socialist and Communist parties and the trade unions embodied, was the Nazi government's foremost objective and chief accomplishment during the first six months of its rule. By July, 1933, neither civil liberties nor active political opposition existed any longer. The burning of the Reichstag building, despite its highly suspicious origins, gave rise to a "red" scare which permitted Hitler's assumption of dictatorial powers, the dismantling of the constitutional guarantees of the Weimar Republic and the legitimated marauding of the Nazi's para-military "Brown Shirts." Although all associations and parties were affected, the left was especially victimized. Its leaders were either arrested *en masse* or driven underground, and its organizations were permanently shut down. Labor dissension persisted throughout the Third Reich, especially when, in the late 1930s, workers sought to extract higher wages from a full-employment economy. Yet there can be little doubt that the Nazi regime succeeded in depriving the working class of effective, autonomous organizations.[3]

The vast number of those arrested required appropriate places of confinement. Concentration camps, such as that opened in the former munitions factory in Dachau, near Munich, were soon erected to accommodate the droves of leftists held in "protective custody." Neither the regular police, nor the existing jails, sufficed to meet the inflated demand. Those camps, not to mention the repressive decrees which accompanied them, laid the groundwork for the S.S. police state; one which initially supplanted the uncontrolled or "wild" arrest and detention activity of the Brown Shirts, but soon grew independent of the regular judiciary and civil administration as well. The concentration camps, furthermore, became experimental laboratories whose results were applied during wartime in the extermination camps situated in the occupied territories east of Germany.[4]

The elimination of organized labor met with little disagreement from middle class, especially lower middle class, Germans. The diverse occupational groups which composed the Nazi electorate not only attributed the defeat in World War I to the Socialist-led cabinet that capitulated to the "dictated peace" of the Allies. They also resented profoundly the expensive social welfare programs and accompanying high taxes which the leverage of the Socialists within the republican system yielded. Although many Nazi voters, as well as the Party's rank and file, articulated a strong hostility to "big" capitalism, embodied in industrial monopolies, department stores, and consumer cooperatives, their esteem for private property, government protection for small producers and national assertivenss translated into a far greater antagonism toward "Marxism."[5]

The attack upon the left, however, demanded direct support at the top in addition to passive approval from below. It could not have succeeded without the consent of the overwhelmingly Protestant conservative "establishment" — the army officers, high-ranking civil servants, estate owners, industrialists, professionals and even Protestant churchmen — whose encouragement of National Socialism was crucial to the installation and stabilization of the regime. Despite the Nazis' impressive electoral strength, the Party never won a parliamentary majority on its own. In order to take power, Hitler needed an alliance with conservative elites.[6]

In important respects, the Nazi Party was as necessary for elites as elites were for Hitler. Although the establishment's influence at the highest levels of government grew in the last years of the Weimar Republic in direct proportion to the decline of parliamentary consensus, internecine conflicts among elites effectively prevented even the most authoritarian of the republican cabinets from reviving an economy undermined by the Depression, enhancing military power against the Versailles Treaty's restrictions and acquiring mass loyalty. The Nazis offered two major assets: first, their platform of aggressive rearmament, revisionism, and especially anti-leftism, promised the removal of the constraints of limited budgets and social programs which, as the Depression worsened, encouraged elites to compete among themselves for scarce resources, as well as with organized labor. Second, the Nazis delivered a mass rightist constituency in support of proposals which, in addition to their intrinsic value to the Nazi electorate, overcame elite divisions as well.

The Cabinet appointed in January, 1933, with Adolf Hitler as Chancellor was, in reality, a coalition that favored conservative retainers from previous Weimar administrations. Although the prominence of elites was intended to restrain the demagogic populism of Nazism, it sanctioned Nazi repression against the coalition's common enemy. In addition to the Chancellorship, the Party acquired the two cabinet posts directly responsible for the police, whose numbers were soon inflated by countless, virulently anti-leftist, Storm Trooper "auxiliaries." No longer would the left, or the republic which gave it influence, impede profitability, military power and conservative unity.[7]

Although not a "political" institution, the Protestant Church effectively illustrates the depth of the establishment's antipathy toward organized labor and its consequences. On numerous occasions throughout the 1930s, the Protestant leadership, composed of bishops, church presidents, well-placed pastors, synodical laymen, theologians and consistorial officials, bitterly opposed the Nazi regime's ecclesiastical and educational policies. It also objected to the racial basis of Nazi anti-Semitism, and, against Nazi sympathizers within the church who argued otherwise, denied that baptized Jews could be excluded from the church on such "secular" grounds. That group, which by and large coalesced into the Confessing Church by mid-1934, often garnered significant public support and the backing of conservative elites within the Reich government. As a result, the Protestant church revealed the limits of the Nazi "totalitarian" ambition to mold all classes and institutions into a tension-free, ideologically cohesive *Volk* community especially when Party zealots intruded upon powerful vested interests and deeply held values. Because the Protestant Church was a major cultural institution which articulated Christian norms against Party ideology, it represented the most common and effective form of opposition in the Third Reich.

Nevertheless — and this point is crucial — the regime profited from the agreement of even its most vociferous conservative critics, including the Protestant leadership, on such issues as the repudiation of the Versailles Treaty, restrictions upon the "excessive" influence of the Jews in public life, and especially, the suppression of the left. That support coexisted organically with opposition, if at times uneasily, and allowed the Nazis to pursue their most radical objectives without serious hindrance.[8]

The poor relations which existed historically between the church and the German working class conditioned Protestant antagonism toward the left. Since the mid-nineteenth century, the Protestant leadership presided over the steady decline in regular Sunday participation among the millions of baptized who comprised the nominal church membership.[9] The statistics for the largest cities were particularly grim, not only because few among the urban educated middle classes identified with church concerns, but also because the indifference of the mass of industrial workers constituted an "alienation" of significant proportions. With increasing determination, Protestant workers distanced themselves from the church as perceptions of a distinctive class identity and outlook took over.[10] For the Protestant leadership, drawing the working class to the church and its message and away from socialism, considered the proletariat's secular ideological surrogate, became the key to the continued vitality of church life in an urbanizing, industrializing and secularizing society.[11]

Several interrelated factors opened wide the gulf between pastor and worker. First, Protestant clergymen enjoyed relatively high social status, salaries, and educational attainment which created a professional ethos and conservative political outlook at least as distinctive and isolating as the class consciousness of the workers. In addition, the Protestant church as a unit was closely identified with the monarchy and with agrarian, bureaucratic and professional elites, many of whom served as lay representatives to the regional synods. Finally, the dominant Protestant theologies — not surprisingly given the social backgrounds of Protestant clerics and the political alliances of the church — stressed obedience, subordination, and above all, the sin of rebellion against political authority.[12]

While not all churchmen were insensitive to the impact of Protestant social commitments upon working class behavior, most leaders preferred to attribute worker disaffection principally to the agitation of socialists and free thinkers. The reinvigorated and intensive preaching of charity, private property, social harmony and anti-Marxism, they believed, would compete effectively with leftist anti-clericalism. Periodic undertakings emerged to lend organizational support to sermons on the "social question." They consisted of Protestant-sponsored trade unions and workingmen's clubs, congresses devoted to the discussion of societal problems, and even a political party — Adolf Stöcker's Christian Social party which enjoyed a brief life-span during the last quarter of the nineteenth century. While those efforts undoubtedly heightened the concern of committed Protestants, they accomplished little in closing the abyss between church and working class.[13]

Thus, as industrialization proceded apace in Germany during the late nineteenth and early twentieth centuries, the Protestant Church confronted a major dilemma. On the one hand, its generous government subventions, its extensive role in education, its status as a legally-recognized corporation, its close ties to the monarchy and the political establshment, not to mention the bureaucratic ranking of its clergymen, signified that Germany was a "Christian" nation whose government endorsed the Protestant obligation to interpret the word of God to a society beset by social divisions. On the other hand, the small percentage of interested listeners, much to the dismay of the Protestant leadership, underlined the disparity between the Protestant mission and the unhappy reality. The working class, with its distinctive subculture and alien ideology, mocked the Protestant aspiration to social mediator and reconciler more graphically than any other popular constituency. It remained simultaneously wood and feared.[14]

The republican interlude which followed the collapse of the monarchy at the end of World War I confirmed Protestant perceptions as to the remoteness of the proletariat and the implacable hostility of its leaders. The emergence of a Socialist-dominated provisional government led to the appointment of the militantly anti-clerical Adolf Hoffman, as Minister of Education, who, in short order, abolished state financial support, ended compulsory religious education and simplified the procedures by which citizens could withdraw from church membership. To be sure, the lobbying of both the Protestant and Catholic churches, accompanied as it was by impressive popular demonstrations, forced the recision of Hoffman's measures. In the end it yielded substantial concessions from the Weimar government, largely by exploiting Socialist moderation and the good will of conservative holdovers from the imperial bureaucracy,[15] that restored virtually all of the past guarantees. Nevertheless, the success with which the Bolshevik Revolution in Russia destroyed the once powerful influence of the Orthodox church constantly reminded German churchmen of just how close Hoffman had come to realizing one of the left's principal historical goals.[16]

Even as the Republic grew to tolerate the inherited prerogatives of the churches, its freer cultural and intellectual climate, not to mention its birth in the ashes of military defeat, registered to priest and pastor alike an aura of decadence, immorality, unregenerated secularism, and national humiliation. The Weimar years witnessed not only the submission to a punitive postwar peace settlement, but also a dramatic increase in the number of church "leavings" combined with the official tolerance of free-thinking and leftist anti-church agitation never permitted by the Empire. Most Protestant leaders only too willingly located the origins of cultural and moral decay in the leftist revolutions of 1918-1919 and the defeat which produced them. Many continued to believe that the postwar system would not permanently assure the Christian foundations of Germany because of the Weimar constitution's neutrality in religious matters.[17] The rapid growth of the German Communist Party after the onset of the Depression convinced many churchmen that the barely tolerable parliamentary democracy would disintegrate into another "godless" Bolshevik experiment.

The left's close identification with the Weimar regime provides the key to understanding why, in 1933, the Protestant leadership welcomed the Hitler cabinet, virtually to the last man, and found little to condemn in its blatant employment of repression. First, the Nazis embraced a mass, principally lower middle class constituency which, in striking contrast to the working class parties, promised to restore the churches to their destined social and cultural role. Point 24 of the Nazi platform, which affirmed the place of "positive" Christianity in German life, and Hitler's periodic assurances regarding the legal status of the churches, assured the Protestant leadership that this state, unlike the Republic, recognized the nation's Christian foundations.[18] As the later opponent of Nazism, Martin Niemöller, explained in retrospect, National Socialism looked upon the Protestant church as a "strong factor in the life of the nation," and grounded its Third Reich on a "Christian foundation." By contrast, the Republic tolerated the anti-church propaganda of union leaders, made divorce easier and facilitated exemptions from church membership.

Sunday attendance declined, as did the number of marriages performed under religious auspices. Financial straits frequently impeded church work and compulsory religious instruction in the schools was abolished.[19]

Second, the Nazi-sympathizing populist "German Christian Movement," whose growth as a significant church faction reflected the strength of Nazism among Protestant voters, crusaded for a religious revitalization within to accompany the national renewal without.[20] In short order, the German Christians would present innumerable problems for the Protestant leadership, but during the early months of 1933, they anesthetized memories of a troubled past. To a German Christian rally in July, Bishop Theophil Wurm of Württemberg recalled his disappointment when as a young, socially aware pastor, his church failed to draw the working class back into the fold. Indeed, he explained the church bore some of the responsibility for not having provided working class parishes with enough pastors. Yet the Socialist leadership was chiefly to blame. "The soul of the German worker was not understood. Rather, it had to be used to implement a *Weltanschauung* which demoralized the *Volk* and church, and because of that, all the efforts of we young theologians to reach and penetrate the heart of the German workers were spurned." But now, remarked Wurm, a momentous change had taken place. "Then, the leaders drove the Volk away from the faith and the church, and today Führer calls the Volk *to* (emphasis mine) the faith and the church." While Wurm implicitly cautioned the German Christians against excessive, divisive, politicization, he nonetheless suggested that the Nazi movement as a whole held the potential for uniting a national rising with a religious awakening, much like the War of Liberation against Napoleon.[21]

Third, the Protestant leadership recognized that the new government was a coalition in which conservative appointments dominated numerically. Thus, the coalition's platform of authoritarianism, revisionism and anti-leftism would subdue the undesirable elements of Nazism — its plebeian Brown Shirts, its virulent anti-Christianity in some circles, and its vulgar, rabid, and violent anti-semitism. Certainly church leaders were aware of Nazi anti-Semitism, but as Martin

Niemöller recalled, "we were, as I must admit, little concerned with that. For we took these new shibboleths merely as slogans which would be useful to attract the masses, which would be dropped as soon as the Nazis attained power and assumed political responsibility."[22] The aging President, Paul von Hindenburg, Junker landowner, war hero and devout Protestant, lent symbolic support to the belief that the new Chancellor's virtues could be cultivated at the expense of his movement's liabilities. As one major Protestant journal argued, the cooperation which appeared to exist between Hitler and Hindenburg promised that church and state would work together toward "the moral and religious renewal of the Volk."[23]

In brief, the Nazis and their surrogates, the German Christians, offered a solution to the chronic Protestant dilemma. Now the church would have *both* formal, legal guarantees *and* mass participation. Thus, the tide of secularization and decay would be stemmed, and the anticlericalism of its perpetrators, the left, would be silenced. In fact, the accession of the Hitler government and the quasi-religious excitement it created, effected a dramatic decline in the number of church "leavings" and an equally stunning increase among those who rejoined.[24]

Small wonder, then, that a church seemingly on the threshold of internal renewal and external restoration refused to confront the consequences of repression as its historical nemesis was systematically undermined in the name of order and internal security. The destruction of organized labor, in addition to being championed for its own sake, occasioned the expression of other, closely related prejudices — especially anti-Semitism, which in the Protestant case, combined traditional Christian anti-Judaism and conservative nationalist anti-pluralism.[25] Prominent Protestant leaders minimized the injustice of such major initiatives in the spring of 1933 as the boycott of Jewish shops and the Reich Civil Service Law, which removed Socialists and Jews from office, usually by reference to the past sins of the left. The central committee of the Protestant umbrella organization, the Church Federation, excused the Civil Service Law as "the first attempt at a solution of the Jewish problem." It conceded acts of violence against Jews, but argued that they were "nothing at all in comparison to the ghastly and shameful events of the 1918 revolution." That declaration concluded that Jews were disproportionately represented in the law, medicine, commerce, the theater, the arts and in the leaderships of the leftist political parties; a state of affairs which threatened the survival of Christian culture in Germany.[26] The numerous Protestant Sunday newspapers, referring to the clear social, economic, cultural and political gains which Jews accomplished during the republican years, implicitly or explicitly blamed the revolution of 1918 and the Socialist influence which resulted.[27]

Similarly, the General Superintendent of Brandenburg, Otto Dibelius, in a famous radio broadcast, lengthily praised the regime's assaults upon "Bolshevism" while justifying the removal of Jews from office as a necessary curtailment of their excessive influence. Not only had the German people suffered through the violent upheavals of the 1918 revolution — even the temporary erection of a communist republic in Bavaria — but they also saw "at closest range how Bolshevism in Russia destroys churches, disintegrates families, annihilates property and renders men the outlawed slaves of a ferocious and despotic government." Dibelius admitted "some excesses," but countered "that cannot be otherwise in a country with 65 million people." Overall, he noted, "the picture of public life in Germany has remained a picture of order and discipline." As for the treatment extended to imprisoned communists, Dibelius was equally firm. "Not one word in the hair-raising reports of the cruel and bloody treatment of Communists in Germany is true. On the basis of such false reports world Jewry has started an agitation against Germany in several countries. To break this boycott the German National Socialists in turn have initiated a boycott movement against Jewry in Germany."[28]

For certain, most Protestant leaders objected to the Nazis' preaching of racial hatred, and resisted especially the application of racial anti-Semitic criteria to church membership, which the most radical of the German Christians espoused. The conflict over the standards for baptism assumed an important place in the struggle between the Confessing Church and its Nazi-sympathizing adversaries. Yet while most leaders acknowledged that the regime's "dragnet" unfairly victimized some, Jews included, very few, if any, challenged the legitimacy of the "dragnet" itself. Even the young Lutheran theologican, Dietrich Bonhoeffer, often credited for having alerted the church as it its responsibilities toward non-Christians, insisted, in the spring of 1933, that there was a Jewish "question," "which our state must deal with, and without a doubt the state is justified in adopting new mehods here."[29]

The Protestant leadership's linkage of the Jewish influence with that of the left found expression elsewhere within the conservative establishment. Most elites looked upon "legal" anti-Jewish measures as either desirable, or at least tolerable, given the regime's defense of property, profits and social privilege.[30] That connection was to have even deadlier consequences later during the Nazi regime's ultimate crusade against the left — the war in the east. There, the army officer corps, having accepted the stereotyped Nazi equation between "Jew" and "Bolshevik," and eager to preserve its status within the National Socialist state, conducted a war of unparalleled brutality and looked aside with few scruples as the S.S. indulged in an orgy of murder.[31]

The Protestant expectation, however, that the Nazi renewal would mean the reaffirmation of the social and cultural place of the church in German life was soon disappointed. The German Christian Movement grew steadily more radical in its demands that the church be "reformed" according to Nazi organizational and racial principles, even to the point of employing the political authority of the Party and state to achieve its goals. Although the Confessing Church, that loose regional alliance of Protestant leaderships who affirmed scriptural integrity and church autonomy from Nazi political interference, forced the regime to withdraw its support from the German Christians by late 1934, assaults against church influence continued, especially in education. Anti-church propaganda proliferated and police harrassment of dissident pastors accelerated.

Thus, the Protestant leadership, like many conservative elites, learned that National Socialism could neither be tamed nor made more "responsible," nor would the repression subside once the left was vanquished at home. Rather, the police power and legalistic props which conservative elites bestowed and the Protestant church supported, profferred the Nazis an apparatus of terror which not only did not disappear, but careened out of control.

NOTES

1. For suggestions to this effect, see W. S. Allen's *The Nazi Seizure of Power. The Experience of a Single German Town 1930-1935* (New York, 1965), pp. 77-78 and Richard Hamilton's summary of the Nazi electoral appeal, *Who Voted for Hitler?* (Princeton, New Jersey, 1982), pp. 361-419.

2. Sarah Gordon, *Hitler, Germans, and the "Jewish Question"* (Princeton, New Jersey, 1984), p. 208. Two short pieces treating this problem are those of Ian Kershaw, "The Persecution of the Jews and German Popular Opinion in the Third Reich," *Leo Baeck Institute Year Book*, 26 (London, Jerusalem, New York, 1981), pp. 261-289; and Lawrence D. Stokes, "The German People and the Destruction of the European Jews," *Central European History*, 6 (1973), 167-191. See also Kershaw's *Popular Opinion and Polictical Dissent in the Third Reich: Bavaria 1933-1945* (Oxford, 1983), pp. 224-277.

3. Volker Berghahn, *Modern Germany. Society, Economy and Politics in the Twentieth Century* (Cambridge, London, New York, 1982), pp. 129-130. For the conflicts between the Nazi regime and the working class, see T. W. Mason, *Sozialpolitik im Dritten Reich: Arbeiterklasse und Volksgemeinschaft* (Opladen, 1977).

4. The "classic" contribution on the SS, now in English translation, is that of Helmut Krausnick and Martin Broszat, *Anatomy of the SS State* (London, Toronto, Sydney, New York, 1982). See also Hans-Günter Richardi, *Schule der Gewalt. Das Konzentrationslager Dachau 1933-1945* (Munich, 1983).

5. The most recent comprehensive analysis of the Nazi constituency is Thomas Childers' *The Nazi Voter. The Social Foundations of Fascism in Germany, 1919-1933* (Chapel Hill, North Carolina, and London, 1983). For the Nazi movement itself, see Michael H. Kater, *The Nazi Party. A Social Profile of Members and Leaders, 1919-1945* (Cambridge, Massachusetts, 1983).

6. David Abraham's *The Collapse of the Weimar Republic. Political Economy and Crisis* (Princeton, New Jersey, 1981), and Michael E. Geyer, *Aufrüstung oder Sicherheit: Die Reichswehr in der Krise der Machtpolitik, 1924-1936* (Mainz, 1980), comprise the best of the recent works on the conservative-Nazi relationship. Both deal extensively with the divisions among elites and their contributions to the Nazi accession.

7. Two new works which discuss the foundations, social bases and ideology of the Nazi "Brown Shirts" are those of Richard Bessel, *Political Violence and the Rise of Nazism. The Storm Troopers in Eastern Germany 1925-1934* (New Haven, Connecticut, and London, 1984), and Conan Fischer, *Stormtroopers. A Social, Economic and Ideological Analysis, 1929-1936* (London, 1983). For the suggestion that the police, under both conservative and Nazi auspices, became an instrument of assault against the left even before Hitler's accession, see Christoph Graf, *Politische Polizei zwischen Demokratie und*

Diktatur. *Die Entwicklung der Preussichen Politischen Polizei von Staatsschutzorgan der Weimarer Republik zum Geheimen Staatspolizeiamt des Dritten Reiches* (Berlin, 1983).

8. The relationship between opposition and consent is an emerging theme in the literature on everyday life in the Third Reich, especially Kershaw, *Popular Opinion and Political Dissent in the Third Reich. Bavaria: 1933-1945* (Oxford, 1983), Detlev Peukert and Jürgen Reulecke, eds., *Die Reihen fast geschlossen. Beiträge zur Geschichte des Alltags unterm Nationalsozialismus* (Wuppertal, 1981), and the series, *Bayern in der NS-Zeit,* now in six volumes (Munich, Vienna, 1979-1983), whose general editor is Martin Broszat.

9. Paul Troschke, *Evangelische Kirchenstatistik Deutschlands,* vol. 6-7 (Berlin, 1930-1932), pp. 32-33.

10. For an analysis of working class attitudes, see Vernon L. Lidtke, "Social Class and Secularization in Imperial Germany, *Leo Baeck Institute Year Book* vol. 25 (1980), pp. 21-40, and Hugh McLeod, "Protestantism and the Working Class in Imperial Germany," *European Studies Review,* 12 (1982), 323-344.

11. The literature on the Protestant Church and the "Social Question" is extensive. See Günter Bräkelmann, *Die Soziale Frage des 19. Jahrhunderts* (Witten, 1962); Gottfried Kretschmar, *Der Evangelisch-soziale Kongress* (Stuttgart, 1972); Klaus-Erich Pollmann, *Landescherrliches Kirchenregiment und soziale Frage* (Berlin, 1973); Manfred Schick, *Kulturprotestantismus und soziale Frage* (Tübingen, 1970); William O. Shanahan, *German Protestants Face the Social Question,* vol, 1, *1815-1871* (Notre Dame, Indiana, 1954); and W. R. Ward, *Theology, Sociology and Politics. The German Protestant Social Conscience 1890-1933* (Berne, Frankfurt/Main, Las Vegas, 1979).

12. For a short statement regarding the social background of Protestant pastors and the composition of Protestant synods, see Friedrich-Martin Balzar, "Kirche und Klassenbindung in der weimarer Republik," in Yorick Spiegel, ed., *Kirche und Klassenbindung* (Frankfurt, 1974), pp. 48-49 and 53-54; see also K. W. Dahm, *Pfarrer und Politik. Soziales Position und politische Mentalität des deutschen evangelischen Pfarrerstandes zwischen 1918 und 1933* (Cologne and Opladen, 1965).

13. See Kurt Nowak, *Evangelische Kirche und Weimarer Republik: Zum politischen Weg des deutschen Protestantismus zwischen 1918 und 1932* (Weimar, 1981), especially pp. 126-137. The Christian-Social Party enjoyed a brief lifetime in the late 1870s, but its support came mainly from lower middle class elements. See Walter Frank, *Hofprediger Adolf Stöcker und die christlichsoziale Bewegung* (Hamburg, 1935).

14. John Groh's *Nineteenth Century German Protestantism: The Church as Social Model* (Washington, 1982), discusses Protestant expectations with regard to the relationship among church, state and society.

15. In addition to Nowak's work, see Jochen Jacke (*Kirche zwischen Monarchie und Republik*) *Der preussische Protestantismus nach dem Zusammenbruch von 1918* (Hamburg, 1976); Claus Motschmann *Evangelische Kirche und preussischen Staat in den Anfängen der weimarer Republik* (Lübeck and Hamburg 1969); and J. R. C. Wright, *'Above Parties:' The Political Attitudes of the German Protestant Church Leadership, 1918-1933* (Oxford, 1974).

16. Klaus Scholder, *Die Kirchen und das Dritte Reich* vol. 1 (Berlin, 1977), pp. 283 327-328, records the reaction of church leaders to the events in Russia

17. Jochen-Christoph Kaiser, *Arbeiterbewegung und organisierte Religonskritik. Proletarische Freidenkerverbände in Kaiserreich und Weimarer Republik* (Stuttgart, 1981). For a summary statement of recent scholarship on the churches in the Weimar Republic see J. S. Conway, "National Socialism and the Christian Churches during the Weimar Republic," in Peter D. Stachura, ed. *The Nazi Machtergreifung* (London Boston, Sydney, 1983), pp. 124-145.

18. Conway surveys the ambiguities in the Nazi attitude toward the churches in *The Nazi Persecution of the Churches* (London, 1968), pp. 1-44.

19. Leo Stein, *I Was in Hell with Niemöller* (London and Edinburgh, 1947), pp. 69-73. See also Manfred Jacobs, "Kirche, Weltanschauung, Politik. Die evangelischen Kirchen und die Option zwischen dem zweiten und dritten Reich " *Vierteljahrschefte für Zeitgeschichte* 3 (1983), 108-135, for a discussion regarding the leadership's expectation of a *völkisch* renewal.

20. For a discussion of the social and theological camps which developed in early 1933, see Shelley Baranowski, "The 1933 German Protestant Church Elections: *Machtpolitik* or Accommodation?', *Church History,* 49 (1980), 298-315.

21. Gerhard Schaefer, *Die Evangelische Landeskirche in Württemberg und der Nationalsozialismus. Eine Dokumentation zum Kirchenkampf,* vol. 2 1933 (Stuttgart, 1972), pp. 430-432.

22. Stein, p. 73.

23. *Allegemeine Evangelisch-lutherische Kirchenzeitung* Nr. 66 (April 7, 1933), 326.

24. For the relevant statistics, see Klaus Motschmann, "Widerstand der Christlichen kirchen im Dritten Reich — aus protestatischer Sicht " *Politische Studien* 34 (1983), 78.

25. The fullest recent account in Richard Gutteridge's *Open Thy Mouth for the Dumb? The German Evangelical Church and the Jews 1879-1950* (Oxford, 1976). See also Kurt Meier's very brief, *Kirche und Judentum* (Göttingen 1968).

26. For the entire text, see Armin Boyens, *Kirchenkampf und Ökumene 1933-1939* (Munich, 1969), pp 299-380.

27. See Donald L. Niewyk, *The Jews in Weimar Germany* (Baton

Rouge and London, 1980), pp. 11-42; Gordon, pp. 7-49; and Ino Arndt, "Machtübernahme und Judenboykott ir der Sicht evangelischen Sontagsblätter," in Wolfgang Benz, ed., *Miscellanea. Festschrift für Helmut Krausnick* (Sutttgart, 1980), pp. 15-31.

28. See Conway, *Nazi Persecution,* pp. 342-344.

29. *No Rusty Swords: Letters, Lectures and Notes, 1928-1936* (New York and Evanston, Illinois, 1947), pp. 222-229.

30. Hans Mommsen, "Hitlers Stellung im Nationalsozialistischen Herrschaftssytem," in Gerhard Hirschfeld and Lothar Kettenacker, eds., *The "Führer State": Myth and Reality. Studies on the Structure and Politics of the Third Reich* (Stuttgart, 1981), pp. 55-57.

31. Helmut See Krausnick and Hans-Heinrich Wilhelm, *Die Truppe des Weltanschauungskrieges. Die Einsatsgruppen der Sicherheitspolizei und der SD 1938-1942* (Stuttgart, 1981), the Militärgeschichtliche Forschungsamt series, *Das Deutsche Reich und der Zweite Weltkrieg,* especially Vol. 4, *Der Angriff auf die Sowjetischen* (Stuttgart, 1983), and Christian Streit, *Keine Kameradan. Die Wehrmacht und die Sowjetischen Union Kriegsgefangenen 1941-1945* (Stuttgart, 1978).

Lutheran Conscience and the Holocaust:
The German and Norwegian Cases

Stephen C. MacDonald

The study of the European Protestant response to the rise of National Socialism and to the Holocaust is beset with formidable obstacles we are only beginning to overcome. Protestantism is a fragmented and multifarious movement. Even in states with large and influential official Protestant establishments there exist constellations of quite independent Protestant denominations. This multiplicity bedevils the historian and cautions us against subscribing to easy generalizations about Protestant Christianity and fascism in the 1930s and 1940s. As this paper suggests, it is the contrast between the responses of various national Protestantisms that is most striking and instructive.

Consider for a moment how different the case is of Roman Catholicism. United by the central authority of the Holy See which imposes doctrinal coherence and mandates clear lines of institutional accountability, Catholicism may more confidently be scrutinized for its attitude toward Nazism and its works since whatever national variations emerge, it is still possible to identify a Catholic – that is, Vatican – position. This is true even when in practice the Catholic Church's circumstances varied dramatically from place to place in Europe during the Second World War. We need only recall that in some states – Slovakia and Croatia, for instance – Catholic authorities collaborated enthusiastically with savagely anti-Semitic, fascist regimes; elsewhere, as in Poland, the Catholic Church found itself a principal target of German repression. These important local differences aside, Roman Catholicism's ability to speak with one voice through the supranational authority of the Pope distinguishes it sharply from the many Protestant denominations. This fact, plus the Catholic Church's great wealth, its enormous membership, and its incomparable prestige — a prestige based in part upon traditions of resistance to the pretensions of the secular power — have caused Catholics and non-Catholics alike to take the Church hard to task for its failure to do more for Hitler's victims, especially the Jews. Much more has been expected in retrospect of the Catholic Church than of the smaller and disparate European Protestant churches.

🙵

The range of Protestant responses to Nazism is illustrated by the contrasting behavior of Protestant churchmen in Germany and Norway. Considerable attention has been paid to those German pastors — Martin Niemoeller, Theophil Wurm, Dietrich Bonhoeffer, among others — who raised their voices against the Nazi dictatorship and who suffered persecution and in some cases death for their actions. It was Wurm, Bishop of Wuerttemberg, who in 1943 issued on behalf of the German Confessing Church an explicit denunciation of the persecution of Jews, the only such protest voiced by a Christian organization in the Third Reich. The protest was as ineffectual as it was unique.

It is the uniqueness of this statement and the exceptional character of those few individuals who chose to resist the regime that is precisely the point. The great majority of German Protestant pastors — like Germans in general — did not resist. The German Protestant establishment at the minimum tolerated and frequently endorsed National Socialist policies. The support of Protestant churchmen was not unconditional, and when the regime went too far and tried to impose an administrative and ideological centralism on the Protestant churches through the Party-sponsored German Christian Movement, the pastors rebelled and formed the Confessing Church as a bulwark against direct Nazi control. But the Confessing Church did not represent an opposition in principle to National Socialism; it merely demonstrated Protestant determination to maintain institutional autonomy within the new state. It marked the boundary beyond which the regime dare not trespass.[1]

Protestant churchmen cooperated with the Hitler regime, especially in the early years of its existence, because though rarely Nazis themselves they shared with the Nazis common cultural anxieties and social preconceptions. Like other German conservatives in the army, the judiciary, the bureaucracy, and the upper ranks of business and industry, Protestant pastors longed for a government that would protect traditional national values, preserve a hierarchical social order threatened (it seemed) with violent dissolution, and restore Christian principles to their rightful place in the functioning of state and society. All these things the Nazis promised to do. After the experience of the "Godless" Weimar Republic whose fitful efforts to separate church and state had only alienated and annoyed many German Christians, Protestant and Catholic, it is little wonder that Protestant leaders should have been comforted by the Nazis' declared intention to make "positive Christianity" central to German life. Moreover, Protestant pastors saw in Hitler's mass party a bridge to Germany's workers the majority of whom had drifted away from organized religion and embraced socialism in the course of industrialization and urbanization. In 1933 Bishop Wurm himself praised Hitler for calling the German people back to religion and the church.[2]

If the acquiescence of the Christian churches in Germany was one of the essential elements in the establishment of the Nazi dictatorship in 1933-1934, the refusal of the Protestant churches in Norway to support Vidkun Quisling's government was a major contributing factor to the wartime bankruptcy of Norwegian fascism. Far from merely witholding support, the Norwegian Protestant establishment took the lead in opposing Quisling and his *Nasjonal Samlung* party in the years 1940-1943.

In the autumn of 1940, following the dual catastrophes of military defeat and foreign occupation, the various Norwegian Lutheran churches laid aside their doctrinal and institutional rivalries to create a Christian Joint Council for the Norwegian Church. The outstanding personality of this Joint Council was the liberal bishop of Oslo, Eivind Josef Berggrav. Throughout 1941 the Joint Council protested publicly the lawless behavior of Quisling's followers and the encroachments by the German occupation authorities in private matters of religion and conscience. When the Germans abrogated the Norwegian constitution and appointed Quisling minister president in February, 1942, all seven of the state church's bishops resigned their positions as civil servants. In April, 1942, 645 of 699 Lutheran pastors followed suit. Thereafter an extralegal Lutheran church, pastored by the resignees and led by an underground "Temporary Church Leadership" ministered to the great mass of Norwegians while a collaborationist state church attempted without success to lend some respectability to Quisling's wretched enterprise.

Hounded by Quisling's police and German security agents, the Temporary Church Leadership twice openly challenged the puppet regime and its protectors. In November, 1942, sixty Protestant pastors sent a letter to Quisling condemning the despoliation and arrest of Jews as illegal and "in sharp conflict with the word of God." In May 1943, the church leadership protested the forced mobilization of Norwegian males for German labor gangs. Finally provoked beyond endurance, the occupation authorities arrested scores of Lutheran churchmen and effectively broke the back of the Protestant resistance.[3]

The November, 1942, protest against the persecution of Norway's Jews is an especially significant document because it raises the issue of modern Lutheran attitudes towards Jews, an important question considering Luther's own virulent opinions. The authors of the 1942 protest argued that Jews were the same as all men, that they possessed equal human value and deserved equal protection under the law. In good Lutheran fashion, the writers turned to Scripture for their authority and cited passages from Acts, Romans, and Galatians to prove their contention that the Bible "from cover to cover proclaims that all groups are of one blood." Luther's own fulminations in *About the Jews and Their Lies* merited no citation in the protest.[4]

All this is worth noting because Luther's hatred of Jews is commonly adduced as one contributing element to European, and specifically German, anti-Semitism. Those searching for antecedents to the Holocaust cannot ignore the typically excessive outbursts from Luther's pen against Jews. Given Luther's role in the development of German intellectual and cultural life, are we not justified in inferring some nexus between the violence of his literary anti-Semitism in the sixteenth century and the terribly literal Nazi anti-Semitism of the twentieth? Perhaps. But the Nowegian example shows that twentieth-century Lutherans are not compelled to heed 400 year-old polemics. The authority of Scripture — as Luther above all men would have had to concede — took precedence over mere human authors. Luther's brilliant and abusive pen cannot explain or excuse the behavior of his coreligionists after four centuries. A contemporary anti-Semitic Lutheran chooses to be an anti-Semite; in 1942 Norwegian Lutherans chose *not* to be anti-Semites.

In this connection it is useful to note the special Norwegian conditions that permitted the Lutheran leaders there to go as far as they did in publicly opposing Quisling. And we must also consider briefly the factors which determined the scale of the destruction visited upon Norway's tiny Jewish community.

Regarding the first question, we may inquire why the resistance leaders among the Lutheran churchmen were not dealt with more harshly. Most of the important opponents of the Quisling regime were not arrested until the spring of 1943, three years after the beginning of the occupation. and those incarcerated were usually spared the draconian treatments that the Nazis regularly imposed on their enemies elsewhere. Berggrav, for instance, after a brief stay in prison was consigned to a relatively comfortable house arrest from 1942 until his liberation at war's end.

There were two principal reasons for Nazi moderation toward the Norwegians. The first was racial. As Nordics and fellow Aryans, the Norwegians were regarded as appropriate human material for important tasks within Hitler's pan-Germanic empire. Himmler was especially anxious to attract Norwegian volunteers into the Waffen SS and to recruit Norweigan farmers as colonists for the vast spaces of depopulated Russia. The Germans were prepared to treat the Norwegians as racial allies, not as despised helots; thus the routine brutalities of Nazi occupation in Poland, Yugoslavia, or the Ukraine were not practiced in Norway.[5]

A second reason for German circumspection stemmed from an erroneous military calculation. Hitler feared, quite mistakenly, that the Allies planned to establish a second front in Norway. The Allies never seriously considered such a plan though the English staged occasional commando raids which deepened Hitler's apprehensions. Until the very end of the war the Germans mantained disproportionally large forces in Norway to guard against an Allied coup. Anxious to keep the population quiescent in what he regarded as an important theater of war, Hitler demonstrated a forebearance toward Norwegian stubbornness that he rarely exhibited elsewhere.

Geographical and political factors both figured significantly in determining the fate of the Jewish population after 1940. Half of Norway's Jews were killed in the course of the Holocaust. This is a substantially lower percentage than perished in another Western, "Nordic" country — Holland — where 75 percent of the Jews died. But it is twice as high a mortality rate as struck the Jews of France. What accounts for the Norwegian death toll?

Of the 1800 Jews living in Norway in 1940, about 900 were able to escape to Sweden with the assistance of sympathetic Christian Norwegians who incurred serious risks by helping their Jewish fellow citizens. Anti-Semitism was not an important force in a country where the culturally assimilated Jewish population constituted only six-one hundreths of one percent of the total. Contiguous Sweden offered a haven with a long border that could not be completely closed to Norwegian refugees. Here the Norwegian situation reminds one of Danish conditions. But there were important differences. Sweden was in fact distant. The Danes were able to save nearly all their Jews not only because they were determined to attempt to do so, but because of the happy circumstance that the Danish Jews were centered in one place — Copenhagen — a quick sea journey from Sweden. The Norwegian Jews also lived in their nation's capital, but Oslo offered no ready access to Sweden and was for all purposes a trap. The Norwegian Jews were unlucky, too, in that Quisling's police and party thugs actively assisted the Germans in rounding up Jews. Unlike Petain in France, Quisling refused to distinguish between the legal status of Jews with Norwegian citizenship and those bearing foreign passports who had already fled the Nazis once in Germany, Austria, and Czechoslovakia. Vichy at least refused to hand *French* Jews over to Eichmann; Quisling delivered up his Norwegian Jews without scruples.[6]

※

There remains the task of explaining the contrasting behavior of the German and Norwegian Protestant Establishments. We have noted a fundamental dissimilarity. Most German pastors supported, with varying degrees of enthusiasm, the National Socialist government; that support did much in the years immediately after 1933 to give respectability to the dictatorship. Most Norwegian pastors refused to support the *Nasjonal Samlung* government and actively protested its actions as being both unconstitutional and unchristian.

Part of the explanation of this dissimilarity lies simply in the fact that patriotism seemed to require different things of German Lutherans and Norwegian Lutherans. Protestant pastors in both countries were usually men of conventional patriotic views. German patriots, pastors included, resented the Treaty of Versailles — especially its portrayal of Germany as solely responsible for the First World War — and they deplored their country's diminished prestige in international affairs. There was nothing exceptional about these views; one did not have to be a man of the Right to entertain them. To the extent that Hitler promised to undo past injustices and then fulfilled his promises with extraordinary successes through 1938, he could count upon that public acquiescence born of restored national pride. Norwegian patriots, unburdened by any analogous collective anguish, required no political messiahs in the inter-war years and sought none. Whatever limited appeal the flattering Nazi doctrines of Nordic racial superiority may have had among Norwegians vanished on April 9, 1940, with the arrival of the invading German army. Thereafter the dictates of patriotism obliged Norwegians to resist the Germans and their Norwegian creatures.

But the obligations of patriotism aside, the behavior of the Norwegian pastors raises an intruiguing theological question: how could these pastors, as good Lutherans, dare resist the authority of the state? For Luther the political authorities are divinely instituted; to rebel against them is to act contrary to the will of God. Government, according to Luther "the most precious treasure and jewel on earth," must be obeyed even when it is unjust or capricious. Just as God commands the Christian to honor and obey his parents, so He also requires the Christian to submit to his prince. The wicked prince, no less than the good one, exercises a God-given power, and it is God, not man, who will sit in judgment of the prince. The Christian may appeal to the conscience of tyrants, but he must not rise up against them. He must continue to obey and, if necessary, suffer.[7]

Luther's political ideas did not develop *in vacuo*; his insistence upon the dignity of the secular arm reflects his rejection of the theocratic pretensions of late medieval Catholicism. And the historical experience of the Reformation confirmed for Protestant thinkers the necessity of preserving the state's authority against threats from below and outside. The great Protestant churches had developed in association with the emerging territorial state in England, Germany, the Netherlands, and Scandanavia. The growth of Protestantism was one aspect of the Western rejection of the universalism represented by the conflicting claims of the Holy Roman Empire and the Roman Catholic Church — a universalism imperfectly and only briefly achieved during the pontificate of Innocent III.

Lutheran churches were explicitly national or territorial institutions. So, in practice, were some of the local Catholic churches — in Castile, for example. But in principle these churches were not territorial or national but international. They were, in a word, catholic. Roman Catholicism was doctrinally indifferent to the creation of the territorial or nation state.

Lutheranism could not afford to be indifferent, for lacking the protection of the territorial state it would have been destroyed in its infancy. Without the intervention of Phillip the Magnanimous, Luther almost certainly would have perished on a Roman pyre. And without the patronage of the territorial princes across northern Europe who quickly perceived the practical uses of the new dispensation, Protestantism could not have enjoyed the rapid expansion it demonstrated through the second third of the sixteenth century. In Germany the permanent religious bifurcation of the country embodied by the Peace of Augsburg proclaimed the unambiguous nexus between the state and the Lutheran church. In the nineteenth century German Lutherans embraced the creation of the German Empire and saw in it the triumph of Protestant Prussia over Catholic Austria. The Lutheran Establishment identified itself closely with the conservative cultural and social ideals of the Hohenzollern Reich where anomalistically the Calvinist Kings of Prussia presided over the territorial Lutheran churches as *summus episcopus*.

The Austrian Catholic Hitler deftly manipulated the symbols of German nationalism and Protestantism in a fashion designed to gain the approval of the Lutheran Establishment. The ceremonial opening of the Reichstag in the Garnison Church in March, 1933, was a masterpiece of political choreography; there admidst the solemn paraphernalia of German High Protestantism and the Prussian military monarchy, Hitler publicly assumed the role of bearer of the state's most hallowed secular traditions. What could have been more natural, more in keeping with its traditions, than the submission of the German Protestant Establishment to the authority of this newly-consecrated prince? Not to have done so would have constituted an unimaginable discontinuity, a disavowal of the doctrine of the dignity of the temporal arm and a rejection of the Lutheran historical experience.

But if Hitler were the legitimate prince, the true vessel of national sovereignty, Vidkun Quisling, was manifestly not. He could make no plausible claim to a public mandate. It was Quisling, and not his opponents, who was the revolutionary, the destroyer of law and order, the rebel against God-given authority. The true prince was in London. Haakon VII, not Quisling, represented legitimate state, and therefore, divine authority. In resisting Quisling and his wicked undertakings the Norwegian Lutheran Church found its historical traditions and its ethical responsibilities to be in complete harmony. There was, happily, no crisis of divided loyalty. Allegiance to the true prince and a vigorous Christian conscience alike led Norwegian Protestants to defy the usurper.

NOTES

1. On the early relationship of the German Protestant churches and the National Socialist regime see Martin Broszat, *Der Staat Hitlers* (Munich, 1969), pp. 283-300.

2. I draw here on a paper by Shelley Baranowski, "From Rivalry to Repression: German Protestantism, Anti-Leftism, and Anti-Semitism, 1933," presented at the Third Annual Conference on the Holocaust, Millersville University, April, 1984.

3. This sketch of the activities of the Norwegian Lutheran Church is based on the paper by Samuel Abrahamsen, "The Relationship of Church and State During the German Occupation in Norway, 1940-1945," presented at the Third Annual Conference on the Holocaust, Millersville University, April, 1984.

4. The complete text of the letter may be found in Abrahamsen, "Relationship of Church and State," pp. 17-19 (typescript).

5. Regarding German wartime policies in Norway see Norman Rich, *Hitler's War Aims: The Establishment of the New Order* (New York, 1974), pp. 121-140.

6. For an excellent brief survey of the fate of the Jews in wartime Western Europe see Michael R. Marrus and Robert O. Paxton, "The Nazis and the Jews in Occupied Western Europe, 1940-1944," *Journal of Modern History*, 54, 4 (December, 1982), 687-714.

7. For a thorough discussion of Luther's political ideas see Paul Althaus, *The Ethics of Martin Luther,* trans. Robert C. Schultz (Philadelphia, 1972), pp. 112-155 *passim.*

The German Catholic Bishops and the Jewish Question:
Explanation and Judgment

Ethel Mary Tinnemann

Since the Catholic church in Germany had given up her right to political activity and to independent economic and social organizations, and had recognized the Nazi government as legitimate and deserving of obedience in 1933, the episcopacy remained the only Catholic organization capable of dealing with the government and of defending Catholics against state oppression. Most young men were in the armed forces or some type of government service by the late 1930s. Individual priests who could reach only a small section of the Catholic population would be jailed at once if they spoke; terrorism and a police system were generally effective against an individual opponent. Unfortunately the episcopacy lacked the experienced and skilled bureaucrats necessary for this task.

Of the twenty-seven German episcopal representatives in the annual conference held at Fulda in 1933, only a half dozen bishops played a major role in church-state relations during the Nazi period. The majority generally backed Adolf Cardinal Bertram, president of the conference, since they, too, desired no break with the state and wished to avoid the charge of treason or the re-incarnation of the 'stab in the back' legend. Most influential among the bishops were Archbishop Conrad Gröber of Freiburg, Michael Cardinal Faulhaber in Munich, Konrad Count von Preysing in Berlin, Clemens August Count von Galen in Münster, Johannes Dietz, who became bishop of Fulda in 1939, and Wilhelm Berning in Osnabrück. The latter and Heinrich Wienken, commissioner for the Fulda Conference, who became bishop in 1937, were supporters of Bertram and the negotiators with the government. Despite his status as a cardinal, Joseph Schulte in Cologne was very reserved in public pronouncements and generally supported Bertram, thus making a revision of the latter's policy almost impossible; Schulte likewise had a heart condition and died in March, 1941. His replacement, Joseph Frings, a supporter of Preysing's view, did not take office until May, 1942, and was too inexperienced to take a major part in episcopal differences.

While many Catholics suffered under Nazism, the Jews, about 1% of the population, suffered more, first by dismissal from jobs, and from terrorism against individuals. Following the April 1, 1933, boycott of Jewish business came the gradual exclusion of Jews from the economic and social life of Germany, thus forcing emigration until the doors were closed in 1941. The Nuremberg laws and the Reich Citizenship law of 1935 deprived the full Jews of citizenship and defined a full Jew as having three Jewish grandparents, irrespective of religion; a Mischling had one or two, was non-Jewish in religion and not married to a Jew; a Mischehen was a Jew married to an Aryan.[1] By 1936 all Jewish children irrespective of religion had to attend Jewish schools. In 1938 the Jews had to report all property, and Crystal Night of November 9-10, 1938, involved the destruction of the synagogues in most German towns and the vandalism of Jewish businesses and homes. In December, 1938, all Jewish property was confiscated. While deportations from Alsace, Baden, and the Saar to Southern France had taken place in July, 1940, the majority of full German Jews were deported to the East between October, 1941, and June, 1942, except for a few in defense plants. The Mischlinge and Mischehen as a general policy faced deportation only in early 1943 although some Catholic Jews were taken earlier, particularly if they had been active politically. For those deported, death from starvation, disease, and mass shootings began at once; the gas chambers were inaugurated in the spring of 1942.

Despite disliking the physical mistreatment of Jews in the prewar period, the German bishops saw no reason to intervene for Jews as distinct from Jewish Catholics who were Catholics, not Jews in the eyes of the church. As Bertram stated about the April 1 boycott, the economic struggle involved did "not relate closely to the interests of the church." Intervention would probably be unsuccessful and might bring "an evil interpretation"; besides the Jewish press had maintained silence on the persecution of Catholics in various countries.[2] Faulhaber of Munich feared that Jewish baiting could turn into Jesuit baiting although he declared that all Catholics should come forward against the persecution of Jews. The Catholic bishops had more important matters to consider: schools, existence of Catholic organizations, and sterilization. The Jews, moreover, could help themselves.[3] The bishops thus took no action against the Nuremberg laws or against the economic boycott and pressure that increased in intensity after the Olympic Games in 1936. No bishop expressed his opposition to Crystal Night despite the growing hostility of the official church to the Nazi regime. Only one priest, Bernhard Lichtenberg, prayed publicly for the Jews after the burning of the synagogues.

Between 1935 and 1941 the Catholic hierarchy endeavored to help the Jewish Catholics to emigrate, but they were not very effective owing to a failure to acknowledge or recognize the determination of the Nazis to get rid of all Jews by one means or another. They were also unable to mount an all-out financial and propaganda drive to get Jews and Jewish Catholics into foreign countries.

The only consistent expression of Catholic hostility to the regime came in the form of attacks on Nazi racist ideology since the latter fit within the religious arena granted to the church by the state. Before and after 1933 the clergy emphasized that God loved all men without distinction of nation or race and desired to save all. Human rights belonged to all as all were created by God. Man was saved not by German blood but by the blood of the crucified Savior, a Jew (until the Nazis forbade this identification). Consequently bishops and priests condemned the glorification of the Nordic race, emphasized the value of the Old Testament and Old Testament Jews, and maintained that Jewish converts to Christianity were Christians, not Jews. But modern Jews, according to the bishops, were no longer the chosen people, not because of race but because they had rejected Christ and in return were rejected by God.

Notwithstanding their hostility to the Nazi radical race ideology, the bishops were not likely to mount an open attack on Hitler, in part because of the split which developed within the episcopacy after 1936. By 1938 the issue of tactics — to negotiate and yield or to speak out in open conflict — was the major divisive factor among the bishops;

it remained so until 1944. Although Bertram personally did not wish to negotiate with Hitler and had no belief that negotiations would yield results, he urged a policy of negotiations and he himself wrote letters.[4] In 1936 the three cardinals favored negotiations, but Preysing considered a *modus vivendi* with the Third Reich an impossibility.

On the invitation of Hitler, Faulhaber met with the Nazi leader at Berchtesgaden in November, 1936; and in his summary for the bishops, he said that Hitler stressed the need for the church to "give up its struggle against the Nazi racial laws."[5] If the church continued the struggle, then National Socialism would have to work without the church. After all, said the Führer, it would be a small thing for the church to give up this attitude in comparison with his goals: to destroy Bolshevism and to make the German people happy.

While Hitler continued to speak emotionally on the position of the church with respect to racial laws, Faulhaber defended the bishops' obligation to speak out against dogmatic and moral errors. He agreed that the country needed to prevent injury to the community, but he differed as to method and asked about substituting internment for those afflicted with hereditary disease. Despite their disagreement in certain moral matters, Faulhaber thought that church and state could reach an accommodation. Overlooking Hitler's claim that the church was to blame for the hostile policy of the Nazi Party toward the church, Faulhaber acknowledged the statesmanlike qualities of Hitler, "a born sovereign."[6]

With the public reading of the papal encyclical, *Mit brennender Sorge (On the Church in Germany)*, March 22, 1937, church-state relations moved into open confrontation. The encyclical strongly condemned Nazi oppression of the church and denounced the divinization of race or state which perverted the order planned by God. "God's sun shines on every human face, so his law knows neither privilege nor exemption."[7] To the Nazis this was treason. Although the church had secretly printed the encyclical and used couriers to distribute it to the clergy, the Gestapo knew about it in advance and confiscated all printed copies.

Following the reading of the encyclical, Preysing began to speak out against the effort of the Party to de-Christianize Germany. This decision to speak occasioned the first serious rift between Preysing and Bertram as Preysing and Galen argued for a common German pastoral and Bertram favored continued negotiations. In October, 1937, Preysing called Bertram's negotiations over teacher education blackmail and refused to participate; he urged Bertram to avoid "delicate diplomacy" and said that attack was the best defense. To Bertram not to negotiate was to be resigned to the attack of the enemy; yet he could not name the values to be gained from negotiations. Responding to Bertram's fear that Catholics would have to face death without a priest, Preysing stated that the "time might come when people would die without a priest because they did not wish one."[8] Preysing, however, recognized that many Catholics would leave the church if a definitive break between church and state occurred. The power of the government against a single bishop was also evident in the ability of the Nazis to exile and effectively silence Bishop Johannes B. Sproll, who refused to vote in the election to approve the *Anschluss* and to elect delegates to the Reichstag.

Notwithstanding the episcopal differences, the Fulda letter of August 1938 to German Catholics spoke out strongly against the efforts of the Nazis to destroy the church, even to exterminate Christianity; and the bishops declared that one must obey God rather than man.[9] Unfortunately foreign affairs dominated men's thinking and most Catholics favored the *Anschluss* so that the letter lacked a powerful effect although it came from a united episcopacy. Reinhardt Heydrich, chief of the Gestapo, wrote that if the foreign successes had not occurred the Catholic church would have called forth the people to resist the state.[10]

With the spring of 1939 conflict between Preysing and Bertram surfaced again, this time over the congratulatory telegram sent by Bertram in the name of the bishops to Hitler on his fiftieth birthday, April 10. Although Faulhaber recognized that the Party did not really want peace, he thought that the bishops must act as if they did not see this and had suggested the telegram as a good-will gesture.[11] As the three cardinals pushed for improved relations, Preysing wrote the new pope to hold firm to the policy of *Mit brennender*

Sorge. He likewise expressed his concern to Bertram about the telegram sent in the name of the bishops, including the exiled Sproll.[12] Despite the telegram, the Nazis on April 18, 1939, ordered the closing of the remaining confessional schools.

The outbreak of war temporarily stilled the controversy, particularly as Pope Pius XII urged unity among the bishops. In April, 1940, the issue of a congratulatory letter to Hitler led to open conflict between Preysing and Bertram. This time Bertram had sent the letter in the name of the bishops without consulting them; he had also in the letter referred to the great successes of the last years although as in other letters he emphasized the loyalty of Catholics and complained about Party propaganda. He asked Hitler to remember that "our striving is not in contradiction to the program of the National Socialist Party and that it finds an echo in your own words of March 23, 1933, January 30, 1934, and your writing of April 28, 1937."[13] Hitler's response included the declaration that he was pleased that Bertram believed there was no contradiction between the church and the program of National Socialism. Preysing at this point resigned as press counselor to the Fulda conference, citing deep differences of opinion over the ecclesiastical-political situation.[14]

In this quarrel which reached a climax at the annual Fulda conference in August, 1940 (which now included the Austrian bishops), Gröber, Faulhaber, and Michael Rackl of Eichstätt had supported Preysing in the latter's demand for an open fight against National Socialism. Faulhaber, however, probably because of health, did not attend the conference and sent the following message which indicated a change of mind: "National Socialism was in 1933 a little brook which could have been guided easily into a Christian channel. Now it is a giant river and the great guilt of the bishops and their advisors is that they then let slip the opportunity to conquer National Socialism by compromise. If the church is to guide or turn the giant river today, she needs to compromise."[15]

Even Gröber was overcome by the bitterness of the quarrel which erupted at the conference and opposed the discussion of the letter to Hitler although Pius XII had written the bishops urging discussion of the issues. When Preysing reported to the assembly, he made no reference to the birthday letter but spoke about his resignation as press counselor and the totalitarian state, with which some believed they could reach accommodation. At the conclusion he referred to the pope's desire that the bishops debate controversial points.

Bertram responded that the bishops could discuss the letter if they wished and immediately left the hall. After a stormy meeting which brought many to tears, they decided against an open discussion. Although the majoirity supported Preysing, they felt that a clarification of the case was inadvisable and no longer necessry. Fearing that aggressive action might destroy the unity of the church and leave her open to destruction, they did not want Bertram to resign and believed that only through compromise could National Socialism be overcome. The only thing Preysing gained at this meeting was the rejection of a declaration expressing gratitude to God for the defense of the Fatherland. No Fulda pastoral was issued, and the split within the episcopacy continued, making a strong and unified public statement impossible. Even when Bertram resigned as president of the conference in 1942, his opposition to a statement was sufficient to block unified action.[16]

Thus the petition policy continued as the warfare against the Jews intensified. During 1941 and 1942 Preysing along with Gröber, Dietz, and Galen urged a stronger defense of church rights; and Preysing, Dietz, and Frings endeavored without success to get a united episcopal statement against the killing of innocent people merely because of race.[17] While evidently accepting the deportation of the Jews, although not the cruelties of transportation or the evacuation of Catholic Jews, Bertram in the name of the German bishops presented a petition, drafted by Preysing, in December, 1941, which spoke for divinely given rights of life, liberty, and property which foreign peoples had as members of the human race.[18] With most bishops seemingly having knowledge of the mass murder of Jews by mid summer or late fall, 1942, Bertram in the name of the bishops intervened and protested on several occasions from November, 1942, through the spring of 1944 over the deportation of Mischehen znd Mischlinge and about the cruelties and poor conditions in camps. In the spring of 1943 and again in 1944 Bertram threatened to speak publicly if his protests were not heeded.[19]

The only general pastorals, however, which indirectly referred to the Jews were the West German bishops' pastoral of December, 1942, and the so-called Decalogue pastoral of September, 1943. The former defended human rights which were independent of the will of man since they rested on eternal law. As the life of an unborn child or the life of the old and weak were sacred, so were the lives of foreign peoples. "Whoever bears a human countenance has rights, which no earthly power may take. . . . All the original rights man has, the right to life, to inviolability, to freedom . . . were not dependent on the state. They can and must not be denied to one not of our blood or of our image. A denial of such rights or even a cruel action against our fellow man is an injustice to foreigners and also to our own people."[20]

The Decalogue letter dealt with the Ten Commandments, of which the remarks on the fifth are pertinent. As usual the bishops encouraged the soldiers to fight for Western Civilization, but said that God's commandment forbade any earthly power from destroying the life of an innocent person; God alone gave and could take away life. "Killing is evil even if allegedly done in the interests of the common welfare"; the letter attacked not only euthanasia but the killing of innocent and disarmed war prisoners and "people of alien race and descent." The state could condemn to death only those worthy of death.[21] Certainly the average German Catholic probably understood the reference to the Jews, but in neither case did the bishops clearly state that the Nazis were killing Jews; nor were the pastoral letters an expression of a united episcopate, and some bishops omitted the phrase about race when reading the letter. Throughout the ten years of Nazi rule the bishops never urged action against unjust laws or measures, even against those which drastically affected Catholics. The Catholics were told to pray, to suffer, and to remain united with the church. Apparently, however, the protests and threat to speak in 1942 and 1943 saved some non-Aryan Catholics from deportation; they also postponed the deportation of other individuals so that the latter had less time to spend in concentration camps and, therefore, greater likelihood of survival.

Basic to understanding the failure of the German Catholics to act for the Jews is a perception of their general attitude. They shared in the latent anti-Semitism of most Germans and accepted the economic and social measures against the Jews as a means of reducing the power of Jewry in Germany and of promoting emigration. As Faulhaber stated in 1933: "We certainly want no dominance which stands in disproportion to the actual number of Jews."[22] Believing in Jewish wealth and the superior economic and political power of the Jews during the Weimar era, Catholics for the most part thought that Jews could defend themselves or emigrate; many associated the Jews with the free-thinkers and atheists whom the Catholics wanted the government to control. Since the majority of Catholics lived in rural areas and knew no Jews as friends or neighbors, they readily concurred with the Nazi idea that Jews were an alien people and possibly state enemies — communists — who should be encouraged to emigrate.[23]

Once the Germans accepted the idea that economic restrictions could rightfully be placed on a people who were different from most Germans in race and religion, then it was difficult for them to reject further steps to complete the separation of Jews from Germans. Few foresaw the ultimate consequences of this policy; and once the Jews were completely separated from the Germans, it was possible for the latter to succumb to the idea that Jews had really been resettled or that no one could do anything about the situation. Psychologically it was difficult for anyone to conceive of wuch a monstrous crime as the extermination of a people.

A theoretical defense of the Ten Commandments and the need to love all men could not undo the radical race ideology of the Nazis or inspire Catholics actively to aid the Jews. Regarding the Jewish problem as a confessional problem, the bishops felt no necessity to speak, particularly in the early years of the regime. The church's goal should be to maintain her identity so as to remain a voice for believers against the ideology of the Nazis. Catholics were also suffering, and the bishops perceived their major tasks as defending schools and religious institutions from confiscation, attacking the sterilization measures, and preventing the de-Christianization of youth through the exclusion of priests from religious instruction; on these issues the church had a legal right to speak. Christians, moreover, had no need to speak out for Jews who had killed Christ and were still hostile to Christianity. Yet Catholics did not hate Jews; the majority just felt no obligation to help them.

At the beginning of the Nazi regime the bishops hoped for accommodation between church and state. As ardent patriots, most Catholics wanted to share in the 'renewal' of Germany; and by 1935 most, if they were not outspoken opponents of the regime, had found jobs and could survive if they remained apolitical. If the bishops failed to speak out when the Nazis murdered the leader of Catholic Action, Erich Klausener, in the June 30, 1934, action, when the church still had a relatively free press and when Catholics were not in full support of the regime, they were unlikely to speak out later.

In harmony with the official Catholic policy in the late nineteenth century which favored monarchical or absolutist regimes rather than popularly based governments, German Catholics feared liberalism with its emphasis on individualism and anti-clericalism which German Catholics had experienced in the *Kulturkampf* of the 1870s. Never very enthusiastic about the Weimar government because of their anti-liberal viewpoint and the signing of the Versailles Treaty, the German Catholics in the late 1920s yearned for an authoritatian regime which would bring order and stability to Germany. Sharing with the laity these views, the Catholic hierarchy also belonged to a hierarchical structure and tradition and were for the most part members of the upper class; many bishops were very nationalistic and had acquired a militaristic outlook as World War I chaplains.

The episcopal background and tradition of respect for authority hindered the bishops from attacking the government. While they might assail the Nazi Party violations of the concordat and the rights of the church, they did not impugn Hitler and government officials except Alfred Rosenberg and a few other Party leaders associated with the racial ideology and with attacks on the church. With the exception of Preysing, the bishops lacked experience in government and a knowledge of the forms of government, and their traditions linked them with the authoritarian Nazi regime. Faulhaber's praise of Hitler's abstention from alcohol and nicotine within a short period after Crystal Night seems to indicate a certain naivete in the political realm.[24] The bishops, too, feared the power of the government and felt the need to accommodate themselves if the church was to survive. As already mentioned, Faulhaber frequently expressed the fear of Nazi Jew-baiting turning into baiting of Catholics. Bertram's decision for or against a proposed letter or petition could be easily influenced by a government accusation that the church was injuring the cause of Germany by her sharp criticism of Nazi policy.

It is no coincidence that the most outspoken and active Catholics were those who had a broad liberal education, some experience in government or political parties, pacifist or peace organizations, or those opposed to anti-Semitism: Preysing; Gertrud Luckner, highly educated convert from Quakerism, member of the peace movement, who aided Jews physically and spiritually until she was incarcerated in Ravensbrück in 1943; Heinrich Krone, active in relief and emigration work, formerly active in the Center Party and in organizations opposed to anti-Semitism, imprisoned after the 1944 attack on Hitler; Bernhard Lichtenberg, pre-war pacifist, and a priest who actively interceded for the Jews, prayed publicly for them after Crystal Night, and directed the Berlin welfare organization until he was imprisoned by the Nazis in 1941; Fransiskus Stratmann, dominican who had to flee Germany and Holland because of his assistance to Jews and who spent the war years in the Vatican; Margarete Sommer, with a background in sociology and in the diocesan pastoral care of women, who became head of the relief services in the diocese of Berlin after Lichtenberg's imprisonment; and Benedikt Kreutz, president of the Association of German Charities.[25]

Another aspect of the episcopal problem in the prewar years was that the Nazi attack on the Jews came in stages. Individual Jews suffered in the early years of the regime, but the majority could survive or emigrate. For this Catholics were probably happy.

Following the outbreak of war, the nationalism, patriotism, and anti-Bolshevism of the bishops and Catholics made it almost impossible for them to attack the government, particularly after the assault on Russia although the bishops recognized Nazi determination to destroy the church after a victorious war. It is difficult to assail one's country in the midst of a war, especially if one's country is losing; and the most critical period of Jewish deportations from Germany occurred when Germans were very concerned with German defeats and with the deaths of family members and friends in both December, 1941 and December, 1942. Since many bishops considered Russian Communist leaders as Jewish, they were doubly opposed to aiding the enemy. As is evident from Faulhaber's notes in March, 1943, and in the discussion of the December, 1941, memorandum-letter controversy, the bishops greatly feared the use of the 'stab in the back' legend against the church. Faulhaber explained the failure of the bishops to intervene by saying: "We could do the opponents of the Catholic church no greater favor than to mount the great guns. Now when they are in difficulties, would they revive at once the story of the 'stab in the back', I think they wait for that opportunity."[26]

Linked with the war situation was the belief that speaking would do no good. Would Catholics follow; Since the Catholics lacked lay organizations to provide lay leaders with a forum and constituency, it was up to the bishops to provide leadership. In 1938, knowing that Catholics were at least latently anti-Semitic and that they now had jobs, Preysing doubted that they would follow if the bishops broke completely with the state. In 1942 and 1943 Catholics were stretched to the limit, and most young men were at the front. Could the bishops really expect that the women, children, old people, and the soldiers on leave who attended the Sunday Masses would leap up to attack the government? Could they expect soldiers in the East to risk death by refusing to obey orders?

Too long had the bishops preached obedience to authority and that priests and lay Catholics should leave negotiations and speaking to the bishops who had never pointed to Hitler as responsible for the evils of the state. Knowing that the Dutch bishops had spoken in vain and that the Scholls had been executed, the bishops may have feared to endanger the few Jews left and the non-Aryan Catholics. Yet the bishops had powerful weapons against injustice within their grasp and were feared by Hitler.[27] As a minority but as the largest cohesive group of Christians in Germany their support for the war was essential. The imposition of an interdict or at least a refusal to allow anything more than the minimum in the form of church services might have caused the state to relax its oppression of the church rather than be faced with discontented Catholics.

Basic to the episcopal approach after 1940 was the fear of disunity which would open themselves and the church to a successful Nazi attack. Led by an old and ailing bishop who opposed any public effort for the Jews or even for the Jewish Catholics and who played off one bishop against the other in the fight with Preysing over tactics, the bishops who urged more vigorous action were unwilling to challenge Bertram.[28]

Born in 1859, Bertram had to acquire some of his seminary training outside Prussian territory because of the *Kulturkampf*; and he did not want ever again to see the German people without priests. After acquiring his doctorate in theology, he became a canon lawyer and was by avocation a church historian. Transferred to Breslau in 1914, he was made a cardinal and in 1920 became presiding official of the Fulda Conference. A shy, studious man with limited ability as a speaker, Bertram chose the well-argued written petition to the government rather than a challenging sermon.

Autocratic in outlook and opposing the expression of ideas contradictory to his, Bertram preferred that even the bishops in Fulda listen to him and not discuss the issues. Tending also to want subordinates who agreed with him, he worked most closely with Berning and Wienken. The papal nuncio. Msgr. Cesare Orsenigo, whose monsignor-secretary was a party member, was no competitor for the authority of the church in Germany and also opposed a break with the state. Because of their belief that Orsenigo spoke for Rome, some bishops accepted this policy of negotiation. For his part, Wienken was a man of good will but blind to the character of the National Socialist state and critical of the clergy who criticized the state.[29]

Like most bishops, Bertram tended to recognize the existing state as legitimate and deserving of obedience in everything not against the laws of God. The anti-Christian character of a state, according to Bertram, was no grounds for dispensing its citizens from obedience; and he opposed the reading of episcopal sermons or letters forbidden by the Gestapo. He firmly believed that a break with the regime would bring worse things for Catholics. While he read and defended the papal encyclical of 1937, he feared to stir the anger of the Nazi hierarchy by attacking the core of National Socialist ideology — its racial program. In 1943 he still claimed to have insufficient information about the sufferings of non-Aryan Catholics for a petition, and in September, 1943, he wrote Faulhaber that "intervention for Poles or Jewish prisoners butt against unconquerable obstacles."[30] The long range interests of the church would not be served by such intervention.

Wilhelm Berning was a member of the Prussian state council and remained so notwithstanding the desire of the Vatican that he resign. In a 1935 memorandum he declared that he had no objection to National Socialism as a state form but only to the New Heathendom promoted by it; he believed that the Nazis would spare the church and that National Socialism and Catholicism could be harmonized. Above all he opposed an open fight with the Nazis. Catholics hostile to the Nazis made much of Berning's visit to a concentration camp in his area in 1936 where prisoners had built a canal. Following a tour of the area, he expressed his admiration. "Here must all be brought who yet doubt the rebuilding work of the Third Reich. What others neglected earlier has today been begun here." He spoke to the prisoners about the "obligation enjoined by faith to obedience and loyalty to nation and government," shared a glass of beer with the guards and uttered a "three-fold Sieg Heil to Führer and Vaterland."[31] During the war years he continued to back Bertram's petition policy.

Cardinal Faulhaber, born in 1869 to a farmer-baker family, was able to attend the local Gymnasium through the aid of the parish priest and later the junior seminary. During his one-year service with the local militia he almost decided for a military career since he liked the discipline and the opportunity offered to one with his leadership ability. He returned, however, to the seminary and was ordained in 1892. Intellectually brilliant, he did archival studies in the Vatican and then taught Old Testament exegesis and Biblical theology at the university until he became bishop of Speyer in 1910.

When World War I broke out, Franziskus Cardinal Bettinger of Munich put Faulhaber in charge of the military pastoral work to which the latter gave himself heart and soul. Upon the sudden death of the archbishop in 1917, the Bavarian state government used its influence to have Faulhaber named to that position and in 1921 to have him promoted to the cardinalate. A confirmed nationalist and monarchist, Faulhaber never completely recovered from the capitulation of the Bavarian monarchy; and he always remained reserved toward he Weimar Republic although he supported it and denounced Nazi ideology when the dangers from the left and right appeared in the late 1920s. His reserve toward Weimar did not depend solely on his royalist views; he feared the centralism of the republic and viewed the central government in Berlin as "red, Protestant, and socialist."[32] As with so many of the bishops, he possessed no understanding of the parliamentary form of party government and easily became disgusted with the party squabbling of the Weimar Republic and its seeming inability to provide order and an effective government.

Perhaps because of his arrival at power rather early by church standards and because of his intellectual capability, he ran the diocesan administration and the meetings of the Bavarian bishops in an autocratic fashion. He had no counselor who could influence him and reigned over the conference of Bavarian bishops as a true prince-bishop. Preysing remarked that "Faulhaber sees himself constantly in a thousand mirrors of self-reflection."[33]

Blind to the influence of Hitler for evil, Faulhaber in February, 1933, reminded the people that the state's authority came from God, not the people; and the citizens must obey the government which in turn should limit the activity of the Godless and Communists. Unless the state violated the laws of God and the church, the citizens were obliged to support the national community and to take no part in revolution.[34] Although he helped draft *Mit brennender Sorge,* he was lastingly affected by his meeting with Hitler in November, 1936 and never took a position against the state or Party and always distinguished between Hitler and his followers.

In his 'yes and no' sermon of February, 1937, he said that the church had given its yes to the new German government, the "highest moral power on earth." The church had made the concordat to obtian peaceful relations, but the state was violating it and attempting to de-Christianize Germany. Yet so long as the bishops tried to improve relations under the concordat, the laity and clergy should keep their opinions to themselves. Acknowledging that some people were asking why the church should keep the condordat since she would hang with or without it, Faulhaber claimed that the church had much to lose if the concordat was dropped: her official legal character, holy days, religious instruction in the schools, and the theological faculties of the universities. In conclusion he asserted that the church would be loyal to its 'yes'. Thus he favored negotiations and had no desire to be known as an opponent of the regime.[35]

Judging by his correspondence, Faulhaber felt no need to speak or act for the Jews and only for the non-Aryan Catholics in the form of a petition for mitigation of the harsh conditions of transport. As spiritual fathers of these Catholics, the bishops owed them this; but like Bertram, Faulhaber considered as hopeless any intervention with the Nazi government for people of Jewish descent.[36] So far as the documentation reveals he did not speak publicly for the Jews except in his Advent sermons of 1933. Whether from illness, personal inclination, or out of deference to Bertram, he did not take a strong position of leadership among the bishops after 1940 although he supported Preysing's effort for a stronger episcopal stand in 1941 and delivered the Decalogue letter.

The most powerful speaker for church rights and the right to life, freedom, and property, Galen, a cousin of Preysing, was born in 1878 and became bishop of Münster in 1933. It was primarily Galen's sermons which forced the Nazis to drop their euthanasia program and to curb the confiscation of religious institutions in the fall of 1941; earlier he had stimulated the peasants to bring about the re-instatement of the crucifixes in the schools of his diocese. In 1936 Galen was the first bishop publicly to condemn the killing of Erich Klausner, leader of Catholic Action, "whose fate had long been felt as unatoned injustice."[37] Allowing that Hitler might not have known of the plan to kill Klausner, Galen charged that the government had not provided a satisfactory explanation and the guilty had not been punished.

Notwithstanding Galen's conflict with the state, it is difficult to arrive at a clear understanding of his position toward the state. He was a nationalist with close ties to the military and probably closer to the Third Reich than to Weimar; he hated both parliamentarianism and Marxism and publicly expressed his joy over Hitler's break with the Soviet Union in 1941. He likewise favored Japan which could keep Communism from the East. When trying to prove the loyalty of Catholics to the regime in 1934, Galen claimed that "neither imperial Germany nor the Weimar Republic represented the divine order for states";[38] but Catholics who opposed secularism and liberalism supported the lesser of two evils. They did not hanker after a return to the Weimar days. According to Preysing, Galen had too great respect for authority which came from God to reject Bertram's position. Nor would he remain firm in opposition to the state; he was overly concerned with the Nazi charge of church hostility to the state.[39] Nevertheless, if anyone had asked Catholics during the Nazi period who was the most outspoken bishop against Nazi oppression of the church, the name given would have been Galen.

To Galen revolt against authority was rebellion against God. When his general vicar was exiled from Oldenburg, Galen submitted. "We stand under force and we accommodate ourselves to force even if we cannot recognize the measures as justified."[40] What Galen ordered until the vicar could return was the non-ringing of church bells and the omission of church prayers for government officials. Never did they wish to "withdraw the power of the church from the state."[41]

To him the Jewish issue was apparently a minor matter. In April, 1940, he delivered a sermon which spoke of the dangers to faith and referred to Jews in a negative fashion, asking the congregation if it would be said of the Germans as of the Jews that the Savior came and they did not accept him. He then pointed to the courage of the Apostles against hostile Jewry and heathendom. In August, 1941, he again referred to God's rejection of the Jews because of their rejection of his Son and asked about God's possible rejection of Germans who had rejected his law.[42]

In October, 1941, however, he intervened with local officials for non-Aryan Catholics in respect to the wearing of the star and against the hardness of evacuation. As a member of the West German Bishops he delivered the December, 1942, pastoral, and a pastoral letter at the end of April spoke of neighborly love which must embrace all men and exclude no one, even enemies; he, too, delivered the Decalogue letter.[43]

Inclined like most bishops to an authoritarian type of government, Conrad Gröber of Freiburg went further than most in his early support of National Socialism; in 1933 he became a member of the Party for a short time and supported Catholic membership in the Party so as to direct it. He was an ardent supporter of Pacelli's desire for a concordat and urged priests to avoid criticism of leading individuals or of the views they represented. Ambitious for leadership he worked to improve relations with the Nazis until horrifed church groups prevailed upon the Vatican to stop Gröber's acitvities.[44] By 1935, however, Gröber had begun to attack the state for its treatment of Catholics and for its violation of the moral law; but he maintained that Catholics were loyal to the state and preached submission to legal authority except in the case of a violation of God's law.

Perhaps the fear of Communism became more dominant in his thinking in the 1940s when he opposed open conflict between church and state. He urged Germans to remain united in their fight against Communism in 1942 and 1943 when the misfortune of a lost war against Bolshevism was a possibility. Believing that it was better to be outside the concentration camps preaching than silent inside, he warned the priests against listening to foreign broadcasts and to keep their opinions to themselves. Probably because he continued to speak up for church rights and to attack the religious-moral errors of National Socialism, particularly the promotion of sterilization and euthanasia, the Nazis continued to view him as a leading opponent of National Socialism. But within the episcopal circle he drew back from open conflict with the state.

Although Gröber had attacked the racial ideology of the Nazis, had proclaimed that all peoples were one and that no one could hate other peoples, and had thought that the church should speak for the Catholic non-aryans at the time of the April 1, 1933, boycott, he still believed that a nation might protect its original racial strand by means within the divine and natural law. In late 1943 he spoke about the devleopment of Christianity from Jewry which became unworthy after the crucifixion perpetrated by Jews; the Jews also had links with the Communists.[45]

Yet he had appealed to the pope, to Caritas, and to Wienken for help for non-Aryan Catholics in Gurs, France. When Luckner was arrested in March-April, 1943, Gröber worked very hard, if unsuccessfully to gain her release; and according to Luckner, the archbishop knew of and supported her efforts to aid the non-Aryan Catholics.[46] Among the important topics for religious instruction, a diocesan conference in the fall of 1942 listed the creation of all men by God so that everyone who bore a human countenance had equal rights. He delivered the West German pastoral in December, 1942, but his preaching in late 1942 and 1943 stressed the importance of the war against Bolshevism and for Germany and Christianity.[47]

Bishop Antonius Hilfrich of the diocese of Limburg, which included the city of Frankfort, presents a rather confused image but perhaps one typical of the average bishop. Although he had endeavored to separate modern Jews from Old Testament Jews in his sermon of February 6, 1939, he pleaded with the nuncio in 1941 to intervene for non-Aryan Catholics who had been deported from Frankfort under frightful conditions; he also asked Wienken to intervene with the government. At the end of January, 1942, his pastoral proclaimed that while men differed as to race they were all made in the image of God with dignity and God-given rights of life, freedom, and property. After reminding his listeners of the fifth commandment and condemning the killing of the innocent, he demanded that the government release individuals wrongfully imprisoned. He told the soldiers that they must obey the laws of God and asked his people to do unto others as they would like done to themselves. He was thus the first bishop to speak publicly for men of a different race although the reference by inference was to baptized Jews. His other letters in 1942 and 1943 followed the general pastorals already cited, but the Decalogue letter was not read in his diocese until January, 1944. At one time Hilfrich sought Vatican financial support for non-Aryan Catholics in his diocese, another instance of the apparent belief of the bishops that only the pope or his representative could achieve anything with respect to the German Jews.[48]

Of all the bishops, manuscript evidence indicates that only Preysing, Dietz, and Frings recognized the episcopal obligation to speak for general human rights and in particular for the Jews. They felt for the non-Aryan Catholics as human beings and wanted to help them, not merely for the sake of appearances or historical judgment; but they could not overcome Bertram's ability to block a common statement. Bertram did not even stand up for non-Aryan Catholics against the star-order, and he continued his protests to the government despite his and Faulhaber's recognition in November, 1941, that petitions in favor of non-Aryans would be unavailing with a government which blindly accepted the racial law and lacked a foundation in supernatural faith. Incapable of speaking up against the government, they felt helpless and so without obligation.[49]

When Frings replaced Schulte, he helped draft the West German pastoral of December, 1942, and the Decalogue letter and in general he supported Preysing. In June and December, 1943, he preached against racial hate by saying: "Whoever kills an innocent and noncombatant intentionally . . . who takes from them life only because they belong to a foreign people, he sins against God's commandment, 'thou shalt not kill'."[50] A sermon in March, 1944, stated that no one should "lose his life or property if he is innocent, perhaps because he belongs to a foreign race. That can only be characterized as an injustice which cries to Heaven."[51]

Preysing, one of the younger bishops, was born in 1880 in Bavaria into a family which was politically active in the Center Party, and became the major opponent of Bertram's policy. Having obtained a broadly based education in literature, art, and foreign languages, he studied law and then served the Bavarian government as a foreign representative in Rome. Returning home to study for the priesthood, he was ordained in 1912 and became secretary to Cardinal Bettinger. When Faulhaber became archibishop in 1917, he named Preysing preacher in the cathedral and a member of the diocesan administration. During this period Preysing came to know Pacelli, the papal nuncio; and soon after Pacelli became secretary of state at the Vatican, Preysing was named bishop of Eichstätt in 1932. In 1935 he took over the Berlin diocese, which was a new diocese in a predominantly

Protestant area and part of the archdiocese governed by Bertram.

Unlike most of the bishops Preysing was an opponent of Hitler from the beginning and saw in him the source of all evil in the Nazi state. Although he saw no occasion for speaking out in Eichstätt where the local Nazis did not cause the church much trouble, he had contacts with the Konnersreuth circle, which included Fritz Gerlich, publisher of *Gerade Weg,* who later died in a concentration camp, and Ingebert Naab, Capuchin, who had to flee Germany. During the war Preysing occasionally met members of the Kreisau circle, another center of intellectual opposition to National Socialism.[52]

Because of the danger to Catholics and because of the time needed to accustom himself to Berlin, Preysing did not begin to speak out against Nazi attacks on the church until the summer of 1937, when he became convinced that negotiations with the state were no longer possible. While favoring the *Anschluss,* he was not dazzled by it or by the success of the lightning war and not split by scruples of loyalty as were Bertram, Galen, and other bishops. As a very reserved individual who did not possess the fighting nature of Galen or his ability as a preacher, Preysing's greatness appears only in the written documents. Unlike most bishops he was not authoritarian in dealing with his subordinates.[53]

Another approach to understanding Preysing's position is to consider his support of Msgr. Bernhard Lichtenberg, a priest noted for his internationalism and pacifism and for his prayers for the Jews after Crystal Night. In 1938 Preysing named Lichtenberg provost of the cathedral chapter and head of the welfare organization. When the latter was imprisoned in 1941, Preysing tried to gain his release and asked the congregation to pray for "one who so often has proclaimed the word of God here and is now imprisoned."[54] After Lichtenberg's death in 1943, Preysing praised those who lived by their principles and became victims to justice in the concentration camps and praised him for speaking the truth even when he was forbidden to speak. Preysing himself took over the leadership of the welfare organization and supported Sommer in her efforts to aid the non-Aryan Catholics and to keep them from being deported.

As bishop of Berlin, where many of the remaining Jews had congregated, Preysing became a key figure in the charitable work for the non-Aryan Catholic residents in that city. He worked very hard to keep Mischlinge and Mischehen from evacuation in November and December, 1943. According to Msgr. Erich Klausener, Preysing protested almost every measure hostile to the Jews to the Reich Chancery and to the responsible ministries. Through an Evangelical pastor he applied pressure on Bertram for a common letter to be read from Catholic and Evangelical pulpits in case the divorce of the Mischehen was announced by the government (to allow the government legally to deport the Jewish partner); Preysing then used the letter in his protest and thus saved thousands of Jews married to Aryans.[55] He contributed personal and episcopal funds to the welfare work and was the moving force in the effort to objtain a common episcopal statement between 1941 and 1943. Preysing probably sent Margarete Sommer's letters of February and July, 1942, about the situation of the deported Jews on to Bertram.

Prior to the pastoral letters of December, 1942, and September, 1943, Preysing in May, 1928, spoke of "true Christian love which did not stop at the limits of a nation; it was unessential whether a neighbor was . . . sinner or holy, he was created by God and therefore was owed love by his fellow creatures. The life of every man had value."[56] In November, 1942, a pastoral for his diocese spoke of the need to love all men, all of whom had the image of God in their souls; this love could not exclude anyone even if he was a member of another race. Nor was it permitted to deprive members of foreign races of thier rights: freedom, property, and marriage.[57]

With the clearest understanding of the Jewish question, Preysing apparently lacked the will to speak out clearly in the light of episcopal disapproval or in the light of the hopelessness of the situation and the danger to the non-Aryan Catholics. As a Protestant city with few Catholics, Berlin did not offer Preysing fruitful ground in which to sow his ideas. The bishop also found his hands somewhat tied in that as a subordinate to Bertram in the archdiocese he had no authority to write to other bishops suggesting various measures. Even the strongest bishop looked to the pope for action rather than speaking out himself.

If no common pastoral on behalf of the Jews was possible, could some bishops or a bishop have helped the Jews? Sermons by an individual bishop would reach very few Catholics, only those at the Mass at which he first spoke; he would then probably be whisked off to jail. Yet his imprisonment might have aroused Catholics to face the need to do something about the mass murder of Jews. Although the priests were very anti-Nazi in 1942 and 1943 and generally hoped for a German defeat as a means of destroying Nazi power, there was no way for the priests to act in unison; one priest in opposition was soon taken off to prison. Thousands of screaming women gained the release of their non-Aryan husbands in February, 1943,[58] but the evidence scarcely indicates that German Catholics would have done the same for the Jews in general. Thus the bishops lacked an effective power base in the German people for a campaign against the extermination policy, and no fiery speaker as Galen in the euthanasia policy arose to spark resistance. Having not urged any type of resistance prior to the war, the bishops in all likelihood could not have galvanized Catholics into action to save the Jews when their own friends and relatives were dying on the Eastern front. The Catholics, like most Germans, were generally unaccustomed to active pariticipation in politics.

In spite of the apparent hopelessness of the situation, should the bishops or a bishop have issued a pastoral denouncing the killing of the Jews by Germans and urged non-cooperation with the government? If Preysing had spoken out clearly in the fall of 1942 or even in 1943 and called things by their right names as he had wanted Bertram to do in 1937, he very likely would have been arrested without achieving the desired result. The Nazis might have also deported all the remaining Jewish Catholics. Should he have risked this and hoped that his pastoral would reach foreign countries so that the latter would act? Perhaps his speaking and imprisonment might have led one or two other bishops and Pius XII to speak. In 1943 and 1944 American and British Jews tried to stimulate their governments to rescue Jews in the East through exchange of prisoners or gifts of trucks and money; there was also talk of bombing railroad tracks leading to death camps. The American and British position, however, was that only with military victory could the Jews by saved. Yet if Preysing's imprisonment and death could have led Pius XII to mount a forceful public attack on the Nazi Jewish policy, possibly American bishops might have led Catholics to join American Jews in applying pressure on their government.

Since the best informed bishops were Bertram and Preysing and since Bertram was by experience and upbringing incapable of speaking, it is on Preysing that the judgment falls. He had the most knowledge and saw the issue of human rights in the Jewish question. If he had spoken in December, 1942, he would probably have achieved nothing for the German Jews; most were already deported; and he might have endangered the Jewish Catholics. Unless he could have reached the army officers, the chances of saving the Jews in the East were practically nil. Yet if his words had received international attention, something might have been done to force Great Britain and the United States to act in favor of the Jews. Actually to achieve anything substantial in favor of the Jews, the bishops would have had to speak before the war; and this was not in their character or background.

Because of the many 'ifs' involved, it is almost impossible to condemn Preysing. To condemn the Berlin bishop, one must also believe that individuals must speak for human rights and for what they know is according to the law of God whether anything will be achieved and regardless of the possibility of causing injury to other individuals. Certainly the Evangelical church did not speak, but the Catholic church as an international church possessed greater freedom from excessive German nationalism and government control and generally had a more international background which should have opened her eyes to the evils of Nazi oppression. The British and American governments share in the guilt for the failure to prevent the destruction of the European Jews, but the Catholic church, unlike most nations in the 1940s, claimed to speak for human and moral rights. If Preysing had spoken it would have been to the glory of the church in Germany and to the support of universal human rights and the brotherhood of man. But this would have asked of Preysing a vision he did not have.

NOTES

1. Although the so-called Aryan race does not exist and although the church did not accept the idea of a superior Aryan race, she sometimes used the language of the day in Germany in her correspondence; and the term, *non-aryan* in this monograph will at times be used to indicate a person of Jewish or semi-Jewish origin.

2. Bertram to archbishops, 31 March, 1933, Gröber NS 10 (Erzbeisshöfliches Archiv Freiburg (hereafter cited as Gröber); Lutz-Eugen Reutter, *Katholische Kirche als Fluchthilfer im Dritten Reich* (Hamburg: Paulus Verlag, 1971), p. 37 (hereafter cited as Reutter, KK); Ludwig Volk, *Der bayerische Episkopat und der Nationalsozialismus 1930-1934*, Commission for Contemporary History, series B, vol. 1 (Mainz: Matthias Grünewald, 1965), p. 77 (hereafter cited as CCH for Commission).

3. Ludwig Volk, ed. *Akten Kardinal Michael von Faulhabers* (1917-1945, 2 vols., CCH, series A, vols. 17 and 26)Mainz: Matthias Grünewald, 1975-1978), 1: 505, no. 300 Faulhaber to Rev. Alis Wurm, 8 April, 1933; pp. 596-697, Faulhaber to Bavarian episcopacy, 5 April, 1933 (hereafter cited as Volk, Akten). A month later in answering a letter Faulhaber explained that the Bavarian pastoral contained no statement on the Jewish question since a "short pastoral message cannot go into all the questions which are certainly in themselves important . . . which, however, in comparison with other issues of the present rank second." (Volk, *Akten,* 1: 725-726, no. 316, to Prof Theodor Steinbuchel, 18 May, 1933).

4. Walter Adolph, *Geheime Aufzeichnungen aus dem nationalsozialistischen Kirchenkampf (1935 1943,* ed. Ulrich von Hehl, CCH, Series A, vol. 28 (Mainz: Matthias Grünewald, 1979), no. 4, pp. 8-9, 12, 14-17, 10-14 May, 1936; no. 25, p. 73, 3 April, 1937 (hereafter cited as Adolph, Aufzeichnungen).

5. Volk, *Akten*, 2: 187, no. 572, 5 November, 1936.

6. *Ibid.*, pp. 184-194; 561/2c, pp. 129-137, Diözesanarchiv Limburg (hereafter cited as Limburg).

7. Claudia Carlen IHM, ed. *The Papal Encyclicals 1903-1939,* 5 vols. (Wilmington, North Carolina: McGrath, 1981), 3: 527.

8. Adolph, *Aufzeichnungen,* no. 113, p. 219, 14 January, 1938, no. 84, pp. 173-177, 20 October, 1937; Preysing memorandum, IA 25 B no. 52 Biblioteka Kapitulna Breslau (hereafter cited as Br).

9. 1938 Fulda Pastoral, Wu 65/42 acc. 32/1973, no. 894, Staatsarchiv Sigmaringen.

10. Heinz Boberach, *Berichte des SD und des Gestapo über Kirchen und Kirchenvolk in Deutschland 1934-1944* (Mainz: Matthias Grünewald, 1971), no. 14, pp. 306-307; Adolph, *Kardinal Preysing und zwei Diktaturen: Sein Widerstand gegen die totalitäre Macht* (Berlin: Morus Verlag, 1971), 135-136;

Hanns Kerrl, minister of church affairs, to Preysing, 26 January, 1939, Paderborn, XXII, Erzbistums-Archiv Paderborn (hereafter cited as Paderborn).
11. *Actes et Documents du Saint Siège relatifs à la seconde Guerre mondiale,* vol. 2, *Lettres de Pie XII aux Evêques allemands, 1939-1944,* ed Pierre Blet et al. (Vatican City: Libreria Editrice Vaticana, 1966), 387-388, Aide Memoir Bertram, 4 March, 1939; 398, Aide memoire Faulhaber, 5 March, 1939 (hereafter cited as Actes et Documents).
12. *Actes et Documents,* 2:70, no. 6, ft. 2, Spring, 1939; Walter Nachlass, 18c, Preysing to Bertram, 1 April, 1939, Pius XII to Preysing, 9 April, 1939, CCH, Bonn; Schulte Pastoral, 23 April, 1939, Limburg, 561/5c, p. 75 and ft. 11.
13. Bertram to Hitler, 10 April, 1940, Gröber Nachlass 20; *Actes et Documents,* 2:85-89, no. 16, Pius XII to bishops, 20 July, 1939; Pfarrer Notbund, 1940, Paderborn XXII, 9, Paderborn.
14. Hitler to Bertram, 28 April, 1940, Möser Nachlass 2, Diözesanarchiv Mainz; Preysing to Bertram, 6 May, 1940, Br IA 25 Z no. 18; also Adolph, Nachlass, 18c.
15. Heydrich to Rosenberg, 10 September, 1940, NS 8, Akten der Kanzlei Rosenberg, Bundesarchiv, Koblenz (hereafter cited as BA); Adolph, *Kardinal Preysing,* p. 162; R58/1099, Akten der Geheimen Staatspolizeiamtes, pp. 7-11, Heydrich's analysis, 20-22 August, 1940, BA; Adolph, *Aufzeichnungen,* no. 134, p. 240, 19 March, 1938.
16. Adolph, *Kardinal Preysing,* pp. 159-162; Adolph, *Aufzeichnungen,* no. 146, pp. 273-275, 10 October, 1940; Adolph, Nachlass 18c, Bertram's conversation, 4 April 1944; Heydrich to Rosenberg, 10 September, 1940, NS 8, no. 256, pp. 24-25; BA; Volk, *Akten,* 2:684-685, no. 789, Buchberger to Faulhaber, 25 August, 1940; Volk, "Adolf Kardinal Bertram (1859-1945):, separate printing from *Zeitgeschichte in Lebensbildern: aus den deustschen Katholizismus des 20. Jahrhunderts,* vol. 1, edited by Rudolf Morsey (Mainz: Matthias Brünewald, 1973), p. 284.
17. Volk, Akten, 2:838, no. 845c, Reasons for the necessity of a pastoral letter, 15 November, 1941, 826-827, no. 845c, 827-835, no. 845a, draft of a letter, 836-837, no, 845b, Guidelines for publication of pastoral, 853, no. 849, 25 November, 1941, 915, no. 886, report of Committee [A Rösch] 3 April, 1942. Robert Leiber thought that Rösch was the compiler of report (Volk, *Akten,* 2:914, ft. 1).
18. Bertram to Dr. Hans Lammers of Reich Chancery with request to give to Hitler, 10 December, 1941, Br I A 25 D no. 1, also Limburg 561/2F, pp. 211-219.
19. Bertram to Reich ministers, 11 January, 1944, and 29 January, 1944, Br IA 25 Z no. 136, 19 November, 1943, Br IA 25 Z no 136, Limburg 561/21, pp. 113-114. Knowledge: Letter 2/18/41, Br IA N no. 12, Sommer

report, Br IA J no. 12, letter, 8/24/43, Br IA 25 Z no 136, "Bericht über die Abwanderung der Juden," Archiv des Bistums Berlin, pp. 1-23; ch. 4 of unpublished manuscript, "Tradition, Division, Stalemate: The Catholic Church in Germany and the Jewish Question during the Nazi Period," by E. M. T.

20. West German pastoral, 13 December, 1942, A O 1.2, Bistumsarchiv Münster (hereafter cited as BAM); Adolph, Nachlass, 18b Nachtrage, 13 December 1942; Adolph, *Kardinal Preysing*, p. 174; Adolph, *Die katholische Kirche im Deutschland Adolf Hitlers* (Berlin: Morus Verlag, 1974), pp. 88-90.

21. Gröber Nachlass 103: copy, Bistumsarchiv Würzburg; read 10 and 17 October, 1943, A O 1.2, BAM; Faulhaber Folder III, Reich, 12 September, 1943, Archiv des Erzbistums München und Freising (hereafter cited as AEM); Adolph, *Katholische Kirche*, pp. 90-91; Limburg, 561/5D, pp. 193-194; R58/188, report, pp. 56-61, 10 September, 1943, BA.

22. Volk, *Akten*, 1:726, no. 316, Faulhaber to Theodor Steinbüchel, 18 May, 1933; Ernst Michel, "Die Überwendung des Liberalismus," *Hochland*, 32d Year, 2 (1935), 193-208; Bernhard Stasiewski, ed., *Akten Deutscher Bischöfe über die Lage der Kirche 1933-1945*, 3 vols., CCH, series A, vols. 5, 20, 25 (Mainz: Matthias Grünewald, 1968-1979), 1:88, no. 23/I, Minutes of meetign of three bishops in Berlin, 25-26 April, 1933.

23. Heinrich August von Winkler, "Die deutsche Gesellschaft der Weimarer Republik und der Antisemitismus," in *Die Juden als Minderheit in der Geschichte*, eds. von Bernd Martin and Ernst Schulin (Munich: Deutscher Taschenbuch Verlag, 1981), pp. 271-289; evidence previously presented.

24. Ernst Helmreich, *The German Churches under Hitler. Background, Struggle and Epilogue* (Detroit: Wayne State University Press, 1975), p. 294.

25. Lutz-Eugen Reutter, *Die Hilfstätigkeit katholischer Organizationen und kirchlicher Stellen für die im nationalsozialistischen Deutschland Verfolgten*, 2d ed. (Hamburg: University of Hamburg Press, 1970), pp. 18-19, 291: Abt Inland I-D, 3/8-20, Chief Geheimstaatspolizei to Foreign Office, 11 November, 1942, Auswärtiges Amt (hereafter cited as AA); Alfons Erb, *Bernard Lichtenberg* (Berlin: Morus Verlag, 1946), p. 8; Walter Adolph *Die katholische Kirche*, p. 68.

26. Volk, *Akten*, 2:826-827, no. 845, Dietz to Faulhaber, 15 November, 1941, 827-835, no. 845a, draft of letter, 836-837, no. 845b, Guidelines for publication of pastoral, 853, no. 849, 25 November, 1941, 851, no. 849, ft. 5, Bertram to Berning, 21 November, 1941, 854, no. 850, Buchberger to Faulhaber, 26 November, 1941, 837-838, no. 845c, Reasons for letter, 15 November, 1941, 850-853, no. 849, Position of Committee, 25 November, 1941, 934, no. 893, report, 14 June, 1942, 915-917, no, 886, Report of Committee; Quotation, 983, no. 915, notes, 30-31 March, 1943.

27. The cessation of confiscation of religious institutions and of the euthanasia program in the fall of 1941 and the decision not to stop the reading

of the March 22, 1942, pastoral are examples of the government's recognition of the power of the Catholic church.

28. Adolph, *Augzeichnungen*, no. 112, pp. 218-219, 12-13 January, 1938.

29. Volk, "Adolf Kardinal Bertram," pp. 274-286; Volk, "Die Kirche in der Weimarer Republik und im NS-Staat," in *Kleine deutsche Kirchengeschichte*, ed. Bernard Kötting (Freiburg: Herder, 1980), p. 112; Volk, "Der Deutsche Episkopat," in *Kirche, Katholiken und Nationalsozialismus*, ed. Klaus Gotto and Konrad Repgen (Mainz: Matthias Grünwald, 1980), pp. 56-57; Walter Adolph, Nachlass, 18, Letter of Robert Leiber, 28 October, 1945; Adolph, *Augzeichnungen*, no. 6, pp. 26-29, 21-24 June, 1936, no. 128, p. 234, 4 March, 1938, no. 9, pp. 39-40, 28 January, 1937, no. 4, pp. 14-15, 10-14 May, 1936, no. 62, p. 133, 19 June, 1937, no. 14, p. 52, 17-19 March, 1937, no. 90, p. 188, 13 November, 1937; Adolph, *Kardinal Preysing*, p. 164; Adolph, *Die katholische Kirche*, pp. 107, 109; Adolph, *Sie Sind Nicht Vergessen* (Berlin: Enka-Druck, 1972), pp. 23-24.

30. Volk, Akten, 2:844-845, no. 846, 1002, no. 926; Bertram to Faulhaber, 17 November, 1941, Br IA 25 J no 12; Bertram to Berning, 19 November, 1943, Br IA 25 Z no. 136, Limburg 561/21, p. 113; Adolph, Nachlass 17P, p. 8; Adolph, *Aufzeichnungen*, no. 11, p. 43, 26 February, 1937; Adolph, *Sie Sind Nicht Vergessen*, pp. 200-202.

31. Heinz Hurten, *Deutsche Briefe 1934-1938: Ein Blatt der katholischen Emigration*, 2 vols., CCH, series A, vols. 6 and 7 (Mainz: Matthias Grünewald, 1936), 2:271-272, no. 93; Pinchas Lapide, *Three Popes and the Jews* (New York: Hawthorn Books, 1967), p. 239; Reutter, II, p. 53; Stasiewski, 3:141, no. 260/II notes, 19 December, 1935; Adolph, *Augzeichnungen*, no. 6, pp. 21-24, June, 1936, no. 9, pp. 39-40, 28 January, 1937.

32. Ludwig Volk, "Michael Kardinal von Faulhaber (1869-1953)", separate printing from *Zeitgeschichte in Lebensbildern: aus den deutschen Katholizismus des 20. Jahrhunderts*, vol. 2, ed. Rudolf Morsey (Mainz: Matthias Grünewald, 1975), 101-113; Volk, "Die Kirche in der Weimarer Republik. . .", pp. 112-113; Volk, "Der deutsche Episkopat," p. 50.

33. Adolph, *Augzeichnungen*, no. 20, p. 63, 31 March, 1937, no. 92, p. 189, 18 November, 1937.

34. Amtsblatt für Erzdiözese München und Freising, 1933, pp. 57-64, 21 February, 1933, AEM.

35. Printed copy, Bischöfliches Ordinariatsarchiv Würzburg; MA 106685, pp. 133-134, 8 March, 1937, 106689, pp. 36-46, Abt II Geheimes Staatsarchiv, Berichte des Regierungspräsidiums, Bayerischen Hauptstaatsarchiv, Munich (hereafter cited as BHAM); Adolph, *Augzeichnungen*, no. 128, pp. 234-235, 4 March, 1938.

36. Volk, *Akten*, 2:824-825, no. 844, Faulhaber to Bertram, 13 No-

vember, 1941, 856 no. 851; Faulhaber to Bertram, 1 December, 1941, Br IA 25 J no. 12.

37. 9 February, 1936, Gröber NS 8.

38. Hans Müller, *Katholische Kirche und Nationalsozialismus Dokumente 1930-1935* (Munich: Nymphenburger Verlagshandlung, 1963), p. 302, no. 159 23 September 1934; Adolph, *Aufzeichnungen*, no. 6, pp. 21-24, June, 1936, no. 103, p. 201, 21 December. 1937, no 122, pp. 228-229, 4 February, 1938; Adolph, *Sie Sind Nicht Vergessen*, p. 183; A O 1.2, 14 September, 1941, BAM; Report, no. 409, 30 September, 1941, Politische Polizei III, Staatsarchiv Münster (hereafter cited as SAM); R43 II/177a, Akten der Reichs Kanzlei, p. 119. Report 1941, BA.

39. Adolph, *Aufzeichnungen*. no. 53 p. 21, 20 April, 1937, no. 88, pp. 185-186, 29 October, 1937, no. 103 p. 202, 21 December, 1937, no. 122, pp 228-229, 4 February, 1938, no. 126, p. 232, 19 February, 1938, no. 129, p. 236, 7 March, 1938; at the time of the quarrel over a follow-up common pastoral to *Mit brennender Sorge*, Bertram remarked that Galen "believes he can command the German episcopacy as he commands his Westphalian peasants." (Adolph, *Aufzeichnungen* no. 59, p. 130, 8 June, 1937).

40. Müller, p. 305.

41. Limburg, 561/2c, pp. 116-118, 3 July, 1938; Adolph, *Aufzeichnungen* no. 98, pp. 194-195, 6 December, 1937; Pastoral, 16 April, 1939, A O 1.2, BAM; Müller, pp. 300-305.

42. R43 II/177a, 11 April, 1940, BA; 3 August, 1941, Gröber NS 8.

43. Galen to Bertram, 27 October, 1941, A - XV-34, Bistums Speyer; Sermons April-May, 1943, A O 1.2, BAM.

44. According to Gröber's postwar account, he and six members of the Freiburg Ordinariat were snared by a cunning recruiter; later he was excluded on account of his hostility to the party (Gröber to Rev. Zeigler, 4 September, 1946, Gröber Nachlass 17; Gröber to Paderborn, 2 December, 1933, p. 2 Gröber Concordat Folder). In July, 1979, the archival director of the diocesan archives in Freiburg suggested that a recruiter might have been given money by someone in the office to get rid of him; the recruiter had to put a name down beside the donation, and the only name he knew was the archbishop's (Dr. Franz Hundsnurscher, July, 1979); Letter to clergy, 28 June, 1933, no. 17 of *Amtsblatt* 30 June, 1933, Gröber to Wienken, 3 March, 1942, Gröber NS 10; Adolph, *Aufzeichnungen* no. 29, pp. 83-84, 7 April, 1937; Gröber, *Hirtenbriefe des Erzbischofs Gröber in die Zeit*, ed. Konrad Hoffman (Freiburg: Herder, 1947), pp. 29-33, 52-58; Ludwig Volk, "Der deutsche Episkopat," pp. 51-52.

45. R43 II/177, p. 143 (p. 16 of mimeogr. copy), January, 1940, BA; Gröber to deanery, 12 November, 1943, Gröber to German episcopate, 18 January, 1943, Gröber to deanery, 5 February, 1942, Gröber NS 102a; General vicar to deanery, 21 October, 1940, Gröber NS 102; Gröber Nachlass 84; Gröber

to Fulda, 15 June, 1944, pastoral letter, 9 May, 1943, Gröber Nachlass 22; Alfred Beer, *Erzbishof Dr. Conrad Gröber: Ein Lebensbild* (Constance: Merk and Co., 1958), pp. 66-74.

46. Reutter, *Die Hilfstätigkeit,* p. 284; Gröber to Wienken, 28 November 1941, Gröber Nachlass 10; Gröber to Bertram, 20, 27, 30 April, 1943, Gröber Nachlass 22; Gröber to Bertram, 1 June, 1943, Br I A 25 Z no 136. An assistant to Luckner who was also arrested said in the police inquiry that Luckner had told her that what she was doing went far beyond what Gröber had permitted; this, of course, may have been Luckner's method of protecting Gröber. (Akten der Geheimen Staatspolizei, Staatspolizeileitstelle, no. 296, Else Heidkamp, Hauptstaatsarchiv, Düsseldorf.

47. General vicar to deanery, Fall, 1942, Gröber to deanery, 12 November, 1942, Gröber NS 102a; 465d, 162, 31 December, 1942, Generallandesarchiv, Karlsruhe.

48. Sermon, 31 January, 1942, Limburg 561/5D, pp. 112-114; Nuncio to bishop of Limburg, 13 January, 1943, 30 March, 1942, pp. 99-100, Limburg 561/21.

49. Volk, *Akten,* 2:824-825, no. 844, Faulhaber to Bertram, 13 November, 1941, 844-845, no. 846; Bertram to Faulhaber, 17 November, 1941, Br IA 25 J no. 12.

50. Ulrich von Hehl, *Katholische Kirche und Nationalsozialismus in Erzbistum Köln 1933-1945,* CCH, series B, vol. 23 (Mainz: Matthias Grünewald, 1977), p. 235.

51. Wilhelm Corsten, *Kölner Aktenstüke zur Lage der katholischen Kirche in Deutschland 1933-1945* (Cologne: J. P. Bachem, 1949), p. 310, no. 233; Adolph, *Hirtenamt und Hitler-Kidtatur* (Berlin: Morus Verlag, 1965), pp. 92-93.

52. Adolph, *Kardinal Preysing,* pp. 21, 35, 117-130; Adolph, *Hirtenamt,* pp. 117-119; Stasiewski, 1:238, no. 44, Preysing to Fulda Conference, 31 May, 1933; Volk, "Konrad Kardianl von Preysing (1880-1950)", separate printing from *Zeitgeschichte in Lebensbildern: aus den deustschen Katholizismus des 20. Jahrhunderts,* vol. 2, edited by Rudolf Morsey (Mainz: Matthias Grünewald, 1975), 88-100; R43, II/178, pp. 175-178, Report of lower officials to Reich minster of church affairs, 14 October, 1938, BA.

53. Adolph, *Aufzeichnungen,* no. 23, p. 73, 2 April, 1937, no. 12, pp. 45-46, 1 March, 1937, no. 129, p. 236, 7 March, 1938; Adolph, *Kardinal Preysing,* p. 17; Volk, "Konrad Kardinal von Preysing," p. 100.

54. Adolph, *Kardinal Preysing,* p. 170; Preysing's preaching, A-XV-34, 2 November, 1941, Bistums Speyer; Adolph, Nachlass, 18b, November, 1943.

55. Preysing to Staatspolizei or RSHA, 7 November, 1941, 24 November, 1941; Erich Klausener, "Margarete Sommer 1893-1965," in Wolfgang Knauft, *Miterbauer des Bistums Berlin: 50 Jahre Geschichte in Characterbildern* (Berlin: Morus, 1979), pp. 175-176.

56. Adolph, Nachlass, 18b, 14 May, 1939.
57. Adolph, *Kardinal Preysing,* p. 174; Klausener, pp. 157, 164, 172.
58. Ruth Andreas-Friedrich, *Schauplatz Berlin: Ein deutsches Tagebuch.* Reprint of Berlin Underground, 1948 (Munich: Rheensberg Verlag, 1962), p. 67.

Racial Eugenics in the Third Reich:
The Catholic Response

Donald Dietrich

I

Like many Germans after 1918, Catholics were trapped in a cruel dilemma. To support the Nazi program in the Weimar era and then in the Third Reich could easily lead to a loss of moral credibility; to oppose Hitler's *Weltanschauung,* however, could result in the assault of Nazi propaganda, and after 1933 the state also could be used against German Catholics. Both accommodation and circumscribed resistance highlight the story of the German Catholic approach to such sensitive and related issues as those of euthanasia and anti-Semitism. The response of Catholics was rooted in their historical politicization and intellectual experiences as well as situationally induced.

Since 1871, Catholics had suffered discrimination in predominantly Protestant Germany; their nationalistic fervor was characterized by many as not genuine. As "outsiders," they had generally striven to be super-patriotic in order to remain in the mainstream of German life. Even before 1871, they also were at least as anti-Semitic and *völkisch* as their fellow Protestant Germans.[1] Historically, then, to position Catholicism in the mainstream of the German intellectual development, clerical leaders made a number of lethal compromises, were indifferent to vital issues, and refused to adhere to the course dictated by positive traditional values. They were Catholics who were German nationalists and intellectuals who tried ot remain relevant in their milieu, supportive of circumscribed racial eugenics and a variety of anti-Semitic orientations.

Analyzing the Catholic reactions to the eugenic-racist policies of the Nazis can help illuminate the nature of the relationship between twentieth century political institutions and the moral norms dominating society. Catholic responses to eugenic theories and Nazi racial policies, inconsistent with the ideal Christian values of brotherhood and love, can also offer a provcative insight into the dynamics undergirding Catholic religious values in the Third Reich and documented resultant behavior patterns. The primary foundation for sustaining these negative values of eugenic-ethnic prejudice in society cannot be found solely in the pathological individual or in the dynamics of interpersonal relationships. Ultimately, negative values are based in the salient historical conditions and the political-economic structures out of which intergroup relationships are developed and sustained. Only in conjunction with specific societal and situational conditions did personal psychological factors become operationalized in eugenic and racial policies.[2] Post-unification Germans in the Empire and subsequently in the Weimar Republic matured in an eugenic and anti-Semitic environment,[3] and ultimately proved unable to mount a decisive opposition against the Nazis.

II

Sounding a radical eugenics theme stressing sterilization and euthanasia in 1895, Adolf Jost asserted that the individual life has no value, but rather was subordinated to the community and to the development of the species.[4] Intellectually, social Darwinism reinforced eugenics but differentiated it from the vulgar racism acceptable in the beerhalls before 1933.[5] By 1930 the eugenics controversy in Germany had led to a scientifically credible set of principles, which would be academically maintained. In the process science helped subvert faith by demoting the status of religious beliefs in the cognitive hierarchy. The result of the scientific debate on the eugenic issue was to separate in a most radical fashion the natural order from the moral. Sterilization and euthanasia, then, were not discoveries of Hitler's. Painless death for the incurably ill had already been recommended, for example, in 1920 by Karl Bindung and Alfred Hoche.[6] Essentially, the eugenic doctrines and practices, ultimately implemented in National Socialist Germany, postulated the existence of genetic differences between races and other categories of man that have much greater importance in determining the worth and performance of members of those groups than anything the individual man can do during his lifetime. Thus, according to this assumption *nature* outweighs *nurture*.[7] The issues emerging in the racial eugenics debate have persisted, of course, beyond the era of the Third Reich.[8]

In the National Socialist ideology and the minds of many Germans, the academic racial eugenics debate was reflected in "vulgar" social Darwinism, a viewpoint co-opted even by the socialists, and the perennial anti-Semitism so popular in Western Civilization.[9] Anti-Semitism became a popular theme for the volkists who turned into political issues questions on sex, ethics, and religion, which really should only be answered in the private arena. These normally private issues, turned into public debates, presented the Church with a forum that was unfamiliar. The Party pursued abstract goals that seemingly could not have any concrete political effects: *Volk* unity, racial purity, *Lebensraum*. For their part, the National Socialists rejected as sterile the problems that politics can resolve, i.e., the development of institutional and legal frameworks within which society can function. In essence, Nazi leaders politicized areas that have usually been reserved for decisions by the individual's conscience.

The eugenic policies of the Nazi regime should not have surprised anyone. Nazi written works, propaganda, and speeches were rife with references stressing the importance of achieving a pure and healthy race. At the annual Party gathering at Nuremberg in 1929 Hitler had held up ancient Sparta's policy of selective infanticide as a model. "If Germany every year would have one million children and eliminate 700-800.000 of the weakest, the end result would probably be an increase in (national) strength."[10] When he assumed power in Germany, Hitler's intentions were a matter of record. His presentation, although vulgar, did not provide a discordant note, since respectable eugenicists had reached similar conclusions, although expressing them in a more aesthetic fashion. Essentially, what emerged in scientifc and academic journals on euthanasia and sterilization was transformed by Nazi politicos into racial purity, a moral-political issue.[11]

There had been a degree of hesitation on the part of Catholic moral theologians when the question of sterilization first emerged in the 1920s. Was it wrong to intervene surgically to prevent the proliferation of undesirable stock and so save the race from degeneration? Two moral theologians confronted one another from the late 1920s until eugenic policies were implemented. The prominent advocate of the axiom that sterilization was forbidden by both the Christian and moral law was Franz Hürth, of the Jesuit Theological Seminary at Valkenburg, later of the Pontifical Gregorian University. His antagonist on this issue was Josef Mayer of the Paderborn philosophical-theological Academy, who defended sterilization as probably licit and certainly still as a debatable academic issue. Ultimately, Hürth was to be sustained by the Holy See and the episcopate. In the 1930 encyclical *Casti Connubi* (*On Christian Marriage*), Pius XI declared that the body of man is inviolable; the State has no authority to sterilize unless for medical reasons or as a punishment for crime; purely eugenic reasons will not suffice. *Casti Connubi* itself was promulgated to confront such views as that of Leo Just: "Without eugenics there can be no solution to the social question"[12] Unconvinced by this encyclical, Mayer went on to defend not only sterilization, but also abortion. Eventually in a Nazi-sponsored memorandum, he justified euthanasia for the mentally ill.[13]

Eugenic sterilization was already keenly debated in Germany by 1927 when Mayer published his *Legal Sterilization of the Mentally Ill*. Opposing Hürth and the majority of moral theologians, Mayer suggested that the chief issue in the controversy was that the sterilized according to canon law, stressing the primary goal of procreation in marriage, would not really have been capable of a proper marital relationship. Marriage, Mayer felt, however, should not focus so exclusively on procreation, but on sanctifying the souls of the partners. The only question that could logically be posed was whether sterilization intended a moral good. He concluded that neither private morality nor the moral world-order was endangered through the sterilization of the mentally ill. The healing of the community was viewed as more important than the physical integrity of the individual. Stressing that Thomas Aquinas accepted castration for sex offenders and that an extensive literature had developed emphasizing that the common good supersedes the individual benefit, Mayer asserted that the state does have the right to control the mentally and medically ill from "haphazard breeding." Since the goal of marriage, he insisted, is not just to beget children, sterilized individuals may certainly be allowed to marry and enjoy the other pleasures of connubial bliss. Mayer was very quick to point out that, conducted properly, legal sterilization measures would not lead to an undue interference of the state into the private lives of individuals.[14] In his scholarly treatise Mayer asserted that it would be licit for the state to enforce sterilization for eugenic societal reasons. A person who is incapable of educating children, he maintained, had no right to beget them. The Jesuit Hürth almost immediately attacked the Mayer thesis, actually directed against his own earlier work.[15] Mayer had argued, for example, that in case of necessity an abortion may be procured. Hürth rejected this view and insisted: "Catholic moral theology sees in the life of a fully innocent person an inviolable good that is immune from a direct human attack by a private person or by the public authority."[16] Until 1933, the eugenics issue was consigned to encyclicals and theological journals.

On 14 July, 1933, Hitler promulgated the "Law Preventing the Transmission of Hereditary Disease." This law for the prevention of progeny with hereditary disease, the basis for Hitler's racial purification program, was not unique, however, but was directly patterned on the model sterilization law proposed by the leaders of the American eugenics movement.[17] The publishing of this law (July 25) was particularly insulting since it contradicted *Casti Connubi* and failed to take into account an earlier episcopal statement, voiced at the May, 1933 Fulda Conference, opposing even voluntary sterilization. Also disturbing to Catholics was the fact that it was approved at the same Cabinet session that had accepted the Concordat, a treaty apparently resolving a plethora of Church-State concerns. This Reich statute, which provided for compulsory sterilization of all persons afflicted with various hereditary diseases or disabilities, including alcoholism, was to take effect 1 January, 1934. Instead of opposing the law, the bishops at their August, 1933, meeting decided to submit a memorandum to the Ministry of the Interior in order to explain the Catholic position. The government was to be asked to frame the implementing ordinances in such a way that Catholic physicians, judges, nurses, and other employees would not be subjected to conflicts of conscience. Catholics, especially parents and directors of asylums, were to be told later how to conduct themselves.[18] Cardinal Adolf Bertram's protest said: "Much as the Church regrets the conflict between Church and state legislation, she cannot pass silently over this violation of the Catholic moral law." Respectable theologians carefully delineated the Catholic position. In an opinion prepared for Cardinal Adolf Bertram, Hürth distinguished between the goal and the content of the 14 July, 1933, law on the prevention of hereditary disease. The goal was approved fom a moral theological standpoint, but the content of the law had to be repudiated because it was against natural and Christian moral law, clearly a confusing response for non-theologians. The challenge would be difficult to handle under the best of conditions. Such was not the case in Nazi Germany where the press was already being carefully censored. Subsequently, Hürth commented that he wanted to publish an article on the new eugenics law, but as Robert Leiber, S.J., informed Pacelli, the Cardinal Secretary of State, it was impossible. Leiber commented that Mayer's 1933 article, published apparently supporting at least a Catholic position, could cause more damage in the long run than public support for the eugenic goals, if not means.[19]

By early November, Bishops Konrad Gröber and Wilhelm Berning could report to their colleagues that the government was willing to exempt directors of Catholic institutions from the duty of applying for the sterilization of patients under their care. The Catholic directors would merely have to report the names of all their patients afflicted with diseases requiring sterilization. In the case of Catholic physicians employed in state institutions the situation was not as hopeful, the bishops thought, though the government was willing to consider the objections of the episcopate. The officials of the Ministry of the Interior, with whom the two bishops were negotiating, had granted the Church the right to inform the faithful of the Catholic position on sterilization. In January of 1934 the faithful were told that according to Catholic doctrine it was forbidden to volunteer for sterilization or apply for another's. Such bishops as Galen and Faulhaber were somewhat more forceful than many of their colleagues in carrying out the injunction of their office.[20] There was, however, no public, frontal attack on the law as such and confusion characterized the Church's responses.

One prominent theologian insisted that it was illicit cooperation in a sinful act for Catholic officials to file applications for sterilization. He felt that priests need not deny the sacraments to officials, however, who were not aware of the sinful character of such applications or who acted in good faith when they complied with the law to keep their positions and support their families. Bertram agreed with the opinion, formulated by moral theologians, on the illicitness of filing applications for sterilization, but expressed strong doubts on how to handle confessions. The Church could be accused of teaching something in theory, but reconciling herself with the same sinful act in practice. The spread of such views "would lead to the loss of all respect for the moral law and for the authority of the Church." It would cause a scandal and thus in the bishop's opinion made it mandatory that the well-being of the official yield to the common good, that is, to "the preservation of morality among the people."[21]

Along with Mayer, other Catholic intellectuals were not convinced by Bertram's insistence on conforming to the official view within the Church. Two Catholic theologians at the University of Braunsberg (East Prussia), Hans Barion and Karl Eschweiler, maintained that the sterilization law was not in conflict with Catholic doctrines. Even though the two professors had been suspended from their faculties by the Church, many lay Catholics, encouraged by their views, complied with the demands of the sterilization law — the path of least resistance. Eschweiler's and Barion's reaction was not isolated. Hürth had already privately written to Father Leiber, Pacelli's confidante, that a number of Catholic theologians were of the opinion that the state did not exist for man, but rather that individuals were to be subordinated to the state. They offered, Hürth pointed out, Thomistic texts based on Aristotle's notion of the polity. Leiber added, however, that if Thomas were correctly interpreted such a position could not be sustained. Bertram himself had already admitted that very few Catholic officials were even bothered by the conflict of conscience that had arisen, and, with this mood of theological uncertainty prevailing, several bishops decided to adopt a more conciliatory position. In particular, it proved impossible to obtain unanimity of opinion as to how confessors were to treat Catholic officials who filed applications for sterilization. A pamphlet published at the Beuron monastery advised priests hearing confession not to pose troubling questions to persons known to be involved with the machinery of the sterilization law. The Cologne Bishops' Conference in May, 1935, suggested that as long as no uniform stand could be reached, no instructions should be issued so that confusion could be avoided.[22] Apparently, the Church had reconciled herself to the fact that most Catholic officials helped enforce the sterilization law, even though theologians generally opposed such eugenic measures.

The theologian, Otto Schilling, for example, had insisted that the Church wanted reason, not medical eugenics, applied to procreation, but within this context the focus should be on the valid welfare of the individual, of the community, and of the race. As an example of applied reason, for example, Pius XI in *Casti Connubi* had urged care in the choice of one's marital partner. The Church could not support artificial birth control or sterilization. Eugenicists, theologians had reminded their readers, recommended noble motives for birth control, but in reality individual selfishness usually dominated. Schilling warned that by reducing the quantity of children, one could also reduce the quality of the whole. With respect to the role of the state in eugenics, Schilling asserted that the state had the strict duty to protect the life of the innocent child, whose helplessness itself was a touching appeal to justice, the foundation of all political life. Naturally Schilling also condemned sterilization by reminding his readers that the sanctity of the family was to be respected by the state. A refined moral education would be necessary for a national eugenics plan to operate within the parameters established by God. In essence, however, man must use his reason while conforming to natural as well as God's law.[23]

In 1935 Karl Frank stated that in a *Volk* descended from a specific race or racial mixture, there were valuable and less valuable offshoots. The current eugenics discussion, he maintained, was concerned with helping the hereditarily better elements attain victory over the inferior. Working with Mendel's laws, he felt that an intelligent approach would actually mean crossing races for a healthier stock. But from the Hitlerian national eugenics standpoint this would be forbidden. Hence, a realistic eugenics policy was not being sought by the Reich. Selfishness, he insisted, should be opposed, and so religious ethics should be highlighted. Moreover, Frank stressed that the recent attacks on the family did not support the realization of eugenic goals. As in nature, those elements of lesser value should never be obliterated. Eugenics, he felt, should reinforce procreation that would strengthen the racial stock while still maintaining the chronically ill. Frank pointed out that the goal of man was to seek fulfillment in eternal life. We must, he insisted, leave to the creator how this goal could be achieved, even by the hereditarily mentally ill, since no one except God had control over all the possibilities inherent in procreation. Catholics, of course, could work to control marriages between the hereditarily ill as well as between the hereditarily ill and the healthy, but the efforts must be guided by rational natural law. Also, constructive economic activities must be provided so that the unfortunates could assist in maintaining themselves.[24] In essence, then, Frank felt that eugenics could be practiced, but only within the confines of divine and natural law and only when motivated by proper charity. Apparently ignorant of Nazi goals, Frank naively maintained that euthanasia was not being seriously discussed in responsible governmental circles. Actually, however, as early as 1935 Hitler had decided on a euthanasia program to improve the quality of race, but hesitated to implement it for fear of the reaction of the Church. In the chaos of a wartime situation, he cleverly reasoned, opposition would not be mounted.[25]

Theologians were discussing the issues of racial differentiation as well. Frank, for example, insisted that all members of mankind from the beginning had been endowed with a rational essence. Culture, of course, merely helps distinguish among human groups. Such a position developed more clearly and promoted vigorously would have obviated the entire concept of the *Untermensch* as well as the stress on racial eugenics either through sterilization or euthanasia. Who could tell when a particular quality could well be necessary for the next specialized formation in the onward development of mankind? Franz Walther felt that euthanasia was rooted in the historical collapse of religion in modern times and could never really improve God's creation. Walther found the deepest roots of the pro-euthanasia movement growing in soil characterized by the collapse of morality, conditioned through the experiences of the first World War as well as a materialistic world view, and powered by the surrender of a belief in God and immortality.[26] Theological opposition to Nazi racial eugenics was developing.

Still, from 1934-1936 approximately 168,000 persons were sterilized. The government was quite aggressive in implementing its law. Priests protesting against sterilization were penalized, frequently losing their right to give religious instruction in the public schools. In 1935 Wilhelm Frick, the Minister of the Interior, during a widely publicized speech, gave notice that the regime would not tolerate any further sabotage of the law. In several notes to the Reich government, Pacelli argued that the Holy See could not grant the state the power to determine the morality of legislation and so reserved the right of the Church to criticize ordinances in conflict with divine law. In fact, however, for all practical purposes, the episcopate was on a path of retreat. The Church's condemnation of sterilization was labeled sabotage of the national renewal and a malicious attack on the state and party. It was seen as an attack on the dynamic and legal foundation of the state.[27] The bishops were uncomfortable whenever their loyalty was attacked and continued their retreat, camouflaged by patriotic speeches focused on such other issues as the Saar plebiscite, which Hitler conveniently provided.

Aided by an intricate casuistry, the bishops had decided that Catholic physicians and social workers might report to the authorities those afflicted with ills calling for sterilization. *Reporting* was "material cooperation" which was lawful, since such an act was morally indifferent and since the Catholic official in question might lose his job. To submit an *application* for the sterilization of a person was "formal cooperation" which, being an essential part of an evil action, was sinful; but the Church did not attempt to enforce this position. When the question arose whether Catholic nurses might assist in sterilization operations, the Church replied negatively. But in 1940 even the Sacred Congregation of the Holy Office ruled that Catholic nurses in state-run hospitals could assist at such operations if a sufficiently important reason were present, such as the replacement of Catholic nurses by staff hostile to the Church, which might prevent the adminstration of the sacraments. The bishops, then, opposed sterilization in theory, but accommodated themselves to the facts of life in the Third Reich, frequently accepting a lesser evil to avoid the greater. Also, they seemed to make decisions to accommodate lay Catholics who could have lost jobs and family stability had the moral idals been strictly enforced. In general, then, they adjusted to the circumstances, applied moral precepts, and avoided burdening lay Catholics with ethical dilemmas. In 1936, the Munich courts decided that an objection to the sterilization law on religious grounds could not be upheld or considered. Further, the legal right of the priest, in distinction from his moral obligation, not to reveal the secrets of the confessional was very gravely qualified.[28] The obvious course, then, was to make sure that matters for the confessional were limited. Sterilization was, of course, only the first step in the racial eugenics program.

The transition to an offensive and aggressive foreign policy in 1937/38 went together with stepping up the domestic struggle against the largely conservative forces in the Army, bureaucracy and judicature. Hitler's speech to the Reichstag on 30 January, 1939, on the occasion of the sixth anniversary of his takeover of power is worth recalling. Not since 1933 had Hitler attacked so fanatically in public the "spiritual weaklings," the decaying "social castes." He argued for the *völkisch* laws and predicted of the Jews that in the event of another world war that "the result will not be . . . a victory for Jewry but the destruction of the Jewish race in Europe." For Hitler war had a purpose more extensive than merely military victory. World War II was a "racial" action which had to be waged at home similar to a second stage of the National Socialist Revolution.[30]

There is an intrinsic connection between the sterilization law of 1933/34 and the euthanasia measures of 1939. The euthanasia policy did not originate in a vacuum but rather had a unique and traceable genesis. Its roots can be found in the medical, juridical, and moral-theological debates from the turn of the century until the 1930s. The infamous euthanasia order was a command to destroy the medically, socially, and, ultimately, the racially unwanted. There is a politico-ideological connection between this euthanasia action and the earlier laws on sound marriage, issued in 1933 and then reinforced in the 1935 Nuremberg laws. For these earlier laws special administrative and court authorities, however, were established with the legally prescribed process of submitting proposals and making decisions. But the cover organizations and secret authorizations concerned with the euthanasia action were deliberately constructed outside the law. Even the sterilization laws, however, had afforded a great deal of latitude of judgment for officials and so themselves had paved the way for the 1939 oral order from the Führer.[31] Departmental cohesion had gradually dissolved; plenipotentiaries subordinate to the Führer had emerged; all the conditions were by 1939 prepared for the euthanasia action and this crucial administrative step on the road to Auschwitz.

Hitler's euthanasia oral order was issued in late October, 1939, after the successful Polish campaign. But it was predated to 1 September, suggesting a connection with the war issues. Certainly it was connected to the race issue, but it also embraced, and now on a very basic level, the power of the State over the individual and highlighted the State, i.e., the Führer, as the ultimate source of justice.[32] Such slogans as "Law is what serves the people" (*Recht ist, was dem Volk nutzt*) or "Common good before private good" (*Gemeinnutz vor Eigennutz*) now were brought to life as the basis for forthcoming arbitrary acts of the government. Euthanasia and its associated procedures embraced a massive assault on traditional morality (Christian and natural) and made the individual the instrument of the State or the race. Compounded with doctrines of racial supremacy, it was the prelude and preparation to the wholesale elimination of *Untermenschen* by any definition. Questionnaires and report forms, for example, provided blanks for information on patients suffering from a variety of diseases or who were criminally insane or who were not German citizens or of German blood. Race and nationality were to be included.[33]

In the same month that Hitler issued his euthanasia order, Pius XII promulgated his first encyclical, *Summi Pontificatus*, which warned of the arbitrariness of political power that assimilated rights that belong to God alone. The state assumption of absolute autonomy "puts itself in the place of the Almighty and elevates the State or group into the last end of life, the supreme criterion of the moral and juridical order, and therefore forbids every appeal to the principles of natural reason and of the Christian conscience." Against the background of the sterilization controversy and Pius' encyclical, the reaction of the German bishops to the 1939 Nazi euthanasia program was predictable; the opposition would be unconditional. Hitler seemed aware that a program to kill the mentally defective would meet strong resistance and so waited until the war began and patriotism made opposition more difficult.[34] Bishop Wurm, Provincial Bishop of the Lutheran Church in Württemberg, accurately prophesied: "There can be no stopping once one starts down this slope."[35] Hitler's order did not immediately touch Catholic institutions. The mentally ill patients had in previous years already been removed from Catholic institutions because of the Catholic opposition to the sterilization laws, and, in view of the intended operations, the institutes themselves had been confiscated.[36]

On 11 August, 1940, Bertram as Chairman of the Fulda Conference wrote to Hans-Heinrich Lammers, head of the Reich Chancellery, and reviewed the long-standing controversies in recent years in the field of eugenics. He stressed that assurances had been formally given that at least euthanasia was still illegal, even if sterilization was not. The point at issue, Bertram asserted, was the practice of government agencies to decree that the incurably insane, the so-called worthless lives, be either destroyed or used as experimental subjects in the search for new methods of curing other diseases. Particularly noteworthy in the Bertram letter are the uncompromising terms. He spoke of the "unqualified inadmissibility of acts of this kind," which were "most strictly forbidden" and "not only by the moral and religious teaching of the Catholic Church but by the religious and moral convictions of all Christians." The slightest exception would lead to grave consequences: "If this principle is once set aside, even with limited exceptions, on the ground of an occasional need, then, as experience teaches us, other exceptions will be made by individuals for their own purposes." The letter overflows with references to the sanctity of human life.[37] On 6 November, 1940, Faulhaber wrote to the Minister of Justice, Franz Gürtner. He reminded Gürtner that in 1934 the German bishops had affirmed the irreconcilability of euthanasia with the Christian conscience. Panic, he continued, has seized the inmates of other welfare institutions, such as old people's homes and tubercular sanitaria. Concluding, he appealed: "But even during wartime one may not discard the everlasting foundations of the moral order, nor the fundamental rights of the individual." Because of the rigorous censorship the outcry was not as great as it might have been. Often important public statements were not printed in the *Amtsblatt* of the diocese for fear of confiscation, but were sent secretly by courier to the local pastors, by whom they were often duplicated again. Some found their way to the foreign press in this form and were never officially printed.[38]

The Pope's own immediate reaction to the euthanasia order was in the arena of doctrine. On 6 December, 1940 *Osservatore Romano* published a decree of the congregation of the Holy Office in the traditional question-answer form:

> Whether it is licit, by the order of the public authority, to kill directly those who, although guilty of no crime worthy of death, nevertheless, because of psychic or physical defects can no longer be of use to the nation and are thought to be an impediment to it and to be an obstacle to its vigor and strength.

The answer was brief, but compelling:

> No. since this is contrary to both the natural and the divine positive law.

Pius gave his own explanation of this decree in a letter (15 December) to Bishop Konrad Preysing:

> About the shattering events which were the object of the courageous letter for Württemberg (Bishop Wurm's 19 July letter), the Holy Office has in the meantime issued a public condemnation on the general principle. We have had our highest tribunal speak as briefly and trenchantly as was possible. We would not think we had done our duty, if we had kept silent about such deeds. It is now for the German bishops to judge what the circumstances of time and place permit to be done.[39]

Such German bishops as Preysing presented the decree in public sermons (9 March, 1941). Clemens August Galen published it in the *Amtsblatt* of the Münster diocese.[40] The Nazis quite clearly were concerned with its publication. On 7 April, 1941, the police and intelligence services were alerted in Düsseldorf, Münster, Aachen, Bielefeld, Dortmund, Osnabrück, and Cologne. The Nazi Police Official, Walter Bierkamp (later head of an *Einsatzgrupp*, an execution squad in the Ukraine), enclosed the translation of the Latin text and forecast trouble: "Since we may expect that discussions and rumors about this problem will increase notably from now on, the respective agencies responsible should follow the situation most attentively and report without delay to the Reich Main Central Office any eventual information, and also in writing to me."[41]

Confidential protests by the bishops resulted in little satisfaction from the Reich authorities. In February, 1941, a new murder clinic was set up at Hadamar near Frankfurt. It was equipped with gas chambers for the extermination of the victims and crematories for the disposal of the bodies. On 24-26 June, 1941, the bishops met at Fulda. Ignoring the campaign against the Soviet Union, they dwelt on the mortal peril facing the German Church. "The very existence of the Church and of Christianity," they said, "is at stake in Germany." They cited among other threats to religion and society, the suppression of those "lives unworthy to live." Bertram was to present their grievances to the government in writing.[42]

Following these varied papal and episcopal responses to the new eugenics crisis, Bishop Galen of Münster created an international scandal by his three famous sermons of 13 and 20 July and 3 August. The third dealt with the suppression of "lives unworthy to live." These unfortunates die, he emphasized, "not because they are guilty of anything but because in the opinion of some doctor, in the view of some committee, they are 'unworthy to live' because in their eyes they belong to the unproductive citizens." Galen focused on the fundamental issue of the entire Nazi era, i.e., genocide as public policy:

> If once it is admitted that people have the right to kill unproductive persons — it concerns at the moment poor, defenseless lunatics — then the murder of all unproductive persons, that is, of incurables, of cripples, of folk maimed by war or work, indeed of us all, when we grow old and feeble and unproductive. . . . None of us will be sure of his life.

Pius praised Galen for his stand in 1941, and, on 24 February, 1943, in a letter to Galen, he wrote: "Perhaps never in modern church history have these three — human dignity, the family, and the Church — been so fatefully linked as today. It is always for us a consolation when we learn of an open and courageous word from a German bishop or the German bishops."[43]

Galen's service is that he produced a great deal of publicity, reinforced a mobilized public opinion, and helped prevent the recurrence of euthanasia at least in Germany. Reich officials also noted that the Church was still a major "uncoordinated" force. Galen's protest gave the Church a renewed public credibility and offered it the possibility of retaining a consistency in its moral theology. Unfortunately, Church officials did not extend and continue their critique once the Nazis moved their racial purification machinery east. The Nazis were clearly upset over Galen's sermons especially that of 3 August, which had an immense effect on the Germans domestically as well as on the soldiers in the field. Indicative of their rage, a Gaustableiter, Arnold F. (Essen), accused Galen of being a paid English agent. But in all of the furor at home and abroad concerning Galen's sermons, it should be recalled that he attacked the National Socialist state and ideology, not his German Fatherland.[44] The bishops seemed able to attack Nazi policies, but not the nefarious political organization from which they emanated. They remained loyal to Germany, even if not to the particular policies of the Reich.

Other protests now followed those of Galen. Anton Hilfrich, Bishop of Limburg, on 13 August sent a letter to the Ministry of Justice condemning the extermination of so-called "lives unworthy of being lived" at Hadamar. He called for an end to further violations of the fifth commandment. Albert Stohr, the Bishop of Mainz, asked in a sermon: "Who gives a man the right to say that a life is unworthy of being lived. . . ? It is wrong to kill directly the life of the innocent." Bishop Franz Bornewasser on 14 September stated that the killing of these so-called unproductive and unworthy but harmless persons "cried to heaven for vengeance." On the feast of Christ the King, Bishop Stohr preached against euthanasia: "Not merely the individual man is not permitted to lay violent hands on his neighbor, but also the community (*Gemeinschaft*) is forbidden to do evil. At no time is it permitted to extinguish a human life." It is particularly noteworthy that Stohr stressed that the community or state could not do that which was forbidden to the individual person by natural or divine law. On 2 November Bishop Preysing warned in a sermon: "Woe to us if the eternal moral law can be changed or set aside for purely expedience reasons. When the right to life of the innocent, the sanctity of life, is denied, then there is no stop in this descending road."[45]

On 10 December, 1941, a most bitter message was sent to the Nazi authorities. Ultimately, the main points were made public. The bishops had catalogued the Hitlerian promises callously dishonored. One compaint stated:

> With deep horror Christian Germans have learned that, by order of the state authorities, numerous insane persons, entrusted to asylums and institutions, were destroyed as

so-called unproductive citizens. At present a large-scale campaign is being made for the killing of incurables through a film (*Ich klage an*) recommended by the authorities and designed to calm the conscience through appeals to pity. We German bishops shall not cease to protest against the killing of innocent persons. Nobody's life is safe unless the commandment, Thou shalt not kill, is observed.[46]

To an extent, although expressed in a very abstract fashion, the German bishops were not exclusively concerned only about the lives of defenseless Germans. In the Fulda pastoral of 12 September, 1943, they urged the defense of all those in danger: "Killing is wrong in itself, even when allegedly exercised in the interest of the common good against innocent and defenseless weak and infirm of mind, on the incurable, those mortally wounded, those with hereditary diseases, infants unable to live, innocent hostages and disarmed war or penal prisoners, or on men of another race and origin."[47] Belatedly, the bishops had observed that eugenic reasons justifying racial purification seemed to be connected inexorably to mass murder. Until it was too late, however, they failed to perceive that the soil had been prepared for this growth by the earlier nationalistic antisemitism and stress on the *Volk,* rarely criticized by Church leaders.

On 24 August, 1941, Hitler's order had reduced the proportions of the euthanasia program in Germany and transferred its functions east. The bishops' protests, in particular those of Galen, and more significantly the reactions of the German people themselves had caused Hitler to reduce the dimensions of the program in Germany. The Nuremberg trials have made clear how Hitler and his doctors prepared themselves for the mass slaughter of the Jews by first killing nearly a hundred thousand of their fellow citizens in Germany.[48] Postwar testimony, a memo from Mayer in 1939 on the Catholic position related to euthanasia, the role of Heinrich Wienken, the bishops' liaison with the government, and the delay of the Catholic response have clouded the historical picture.

The defense strategy in the 1967 euthanasia trials was to show that the killing of the insane and the hopelessly ill was thought to be respectable and had also been practiced in other countries. An opinion by Josef Mayer was introduced through the testimony of Albert Hartl, a former SS Officer and Gestapo official, who insisted that he had commissioned from Mayer a memorandum on the subject in 1939. Mayer responded with a 100+ page theological opinion in favor of euthanasia. Hartl allegedly circulated the document to those engaged in the euthanasia program. A Catholic moral theologian was thus brought in to ease the political consciences of the Nazis at the very inception of the extermination program. The chief of the Catholic section of the SD (secret intelligence), Albert Hartl, declared that on Hitler's order he had asked Mayer for an opinion on the euthanasia problem from the Catholic viewpoint. The theologian, said the witness, anticipated no fundamental objection from the Church. In Hartl's words, "Only then did Hitler decide to begin the 'mercy killing' program."[49]

There is no need to doubt whether Mayer could have given such an opinion. His earlier views on sterilization and abortion had already predisposed him for such a conclusion and were indeed the reason why he was approached by the Nazis. Still, if Hartl had really wished to provide his Nazi superiors reliable information on the views and potential reactions of the bishops, he obviously misled these leaders. Mayer's opinion was completely out of harmony with Catholic doctrine. It also seems unlikely that Hitler would have personally wished to sound out legitimate Catholic opinion about Action "T-4." Likewise, he would scarcely have needed the assurances of the *Pfaffen* before proceeding on his course. The text of the alleged Mayer *Gutachten* has never been found under Mayer's name.[50] Mayer himself ultimately left the Paderborn Academy after 1945 and ceased writing on moral issues. The reasons for his departure are obscure, but perhaps relate to his links as a spy to Hartl. Mayer appears to be not merely a supplier of learned dissertations to the Nazis, but also other information as well. He also appears to have been a Nazi informer all during the war.[51]

Based on past ecclesiastical adaptation, some Nazis apparently thought that the Church would not be so unequivocably opposed to euthanasia if specific concessions could be made. Hans Hefelmann was the executive assistant to Victor Brack, a member of the Führer's personal chancellery. On 7 April, 1964, Hefelmann affirmed during his trial that the Catholic bishops were willing to moderate their stand if opportunities to perform pastoral functions were made available.

At least according to Hefelmann, Catholic bishops had been willing to tolerate a limited euthanasia restricted to certain categories of persons. Hefelmann alleged that he was himself present at two interviews between Bishop Heinrich Wienken (the Fulda bishops' liaison with the government) and the Minister of the Interior, Wilhelm Frick. He said that the arrest of Bishops Galen and Hilfrich was averted because Wienken, authorized by the bishops, had agreed to accept specific government regulations, i.e., only the completely insane persons would be eliminated. Little credence need be attached to the Hefelmann testimony. To the bishops, the lives of the mentally ill were sacrosanct and inviolable. Hence, no "limited euthanasia" could be permitted. No other evidence substantiates Hefelmann's testimony, and he contradicted it himself several weeks earlier. In the middle of March he claimed that the arrest of von Galen and Hilfrich, demanded by Heydrich and Himmler, had been avoided by Victor Brack's intervention with Hitler — that is, not by any "concessions" on the Catholic side. He also testified that Hitler had personally taken the decision to suspend the program in order not to give the Churches any further occasion for public protest. There is no indication that the Church representatives were willing to compromise.[52]

The testimony of Hefelmann, Hartl,[53] and Wienken during the euthanasia trials of the 1960s has offered additional insights, however, into the Church's relatively slow response to Hitler's back-dated order. The suggestion of a "deal" being made by Wienken, in the light of other published materials, does not seem too likely. Wienken was an unobtrusive, diligent church bureaucrat with an enormous capacity for optimism in his role as liaison officer between the German Catholic hierarchy and the Nazi state. Determined not to provoke any quarrels and believing in the compatibility of loyalty to Christ's Church and Hitler's Germany, both Bertram and Wienken were cut from the same cloth. Wienken weathered the storms of political controversy, but at no little cost to his personal image of integrity. The most controversial issue over which he is alleged to have capitulated was that of the Nazi euthanasia program. Indeed, Wienken's optimism that problems could be negotiated opened the way for ambiguous interpretations even though he did not compromise on the episcopal position that euthanasia violated the Fifth Commandment.[54]

As the Fulda representative, Wienken had to deal with the National Socialist government at a particularly important time. The *Blitzkrieg* had been an almost unprecedented victory. The campaigns in the West had astounded the world. In this victorious Germany, Wienken was certainly susceptible to Nazi blandishments. By November, 1940, Wienken had several times discussed the euthanasia theme. But the development of the Church's case was interrupted in early autumn by the insistence of the Propaganda Ministry representatives that all churches respond more carefully to the political needs of wartime Germany. To insure pastoral care under wartime conditions, Wienken recommended to the episcopate great care in the handling of the wartime doctrinal decisions of the Church and renunciation of anything injurious or harmful to the political welfare of wartime Germany.[55] Wienken's discussions of euthanasia and its problems are not understandable without understanding his personality. He wanted to remain in contact with the opponents of the Church, while hoping to avoid conflict without capitulation. Counterbalancing what appears to be an overzealous desire to compromise, Wienken during these same weeks petitioned against the beginning Jewish deportations and for the alleviation of the sufferings being endured by the priests in Dachau. To the aggressive Bishop Preysing, Wienken on 5 November, 1940, confided what probably was his own motivation. Wienken maintained that there were in the Nazi Party two camps — one was anti-Church and anti-Christian and one hoped to use the Church to support the regime. He hoped to strengthen the compromise party, but was unsure where the Führer stood. The precise role of Wienken is obscured because his sole accuser, Hefelmann, has taken a variety of positions and was not privy to all of the discussions.[56]

Whether Mayer performed his role of informer and spy willingly or unwillingly, under blackmail fear or personal conviction, he was certainly no representative of German Catholic clerical thought or action.[57] This murder ethic of the Nazis was possible only in their concept of the absolute power of the State, unanswerable to any moral claims except the imperatives of race. Once on this slope there could be no internal corrective or brake. Mayer promoted sterilization, but did not maintain that it would be licit to kill the mentally ill in his 1927 book. The bishops did not initially launch a full-scale assault against sterilization except in theory; they compromised on a pastoral level. Human rights were being hierarchically scaled by Catholic leaders in a Nazi Germany where no human rights were sacrosanct. Wienken hoped that a patriotic Church could reshape radical Nazi policies. On 28 April, 1972, Georg Siegmund of Fulda during a broadcast over Vatican Radio cited a proverb that epitomizes what occurred in the Church during these years: "If you give the devil your finger, he will take your hand."[58] Success in the nearly total elimination of the domestic euthanasia program, however, can in part be credited to the Catholic Church, tarnished by its noteworthy failure in the "Jewish Question."

III

Instead of emphasizing a spontaneous eruption of popular anti-Semitism in the socio-psychological crisis of Weimar, recent interpretations have stressed the conscious manipulative exploitation of anti-Semitism, which the Nazis used as a tool of integration and mass mobilization. In some interpretations anti-Semitism served the interests of finance capital; in others it seemed as a cementing element which diverted attention from the failures of Nazi socio-economic policies and held together the antagonistic forces of the Nazi movement.[59] But as Kershaw has recently noted, public opinion did not support radicalized anti-Semitism. In essence popular opinion was indifferent and guided by latent and historically rooted anti-Semitism. Such opinion, however, did supply a climate within which Nazi ideology and programs could advance unchallenged.[60]

The Catholic anti-Semitic experience during the *Kulturkampf* may be seen as a phenomenon that at least reinforced an existant anti-Semitism and simultaneously aided Catholics in their struggle for integration into a potentially hostile authoritarian Reich. Parliamentary liberalism, viewed by many as a Jewish political group, was not accepted in the 1870s nor would it be approved thereafter enthusiastically by many Catholics. Even if most Catholics were not racially anti-Semitic, therefore, they could hardly be jaundiced toward the Nazis in light of their own post-1871 experiences. Anti-Semitism served the Catholic Center Party as a functional mechanism for political mobilization to the right. After 1880, it could be directed against liberal Jews, Social Democrats, or against any problem that seemed insoluble or rooted in an "anti-German" conspiracy.[61]

After 1918 a variety of clerical Catholic leaders assaulted the Jews with theological and political diatribes. The Jesuit Gustav Gundlach argued for a mild political anti-Semitism and contended that fighting the Jews' "exaggerated and harmful influence" was permitted as long as it used moral means. Vicar General Mayer of Mainz, anti-Nazi in other respects, maintained that *Mein Kampf* had outlined the bad influence of the Jews in the press, theater, and literature. Father Senn called even German Catholicism *verjudet* and labeled the Hitler movement radical, but really the last good opportunity to throw off the Jewish yoke.[62]

During the Weimar years, the German bishops preached against the Nazi glorification of race and blood, but generally had almost nothing specific to say about the widespread anti-Semitic propaganda. On 27 August, 1922, Faulhaber characterized the November revolution as perjury and high treason, an unfortunate condemnation since in the minds of many this political system was part of the liberal-Jewish conspiracy. In 1923 Cardinal Faulhaber, for example, declared that every human life was precious, including that of a Jew — a backhanded compliment. Faulhaber also noted in 1924 that even if Hitler's subordinates did not realize that the German nation required the support of Christianity, the Führer did. Other Catholics, most notably those in the *Katholikenbund,* urged combat against the enemies of Germany and the Church — Marxists, Freemasons, and Jews.[63] Clearly, then, many Catholics could see in Nazism at least some programs they could support. Still, for the most part the "Jewish Question" was important only to a minority of Germans. The general population was never actively instrumental in driving Jews from Germany or in their annihilation. Hitler and his radical followers pursued the "Final Solution."[64] After 1933 moderate anti-Semitism appears to have been a success, because the population accepted legal and "moderate" measures against the Jews in Germany. Extreme anti-Semitism was apparently a failure in terms of public opinion after 1933. But the simple fact that Hitler could find enough collaborators to exterminate most German and European Jews seems to indicate that public opinion, at least in this area, had become irrelevant during the war,[65] since sensitivity toward Jewish rights had been undermined in the past. Although the ambivalent attitude of the Papacy and of the Catholic hierarchy to the Jewish Question has been subjected to a thorough alanysis, the stance adopted by the theologians and parochial clergy has not been thoroughly delineated.[66] In all likelihood, of course, it was the parish clergy who were most able to exert a direct influence upon their flock.

Almost universally by 1933, Catholic thinkers were seeking a rapproachment with the new Nazi state. Friedrich Muckermann contended that there was a natural organic root to the *Volkstum* and another organic principle directed the supernatural development of the Church. Frequently, both *Volk* and *Kirche* were enlisted to support one another. *Volkstum, Reich,* and *Rasse* intermingled at the base of the institutional state. The dominant signal being sent by the Catholic publicists was for reconciliation; they generally failed to explicate analytically the overt and covert meanings of these loaded "German values." Even liturgy journals typically avoided articles that offered scholarly analyses of the Jewish origins of early Christian liturgical developments. In the Christian perspective the real enemy was not the heathen or pagan, but rather the Jew. The *völkisch* Christians saw the hostile Church and loyal Christians as enemies on the side of the Jews. Clearly then, Church leaders had to emphasize their disdain or even outright hatred of the Jews. Their institutional survival seemed dependent on this. Anti-Semitism had a role in the relationship between the Catholic populace and the Nazis. Stressing a common political hostility toward the Jews, connected to anti-liberal and anti-Socialist resentment, a solidarity existed between the Catholics and Nazis. This congruence had a greater impact on the Catholic laity than did abstract theological ruminations. The latter elements played a central role mainly in the official reactions of leading Catholics to the Nazis, but even here common ties were also highlighted in the early reconciliation phase.[67]

Karl Adam, one of the foremost theologians of the twentieth century, claimed that it was the right and duty of the state to preserve the blood purity of the *Volk*. Apparently even at this early date having second thoughts, Adam did not conclude his essay in any of the subsequent issues of the *Theologische Quartalschrift*. The expulsion of the Jewish mentality apparent in the press, literature, science, and art was to be undertaken by the state as a necessary measure, although the Christian conscience had to insist that the legal ordinances be implemented in a spirit of justice and love.[68]

An article (1935) on the revolution of 1918 in a paper serving Bavarian priests exposed the role of the Jews in the *Dolchstoss* of the undefeated German army, thereby revivifying a seventeen year old accusation. "While the front made superhuman sacrifices and fought with admirable bravery against a world of enemies, the Jew Emil Barth equipped his *Untermenschen* (subhumans) with hand grenades and automatic pistols in order to attack the national defense from the rear. . . ." These acts of treason, the article suggested, actually began in 1914, when the Jew, Karl Liebknecht, refused to vote for the war appropriations.[69] The anti-Semite theme persisted. The Jews had had a "demoralizing influence on religiosity and national character."[70] The Jews, as a spiritual community, had brought the German people "more damage than benefit."[71] The Jews had killed Jesus in their boundless hatred of Christianity, and were still in the forefront of those seeking to destroy the Church.[72] These articles, written by priests, appeared in various journals and suggest the extensive network of prejudice entwined in support of the *Volk*. Some Catholic theologians attempted to promulgate a more intellectualized *völkisch* anti-Semitism that could be acceptable to intellectuals with their refined sensibilities.

In *Theologie und Glaube* (1934) Konrad Algermissen perceived a synthesis emerging between *Volkstum* and *Christentum*. Just as the renewal of the *Volk* came from Christianity, so a vibrant Christianity was internally to develop within and grow from the living essence of the *Volk*. Part of this rebirth of the spirit in God had to be rooted in race and blood. In his view a baptized Jew remained a Jew according to race and blood, although for the moral worth of the individual the race roots were insignificant compared to free-will acts. This modified racism still gave credence to the distinction contained in the insider-outsider array of values. Algermissen did, however, insist that Article 24 of the Nazi Program was not totally valid since the *Volkstum* could not be the ultimate source of value, i.e., God Himself. Essentially, the *Volk* and Christianity belonged together as nature and supernature. They were complementary. Algermissen contended that it was God's will that Christianity in Germany should appear in a form congenial and corresponding to the deepest values of the German *Volk*. Finally, Christianity had never destroyed anything worthwhile in the German soul, but rather had merely perfected everything beautiful and natural which lay at the origins of the race.[73] Supporting the intrinsic connections between Christianity and the German people could help, of course, serve to isolated the Jewish community.

Karl Eschweiler strengthened the Catholic consensus which seemed to be emerging and which helped reinforce the gradual episcopal adaptation. The NSDAP and the state had become *de facto* unified. In his view, the Reich was once again to become the strong bulwark for the Christian West or civilization would sink into a *Volksgesellschaft*, characterized by a lack of faith, in which there would be no place for the chair of Peter. Article 24 so consistently attacked by Catholics was now given a new interpretation. Its stress on the moral feeling of the German people was meant to oppose the cleavages being created in human nature, i.e., individualism vs. communism, materialism vs. spirtualism. The grace of divine faith in Germans did not destroy their unique God-created natural dispositions. Grace was support for and presupposed nature. Referring to an earlier Bavarian episcopal letter, Eschweiler agreed with the bishops' conviction that the true renewal of the *Volk* could be derived solely from faith. Christianity should reinforce the natural life of the *Volk*. When he went so far as to approve the compulsory sterilization law enacted on 14 July, 1933, Eschweiler was suspended and barred from teaching until he submitted to censure by Rome. His accommodation was too extensive. After his death (1936) an obituary in Alfred Rosenberg's gazette called him a "martyr to the Roman system."[74] The fact that all of these prominent men aligned themselves with the new regime could in all likelihood be viewed by "average" Catholics as proof that National Socialism, despite superficial faults, could not really be so evil as some had earlier suggested.[75] Practically all of these works, moreover, appeared with the approval of Church authorities and thus carried the stamp of orthodoxy. Theologians argued abstractly from a pro-*Volk* position, simultaneously putting forward the moderate anti-Semitic arguments that had become common currency among the Catholic hierarchy and theologians. Theirs was a latent, not blatantly radical anti-Semitism. Both the bishops and the theologians were intellectual anti-Semites. But what were the opinions of local priests and their congregations? In his popular sermons in the *Frauenkirche* in December, 1936, the Jesuit Hermann Muckermann concluded that Christ's teaching was not Jewish in origin, but opposed Jewry. He expressly maintained "the facts of heredity and race" and insisted that, at least in principle, the Church could support the eugenic and racial policies of the regime. He had already in the spring of 1936 in Bamberg described a "healthy racial stock" as "a lofty magnificent gift of heaven" and regarded it as a Christian duty to strengthen and multiply the home race (*Heimrasse*). Though not opposed to God's plan as such, combining the home race with alien races should be rejected.[76] Muckermann was concerned with theoretical racial and eugenic problems, not prepared to see the crucial issues at hand.

A few clergymen spoke out publicly on the "racial problem" from the Nazi perspective. A Catholic Redemptorist from Cham in 1939 praised the Nazi State, mentioned the Jewish Question, and portrayed Jews as the murderers of Christ. A Catholic priest from the Bamberg district in March, 1939, offered such a pro-Nazi sermon that about thirty people left the Church in protest. He called out as they went: "Let them go, they're nothing but Jew-servers."[77] But Nazi racial views as such were rare among the parish clergy. Although not preaching racial hatred, however, some priests did reveal a racist attitude and a basic acknowledgment that there existed a racial problem. Frequently, Catholic clergy opposed the radical racial policy of the regime and occasionally even sided openly with the persecuted Jews. Allegedly, a speaker in Bamberg declared in a sermon: "For God there is no *völkisch* matters and no national laws . . . . For him there are no racial differences."[78] A Catholic priest in Neustadt an der Saale in October, 1934, condemned human hatred and a lack of charity with respect to anti-Jewish actions and repudiated anti-Jewish songs in the *Hitlerjugend* since these produced hatred towards the Jews and implanted prejudice in young people.[79] One Catholic priest in the district of Neustadt an der Aisch in Middle Franconia was presented a summons in the summer of 1940 for allegedly saying in his sermon that "the Jews should not be cast out since they too are human beings."[80] Following the "Crystal Night" of 1938 a priest in Neumarkt in der Oberpfalz compared those who smashed Jewish windows with the purest Bolsheviks.[81] Disorder, not necessarily anti-Semitism, was to be condemned.

In Bavaria the attitudes of the clergy toward the Jews suggests divison on the "race question." Some clergy approved the exclusion of Jews from German society. Most rejected the Nazi dogma of hate toward a particular part of mankind. Still latent anti-Semitic feelings were expressed. A number of government reports show, for example, that local clergy did not condemn the discrimination itself, but rather the deplorable excesses of the Jewish persecution. In the final analysis, the evidence illustrates that the overwhelming majority of priests and pastors, modeling their superiors, made few public comments and silently watched the persecutions.[82]

A variety of reasons can be offered to explain the surprising lack of response. Clearly the vulnerable position of the priests in the Third Reich, the power of the police state, and the generally pervasive atmosphere of fear and repression explain a great deal. Defense of the Church itself had a high priority ranking, but the Jewish Question, in the opinion of Church leaders a political matter, was scrupulously avoided after 1933. Moreover, the Jewish Question did not seem to be regarded by the clergy as a central theme to be addressed. The parish priest could generally count on the popular support of his flock in response to Nazi interference in local Church affairs as well as full support from his superiors. In the Jewish Question, however, the clergy encountered primarily indifference or at the most abstract and latent anti-Semitism.[83] In Munich, for example, the police interpreted the considerable success of the annual sales at Jewish department stores as a sign that many women still "had not understood, nor want to understand, the lines laid down by the Führer for solving the Jewish Question."[84] Such complaints were common throughout Germany in these years before the war.[85] Intimidation helped reinforce the anti-Semitic ideology. Businessmen saw a chance to ruin rivals by reporting their Jewish background to the Party peasants deaf to a racial consciousness,[86] businessmen greedy for money, intellectuals mired in anti-Semitic traditions, all combined to negate any effort to oppose vigorously Nazi racism. For the peasants, economic self-interest can explain the unwillingness of rural Catholics to accept Nazi racial dogma In the Jewish Question the clergy tended to follow and reflect rather than mold popular opinion. Priests certainly rejected Nazi inhumanities, but living in a historical as well as socio-economical climate hostile to the Jews, they mirrored the anti-Semitism and indifference of their fellow-Germans. Blatant, ideological hatred of the Jews was absent in both the clergy and the laity. Certainly Christian precepts of humanity were present as well as the widespread rejection of the Nazi Party for its assault on the Church, which resulted in a rejection of Nazi values.

The hierarchy, theologians, and parish priests did little to construct anti-racist attitudes. The ambivalent attitude of the Church toward race, however, allowed the retention of anti-Semitic views by the faithful. In essence, Jews were not to be hated, but they did not necessarily have to be loved.[87] Nazi paganism was rooted in racial inequality which should have been diametrically opposed to God's commandments and the expressed values of the Catholic Church. Defending themselves against Nazism, Catholics should have rejected racism. In the real world of the Third Reich, however, the Church saw the ideological struggle mainly as a struggle for the faithful in a religious sense exclusively and as a defense of Church institutions. The real racial issue as a question of human values was only touched upon tangentially. Voices of protest were not significant in the "Church struggle" nor did they find support from the hierarchy. The Jewish Question was basically a matter of indifference to the clergy as well as to most Catholic parishoners.[88] As Kershaw has recently noted in his study of Bavaria, popular opinion was largely neutral to the fate of the Jews but infused with a populistic anti-Jewish feeling, consistently reinforced by Nazi propaganda. Such a condition provided the environment within which Nazi legal and then murderous assaults on the Jews could take place unchallenged, especially as the war began to take its physical and psychological toll on Germans. With respect to the Church, Nazi racial policies, based on universal hatred, were ignored, and Catholics seemed indifferent toward the larger human issues.

IV

Public opinion followed by the forceful reaction of the Catholic Church were the key factors in Hitler's decision to abandon the euthanasia program. The episcopal public protests helped form and consolidate public opinion and contributed to the general feeling of outrage which eventually led the Führer to suspend the domestic euthanasia program. Here is an example of the strength, power, and influence of public opinion in Hitler's totalitarian state, occurring at a time when Hitler stood at the zenith of his military success. Had German public opinion responded similarly against such other crimes as the Final Solution, the results might well have been similar. Euthanasia and the Final Solution were concrete manifestations of Nazi ideology and became gradually institutionalized after 1933. The reproduction of the experiences of the T-4 organization, the bureaucracy in charge of euthanasia, and the continuation of the purification of the German *Volk* from less worthy strains into the purification of Europe from inferior races form a continuum.[90] Euthanasia in Germany was protested; the Final Solution in the East received little vehement and meaningful opposition.

The majority of people who had been outraged over the euthanasia issue, because it touched their friends and relatives, failed to react sufficiently when their Jewish neighbors were exposed to discrimination, ghettoization, deportation, and execution. The disaster befalling the Jews, the culmination of years of antisemitic propaganda, did not stimulate similar humane feelings.[91] That German public opinion and the Church were a force to be reckoned with in principle and could have played a more positive role in averting the Jewish disaster as well — that is a lesson to be derived from the fate of Hitler's euthanasia efforts. But the power of the Church and public opinion should not be overestimated. Sterilization and euthanasia were merely components of the intricate, Nazi racial eugenic policy, almost unbelievable in magnitude until the war was well underway. Rumors of extermination camps were probably believed by many Germans. The Jewish Question for most Germans, however, was hardly a topic of concern.[92] By 1941 the Final Solution along with *Lebensraum* as the twin goals of the regime were being implemented, although ultimately the latter would be surrendered to insure the success of the former. Hitler could afford surrender on the relatively minor euthanasia program to achieve his major ideological goal. Success in war and the Final Solution would allow him to focus later on the Church, and his intentions there were clearly to destroy that institution which he had not yet fully subverted.

Nazi eugenic policies led from sterilization to the death camps in a logical progression. First, those who were thought likely to pass on hereditary defects were deprived of their procreative powers. Their children and those members of "inferior races" could be legally aborted. Then defective Germans were put to death. But since membership in an "inferior" race was considered in itself to be a hereditary, transmissable defect, the euthanasia program was simply broadened to become the mass extermination of entire populations. A number of individuals who had worked in the Euthanasia *Aktion,* for example, eventually cooperated in the Final Solution.[93] In the final analysis, the dynamic hatred of the masses proved unnecessary. Latent anti-Semitism, reinforced by and combined with compromises over the sterilization issue and concern only over fellow Germans in the euthanasia controversy as well as apathy toward such issues during the war allowed the criminal and dynamic Nazi hatred to implement the holocaust.

NOTES

1. David Blackbourn, "Roman Catholics, the Centre Party and Anti-Semitism in Imperial Germany," in Paul Kennedy and Anthony Nicholls (eds.), *National and Racialist Movements in Britain and Germany before 1914* (London, 1981), pp. 106-129; Uriel Tal, *Christians and Jews in Germany: Religion, Politics and Ideology in the Second Reich, 1870-1914* (Ithaca, New York, 1975); Werner Mosse, ed., *Entscheidungsjahr 1932. Zur Judenfrage in der Endphase der Weimarer Republik* (Tübingen, 1965).
2. Howard J. Ehrlich, *The Social Psychology of Prejudice: A Systematic Theoretical Review and Propositional Inventory of the American Social Psychological Study of Prejudice* (New York, 1973), pp. 160ff.
3. P. G. J. Pulzer, *The Rise of Political Antisemitism in Germany and Austria* (New York, 1964); Alfred Kelley, *The Descent of Darwin: The Popularization of Darwinism in Germany, 1860-1914* (Chapel Hill, North Carolina, 1981).
4. Adolf Jost, *Das Recht auf den Tod* (Göttingen, 1895).
5. Loren Graham, "Science and Values: The Eugenics Movement in Germany and Russia in the 1920s," *The American Historical Review*, 82 (1977), 1134; for an outstanding survey of pre-1933 and the National Socialist literature on virtually every aspect of racial eugenics, see Klaus Dörner, "Nationalsozialismus und Lebensvernichtung," *Vierteljahrshefte für Zeitgeschichte*, 15 (1967), 121-152; for a recent analysis of euthanasia in the Third Reich, see Ernst Klee, *'Euthanasie' im NS-Staat. Die 'Vernichtung Lebensunwerten Lebens'* Frankfurt, 1983). Klee has presented how the mass murder of the mentally ill was interwoven into the tawdry history of the Third Reich.
6. Karl Bindung und Alfred Hoche, *Die Freigabe der Vernichtung lebensunwerten Lebens, Ihr Mass und Ihre Form* (Leipzig, 1920); see also E. Meltzer, *Das Problem der Freigabe der Vernichtung lebensunwerten Lebens* (Weimar, 1925), Ernest Gellner, *Legitimation of Belief* (London, 1974), ch. 8.
7. For a well-documented, although somewhat biased perhaps because of its East German orientation, presentation of the sterilization issues before and after 1933, see Kurt Nowak, *Euthanasie und Sterilisierung im Dritten*

Reich (Göttingen, 1978). Nowak has carefully analyzed the contributions made to the ongoing debate by jurists, medical doctors, and theologians. His development of the pre-1933 Catholic position, however, is decidedly one-sided, since he never cites the works of Franz Hürth (see below) and his debate with Joseph Mayer.

8. For the most recent official Catholic position on euthanasia, see *Declaration on Euthanasia* issued by the *Sacred Congregation for the Doctrine of the Faith*, Publication No. 704, United States Catholic Conference.

9. Paula E. Hyman, "The History of European Jewry: Recent Trends in the Literature," *Journal of Modern History*, 54 (1982), 303-319. The literature on anti-Semitism in Germany is massive. Some coherent scholarly accounts of the intricacies involved in creating such an attitudinal dimension may be found in Pulzer, *Political Antisemitism* and Jacob Katz, *From Prejudice to Destruction: Anti-Semitism, 1700-1933* (Cambridge, 1980). Anti-Semitism, of course, was hardly peculiar to Germany, see Martin Blumenson, ed., *The Patton Papers: 1940-1945* (Boston, 1974), p. 751; on 17 September, 1945, Patton made the following comment on displaced persons in his Bavarian command: "(Earl G.) Harrison (State Department) and his ilk believe that the Displaced Person is a human being, which he is not, and this applies particularly to the Jews who are lower than animals."

10. *Völkischer Beobachter*, no. 131, 7 August, 1929; the evolution and institutionalization of the Nazi eugenics policy can be seen in Larry V. Thompson, "Lebensborn and the Eugenics Policy of the Reichsführer—SS," *Central European History*, 4 (1971): 54-77

11. Horowitz also convincingly argues that to raise the issue of "personality," the key to this entire issue, is to present the case for the restoration of individualism on a new basis; Irving Louis Horowitz, *Taking Lives: Genocide and State Power* (New Brunswick, New Jersey, 1980).

12. Albert Niedermeyer, *Handbuch der speziallen Pastoralmedizin* (Vienna, 1950-1953), 4:222; K. Just, *Eugenik und Weltanschauung* (Berlin, 1932).

13. Robert Graham, "The 'Right to Kill' in the Third Reich. Prelude to Genocide," *The Catholic Historical Review*, 62 (1976): 56-76; in Volumes 4 and 6, Niedermeyer has presented a thorough review of the literature covering the debates and opinions on sterilization, abortion, and euthanasia in Weimar and Nazi Germany. Before *Casti Connubi*, for example, the well-known Catholic priest-eugenicist at the Kaiser Wilhelm Institute, Professor Hermann Muckermann, supported sterilization legislation.

14. Josef Mayer, *Gesetzliche Unfruchtbarmachung Geisteskranker* (Freiburg, 1927), pp. 113-121, 124-125, 128, 352, 373-386, 422, 434; Mayer was already attacking Hürth's position, see p. 352 in Mayer, *Gesetzliche*.

15. After Mayer's 1927 work, the parameters of the debate may be seen in the following: Franz Hürth, "Die 'aequalitas institutiae in ihrer Beziehung zur 'aequivalentia obiectorum' bei strengen Reichtsverbindlichkeiten," *Scholastik*

3 (1928): 481-505; Josef Mayer, "Sexualprobleme zur Strafrechtsreform," *Theologie und Glaube* 21 (1929), 137-162; Franz Hürth, "Zur Frage des Tötungsrechtes aus Notstand," *Scholastik*, 4 (1929), 534-560. The 1927 Mayer book was later cited in a bibliography of the most important writings on the subject, in an analysis of the 1933 sterilization legislation, published by four Nazi doctors, Fran Rüdin, et al., eds., *Zur Verhütung erbkranken Nachwuchses-Gesetz und Erläuterung* (Munich, 1934).

16. As late as 1933 Mayer was still pleading for support of sterilization legislation, see Josef Mayer, "Zum Gesetz gegen erbkranken Nachwuchs," *Germania* no. 221, 13 August, 1933; see the warning of Leiber to Pacelli, cited in Ludwig Volk, Das Reichskonkordat vom 20 Juli 1933. Von den Ansätzen in der Weimarer Republik bis zur Ratifizierung am 10 September 1933 (Mainz, 1972).

17. Martin Broszat, *The Hitler State: The Foundation and Development of the Internal Structure of the Third Reich* (London, 1981), pp. 284ff.; Allan Chase, *The Legacy of Malthus* (New York, 1977), p. 349; *Reichsgesetzblatt* 1933, I, 529-531.

18. For a variety of quotes which consistently oppose euthanasia from Faulhaber in 1934 to Bertram in 1943, see Friedrich Stöffler,"Die 'Euthanasie' und die Haltung der Bischöfe im Heissischen *Reum 1940-1945*," *Archiv für Mittelrheinische Kirchengeschichte* 13 (1962), 321-323; see also, Hermann Berg, ed., *Albert Stohr, Gottes Ordnung in der Welt* (Mainz, 1960), pp. 25-28, 59; *Protokoll der Verhandlungen der Plenar-Konferenz der deutschen Bischöfe vom 29 bis 31 August 1933*, p. 12.

19. Bertram in Günter Lewy, *The Catholic Church and Nazi Germany* (New York, 1964), p. 259; see Niedermayer, 4:280 for Hürth's *Gutachten* submitted to Bertram; Mayer's opinions at this point can also be found in Josef Mayer, "Zum Gesetz gegen erbkranken Nachwuchs," *Germania*, n. 221, 13 August 1933; Josef Mayer, "Vorschlage für ein eugenisches Aufbauprogram," *Schönere Zukunft*, 21 Mai 1933;814-815; 28 Mai 1933:837-839; Leiber in Volk, *Das Reichskonkordat*, p. 248.

20. Lewy, pp. 259-260; Wilhelm Corsten, ed., *Kölner Aktenstücke zur Lage der Katholischen Kirche in Deutschland* (Cologne, 1949), pp. 17-18.

21. Bertram to the German bishops, in Lewy, p. 261.

22. *Münchener Katholische Kirchenzeitung*, no. 49, 2 December, 1934, p. 714; *Ecclesiastica*, 14 (1934): 345-346. Both Barion and Eschwiler had joined the Nazi party in May, 1933, and have files in the Berlin Document Center; Leiber to Pacelli in Volk, *Reichskonkordat*, 17 August, 1933, p. 247; *Sterilisierung und Seelsorge* (Beuron, 1935); Lewy; pp. 261-262.

23. Otto Schilling, "Richtiges und Falsches bei der sog. Eugenik," *Schönere Zukunft*, 7 (1932), 570-572, 597-598.

24. Karl Frank, "Zur Eugnik," *Stimmen der Zeit*, 128 (1935), 316-324.

25. Alexander Mitscherlich and Fred Mielke, *Doctors of Infamy* (New York, 1949), p. 91.

26. Karl Frank, "Rassenkunde und Rassengeschichte der Menschheit," *Stimmen der Zeit,* 127 (1934), 110; Franz Walther, *Die Euthanasie und die Heiligkeit des Lebens. Die Lebensvernichtung im Dienste der Medizin und Eugenick nach christlichen und materialistischer Ethik* (Munich, 1935), p. 22; Nowak, p. 128.

27. Lewy, p. 262; Norman St. John-Stenas, *Life, Death and the Law* (Bloomington, Indiana,1961),p. 174; Niedermeyer, 4:265.

28. Protokoll der Verhandlungen der Plenar-Konferenz der deutschen Bischöfe in Fulda am 5., 6. und 7. Juni 1934, p. 6; expert opinion of Professor Wehr, Trier, 4 December, 1935, DA Trier, 59/23, Lewy, p. 262; for an extensive treatment of the distinctions between material and formal cooperation as well as the other moral precepts that could be applied by pastors in handling the sterilization issue, see Niedermeyer, 4:288ff.

29. Karl Schleunes, *The Twisted Road to Auschwitz: Nazi Policy Toward German Jews, 1933-1939* (Urbana, Illinois, 1970).

30. Max Domarus, *Hitler. Reden und Proklamationen 1932-45* (Munich, 1965), 2:1058; A. Mitscherlich and F. Mielke, eds., *Medizin ohne Menschlichkeit. Dokumente des Nürnberger-Arzteprozesses,* (Frankfurt, 1948), p. 184.

31. Nowak, pp. 64ff., 87ff.; for a discussion of the euthanasia categories used by the Nazis, see Helmut Ehrhardt, *Euthanasie und Vernichtung "lebensunwerten" Lebens* (Stuttgart, 1965), p. 43. Ehrhardt also offers a succinct analysis of the medical, historical, and psychological roots of euthanasia as well as a careful analytical treatment of Nazi policy.

32. A trenchant exposition of the plight of lawyers has been provided by Lothar Gruchmann's "Euthanasie und Justiz im Dritten Reich," *Vierteljahrshefte für Zeitgeschichte,* 20 (1972), 235-279. The article exposes the operations of both Gürtner and Lammers as they tried to handle legally Hitler's oral order which in reality had the force of law. The legal problems were certainly exposed when Nazi lawyers wanted to respond to Galen and his sermons. How does a government ministry, for example, prosecute a person for breaking an unpublished law? By keeping his order secret, Hitler made it difficult to restrict opponents of the regime. But to publicize the order would mobilize public opinion against the government.

33. Graham, "Right to Kill," p. 57; W. Catel, *Grenzsituationen des Lebens. Beitrag zum Problem einer begrenzten Euthanasie* (Nürnberg, 1962). There is probably no way in which to achieve limited euthanasia; see Mitcherlich, *Medicine,* p. 98; the opposition of the Catholic Church is recounted in Nowak, pp. 158-177. The focus of the program was on eliminating those who were diseased as well as ultimately those who were socially unfit. Even under the pressure mobilized by the state, however, a majority of the German doctors

during this period repudiated the entire concept of the elimination of the *lebensunwerten Leben*; see, Georg Zillig, "Über Euthanasie," *Hochland* 42 (1949/50), 351.

34. *Acta Apostolica Sedis*, 31 (1939), 466, par. 48; United States vs. Karl Brandt et al., Nuremburg Trials, transcript, Vol. 7a, p. 2413, in Graham, "Right to Kill," p. 60.

35. *Nazi Conspiracy and Aggression* (Washington, D. C., 1947), Supplement A, pp. 1218-1225.

36. Friedrich Stöffler, "Die 'Euthanasie' und die Haltung der Bischöfe im hessischen Raum, 1940-1945," *Archiv für mittelrheinische Kirchengeschichte*, 13 (1961), 317.

37. Johann Neuhäusler, *Kreuz und Hakenkreuz* (Munich, 1946), 2: 357-359.

38. *Ibid.*, 359-363.

39. *Actes et documentesdu Saint Siege relatifs a la Seconde Guerre Mondiale*, Vol. 2: *Lettres de Pie XII aux Eveques allemands, 1939-1945* (Vatican City, 1966), pp. 102-103.

40. *Ibid.*, pp. 208-209.

41. National Archives, Washington, D. C., T 175/409/293 z 690-692.

42. The letter (16 July, 1941) was considered too weak by many of the bishops and too strong by the Minister for Church Affairs, Hans Kerrl, who on 4 August, 1941, rejected it. See *Actes et Documentes*, 2:224. See also Ludwig Volk, "Die Fuldaer Bischofskonferenz von der Enzyklika *Mit Brennender Sorge* bis Zum Ende der NS — Herrschaft", *Stimmen der Zeit*, 178 (1966), 241-267.

43. Heinrich Portmann, ed., *Bischof Graf von Galen Spricht! Ein Apostolischer Kampf und Sein Widerhall* (Freiburg, 1946), pp. 66-76; *Actes et Documentes*, 2:230, 308.

44. Gitta Sereny, *Into that Darkness: From Mercy Killing to Mass Murder* (New York, 1974), p. 295. Sereny offers the purported opinions of the now dead Burkhart Schneider, S.J., one of the editors of the materials of Pius XII. If made, Schnieder's comment is unfounded, at least with respect to content; Martin Höllen, "Katholische Kirche und NS — 'Euthanasie.' Eine vergleichende Analyse neuer Quellen," *Zeitschrift für Kirchengeschichte* 91 (1980), 81. Nowak, p. 163, 169.

45. *Nazi Conspiracy and Aggression*, 3:449-451; Stöffler, pp. 324, 342ff.; Neuhäusler, *Kreuz*, 2:371-373; *Actes et Documentes*, 2:253.

46. Konrad Hofmann, *Zeugnis und Kampfe des deutschen Episkopats. Gemeinsame Hirtenbriefe und Denkschreiben* (Freiburg, 1946), p. 72; the letter was repeated in a variety of sermons during early 1942, see Corsten, pp. 260-277 and Neuhäusler, *Kreuz*, 2:373.

47. Neuhäusler, *Kreuz*, 2:373ff.

48. Graham, "Right to Kill," pp. 72-73.
49. *Süddeutsche Zeitung,* 15 February, 1967.
50. An Erich Warmund did issue a memo, *Euthanasie im Lichte der katholischen Moral und Praxis* (Vienna, 1940). Even though the date of 1940 does not agree with the 1939 date given by Hartl, the work appears to be the "lost" memo of Josef Mayer issued not surprisingly under a pseudonym. The textual content matches the brief summary of the *Gutachten,* given in 1947 by Albert Hartl (*National Archives,* RG 238, Records of the National Archives, Collection of World War II War Crimes, C1-P1R/106, C1-11R/S3, C1-F1R/123). No records of Erich Warmund can be located at the Berlin Document Center, where they most likely would be stored, as indicated in a letter (2/14/84) from the Director of the Center to this author.
51. Hartl estimated that he had about 200 informers, both Catholic and Protestant, in ecclesiastical circles; see, Reinhard Henkys, *Die Nationalsozialisten Gewaltbrecher* (Stuttgart, 1964), p. 178.
52. Graham, "Right to Kill," pp. 73-74; see New York *Times,* 19 March, 1964, for the early reports on the trial.
53. The most recent study of the role of Albert Hartl in the SS and in his dealings with the Catholic Church is being one by Georg Denzler. See Georg Denzler, "SS — Spitzel mit Soutane," *Die Zeit,* no. 36, 3 September, 1982, pp. 9-10.
54. Martin Höllen, *Heinrich Wienken, der 'unpolitische' Kirchenpolitiker. Eine Biographie aus drei Epochen des deutschen Katholizismus* (Mainz, 1981), pp. 86-100. Höllen is convinced that one can only speculate whether an earlier or more decisive protest by the Catholic hierarchy could have been effective.
55. Heinrich Missalla, *Für Volk und Vaterland. Die kirchliche Kriegshilfe im Zweiten Weltkreig* (Königstein, 1978), pp. 115ff.
56. Ulrich Hehl, ed., *Walter Adolph, Geheime Aufzeichnungen aus den Kirchenkampf, 1935-1943* (Mainz, 1979), pp. 276ff.; Höllen, "Katholische Kirche," p. 73.
57. Robert Graham, "Spie Naziste attorno al Vaticano durante la Seconda Guerra Mondiale," *La Civilta Cattolica,* 121 (1970), 1:21-31; Hartl's indiscreet revelation on Mayer was made to Sereny, pp. 64-76.
58. Siegmund's comment in Graham, "Right to Kill," p. 76.
59. Ian Kershaw, *Popular Opinion and Public Dissent in the Third Reich in Bavaria, 1933-1945* (Oxford, 1983), 224-225; K. Patzold, *Fascismus, Rassenwahn, Judenverfolgung* (Berlin, 1975), pp. 28-32; M. Broszat, "Soziale Motivation und Führer — Bindung des Nationalsozialismus," *Vierteljahrshefte für Zeitgeschichte,* 18 (1970), 400ff.
60. Kershaw, p. 277.
61. Carl Zangerl, "Courting the Catholic Vote: The Center Party in

Baden, 1900-1913," *Central European History,* 10 (1977), 220-221, 238-240; David Blackbourn, "Class and Politics in Wilhelmine Germany: The Center Party and the Social Democrats in Württemberg," *Central European History,* 9 (1976), 220-249; Ernst Heinen, "Antisemiitsche Strömungen im politischen Katholizismus während des Kulturkampfes," in Ernst Heinen and Julius Schoeps, eds., *Geschichte in der Gegenwart* (Paderborn, 1972), pp. 259-299.

62. Gustav Gundlach, S.J., "Antisemitismus," in *Lexikon für Theologie und Kirche,* 2nd rev. ed. (Freiburg, 1930), 1:504; Lewy, p. 271; Wilhelm Maria Senn, *Katholizismus und Nationalsozialismus* (Münster, 1931), p. 80.

63. Michael Faulhaber, *Deutsches Ehrgefühl und katholisches Gewissen* (Munich, 1925), pp. 13, 19; *Münchener Katholische Kirchenzeitung,* no. 31, 31 July 1932, p. 332; *Der Rütlischwur,* 114 (1924), no. 1, p. 4.

64. Uwe Adam, *Judenpolitik im Dritten Reich* (Düsseldorf, 1972); Eberhard Jäckel, *Hitler's Weltanschauung: A Blueprint for Power* (Middletown, Connecticut, 1972).

65. Sarah Ann Gordon, *German Opposition to Anti-Semitic Measures between 1933 and 1945, with Particular Reference to the Rhine-Ruhr Area,* Ph.D. dissertaion, Buffalo, New York, 1979, pp. 410-411.

66. Lewy, ch. 10; John Conway, *The Nazi Persecution of the Churches, 1933-1945* (London, 1968); B. van Schewick, "Katholische Kirche und nationalsozialistiche Rassenpolitik," in K. Gotto and K. Repgen, eds., *Kirche, Katholiken, und Nationalsozialismus* (Mainz, 1980), pp. 83-100; Donald Dietrich, "Historical Judgments and Eternal Verities," in "The Papcy and the Holocaust: Symposium Article," *Society,* 20 (1983), 31-35.

67. Friedrich Muckermann, *Vom Rätsel der Zeit* (Munich, 1933), p. 102; A. Baumstark, "Wege Zum Judentum des neutestamentlichen Zeitalters," *Bonner Zeitschrift für Theologie und Seelsorge* 4 (1927), 24ff.; Lorenz Dürr, "Das Unsemitische und Übersemitische in der semitischen alttestamentiken Religion," *Bonner Zeitschrift für Theologie und Seelsorge* 8 (1931), 1ff.

68. Robert Grosche, "Die Grundlagen einer christlichen Politik der deutschen Katholiken," *Die Schildgenossen* 13 (1933/34), 48ff.; Rudolf Grober, "Deutsche Sendung. Zur Idee und Geschichte des Sacrum Imperium," *Werkblätter von Neudeutschland. Alterenbund* 6 (1933/34), 169ff.; 232ff.; Karl Adam, "Deutsches Volkstum und katholisches Christentum," *Theologische Quartalschrift* 114 (1933), 40ff.; Lewy, p. 279.

69. "Vor 17 Jahren: Marxismus über Deutschland," *Klerusblatt* 16 (1935), 785-788.

70. F. Schülein, "Geschichte der Juden," *Lexikon für Theologie und Kirche* (2nd rev. ed.; Freiburg, 1933), V:687.

71. Gustav Lehmacher, S.J., "Rassenwerte," *Stimmen der Zeit* 126 (1933), 81.

72. Theodor Bogler, O.S.B., *Der Glaube von Gestern und Heute* (Cologne, 1939), p. 150.

73. Konrad Algermissen, "Christentum und Germanentum," *Theologie und Glaube* 26 (1934), 302-303, 312. 219, 321-322, 328.

74. Karl Eschweiler, "Die Kirche im neuen Reich," *Deutsches Volkstum* 15 (1933), 451, 453, 455-456: *Mitteilungen zur Weltanschaulichen Lage*, II, 2 (2936), 1. Eschweiler had joined the NSDAP on 1 May, 1933 and remained a member until his death, see Berlin Document Center, file Karl Eschweiler.

75. Lewy, p. 109.

76. H. Witetschek, ed., *Die kirchliche Lage in Bayern nach den Regierungspräsidentenberichten, 1933-1943*. Vol. I. *Regierungsbezirk Oberbayern* (Mainz, 1966), pp. 175ff; H. Witetschek, ed., *Die kirchliche Lage in Bayern nach den Regierungspräsidenten 1933-1943*. Vol. II. *Regierungsbezirk Ober-und Mittelfranken* (Mainz, 1967), p. 80.

77. Witetschek, *Kirchliche Lage*, 2:317; *Ibid.*, 1:175ff.

78. Witetschek, *Kirchliche Lage*, 2:218.

79. Kershaw, p. 252.

80. Witetschek, *Kirchliche Lage*, 2:353.

81. W. Ziegler, ed., *Die kirchliche Lage in Bayern nach den Regierungspräsidentenberichten, 1933-1945*. Vol. IV. *Regierungsbezirk Niederbayern und der Oberpfalz* (Mainz, 1973), p. 224.

82. Kershaw, pp. 253-255.

83. Schleunes, pp. 88-89; P. Hanke *Zur Geschichte der Juden in München zwischen 1933 und 1945* (Munich, 1967), pp. 83-86; Kershaw, pp. 245-246, 254.

84. Kershaw, p. 245.

85. Ian Kershaw, "The Persecution of the Jews and German Popular Opinion in the Third Reich," *Leo Baeck Institute Yearbook*, 26 (1981).

86. B. Z. Ophir and F. Wiesemann, *Die judischen Gemeinden in Bayern 1918-1945. Geschichte und Zerstörung* (Munich, 1979), p. 472; Kershaw, *Popular Opinion*, p. 246.

87. Van Schewick, pp. 90-91.

88. Kershaw, *Popular Opinion*, p. 247; H. Witetschek, ed., *Die Kirchliche Lage in Bayern nach den Regierungspräsidentenberichten, 1933-1943*. Vol. III, *Regierungsbezirk Schwaben* (Mainz, 1971), p. 28.

89. Kershaw, *Popular Opinion*, p. 277. Because the study focused on Bavaria, its conclusions are certainly tentative with respect to to the rest of Germany, but are certainly suggestive and probably accurately reflect the multiplicity of Catholic and non-Catholic responses during this period; cf. Heinz Boberach, *Berichte des SD und der Gestapo über Kirchen und Kirchenvolk in Deutschland, 1934-1944* (Mainz, 1971).

90. Klaus Dörner, "Nationalsozialismus und Lebesvernichtung," *Vierteljahrshefte fur Zeitgeschichte*, 15 (1967), 152.

91. Leon Poliakov, *Harvest of Hate* (London, 1956), p. 283; the Final Solution program was reasonably well-known in Germany; see Lawrence Stokes,

"The German People and the Destruction of the European Jews," *Central European History*, 6 (1973), 167-191. Intimidation and passive security militated against any resistance to this outrage.

    92.   Stokes, 184-185; M. G. Steinert, *Hitler's Krieg und die Deutschen* (Düsseldorf, 1970), pp. 258-259.

Perverse Witness to the Holocaust:
Christian Missions and Missionaries

Robert W. Ross

Missionary work among Jews in the United States and also in Europe was being actively carried out in the period of the Nazi era, 1933-1945. Such work was carried on by Jewish evangelistic efforts within Protestant denominations who sponsored missions, appointed missionaries for Jewish evangelization, and who, sometimes, had a denominational official assigned to this area of responsibility. One example of such a denominationally sponsored program would be that of the Presbyterian Church in the United States with its Office of Jewish Evangelization, Board of National Missions headed by John Stuart Conning until 1936, when he was succeeded by Conrad Hoffman, Jr.

Prior to becoming Secretary of Jewish Evangelization, Board of National Missions, The Presbyterian Church in the United States, Hoffman had served as Director of Jewish Work for the International Council and Director of the International Missionary Council's Committee on the Christian Approach to the Jews. In his new position with the Presbyterian Church in the USA, he continued as Director of the IMC's program on a shared , or part-time basis.[1] Conrad Hoffman was a frequent traveler in Europe, and had extensive contacts through the International Missionary Council.

In 1939, Hoffman wrote an article, "To Be a Non-Aryan in Germany," published in *Women and Missions* (January, 1939), which was reprinted and distributed by the Advisory Committee on the Christian Approach to the Jews of the Board of Missions of the Presbyterian Church USA. In the article Hoffman details the effect of the Nuremberg Laws of September 15, 1935, and the subsequent "decrees" issued periodically from 1935 on, that restricted and harassed Germany's Jews. He cites loss of citizenship, loss of civil rights, loss of privileges, loss of professions, loss of businesses, loss of access to government services for assistance in emigrating, public humiliation and degradation.

> More and more you realize you are an outcast. You slink through the streets, hurry home to hide yourself away from public gaze and humiliation. . . . You dare not complain or protest; to do so and be overheard may mean arrest and concentration camp for you. And the mere mention of Dachau strikes terror in you, because of the nameless torture which you know has gone on there.[2]

In 1941, Hoffman wrote a study guide for Jewish-Christian relations, *The Jew Today*. Chapter 1 is devoted, in part, to a detailed analysis of the situation for Jews in Germany, and also in the newly occupied countries under Nazi rule. In the Foreword, Hoffman stated, "It is recognized that with the rapid shifts taking place in our present-day world, some conditions referred to here are sure to change even before the manuscript can be printed."[3]

Hoffman then described what he calls the "cold pogrom" and its effect on the 4,000,000 Jews under Hitler's domination by the end of 1940. He then wrote, "With the spread of . . . racial discrimination, the Jews of the world have entered a new era of shock and despair . . . , For the Jews the situation is freighted with menace. . . . No other people are so radically and universally affected by events of our day."[4] Hoffman further stated, "Great shiftings of Jewish populations are ruthlessly enforced; panic-stricken, desperate Jews seek to escape the relentless and brutal pressure of persecution."[5]

Hoffman then referred to "evacué camps" in Southern France, ". . . where indescribable hardships brought death to hundreds."[6] Conditions in Poland including the ghettoizing of Jews, in Rumania, in Hungary, in Czechoslovakia, Italy, in France, and in Holland are then described.

> This relentless pursuit and hounding of the Jews throughout Europe has caused increasing impoverishment of millions. . . . Families are wrecked; the individual members are often

scattered and hopelessly lost. Many have died in concentration camps. Others have committed suicide."[7]

The majority of the remaining text focuses on the failure of the nations to accept Jewis refugees, Great Britain's failure to make Palestine available, and the persistent presence of anti-Semitism in the Church (Christian) throughout Europe and in America, and as policy among the nations in the West.

Late in the text (pages 61-62) Hoffman discusses Jewish missionary work by Christian organizations. Such work was first done by the London Jews' Society founded in 1809. He noted the number of countries in which mission societies working among Jews existed (7) excluding the United States. He noted the work of the Church of Scotland, then mentioned those American denominations having official Jewish missionary offices or departments. Besides his own, the Presbyterian Church, U.S.A., the Lutheran Church, the Southern Baptist Church, the United Church of Canada, the Church of England in Canada, and the Women's Home Missionary Society of the Methodist Episcopal Church were noted. He also noted most missionary work among Jews was carried on by independent missionary organizations not affiliated with any denomination.[8]

Hoffman mentioned the Lutherans. In the Minneapolis-St. Paul, Minnesota, area there was a Lutheran cooperative ministry to Jews. It was cooperative, in that five Lutheran bodies, otherwise functioning as separate denominations, jointly supported the Zion Society for Israel missionary work.[9] Included in the work of this missionary organization was contact with missionaries in Europe's cities who worked among Jews. Also, the organization published a monthly magazine, *The Friend of Zion*. Customarily, news about the plight of the Jews in Germany and in Europe's occupied countries was carried in this magazine. Three sources for such news predominated. The first was correspondence from missionaries working in Europe who sent letters with the intention of having all or part of them published. The second source was the news services or news wires from which information would be taken, generally with acknowledgment, and printed in the magazine. The third source was persons working in

Jewish evangelization who were well-known in this area of mission endeavor who would write an article, or whose article in another periodical would be reprinted, with permission, in *The Friend of Zion*.

By March, 1934, and consistently, month by month through World War II and beyond the plight of the Jews under the Nazis was a regularly reported upon subject. The first reports were about the "Aryan paragraph" of April 7, 1933, and its meaning for Jews, particularly those who called themselves, or were called "Hebrew-Christians" or Jews who had converted to Christianity. A news note in *The Friend of Zion* for October, 1934, calls the outlook for Jews in Germany hopeless ". . . even if Hitler should be overthrown. . . ."[10] In the early years, anti-Semitism in a variety of forms was written about, or discussed. An article, translated from Swedish, focused on the "non-Aryan" legislation in Germany as a gross form of anti-Semitism, "Anti-Semitism – the Most Serious Obstacle to Jewish Evangelization."[11] In the same issue a small news item was titled "Nazi Fury Breaks Out Again Over German Jews."[12] In December, 1935, the following appeared:

> The fate of the Jews in Germany grows more instead of less tragic every day. All protests, all appeals to Germany's 'better nature' all the stir created throughout the civilized world by the anti-Semitic barbarities of the Nazis have not made any difference. One reason may be that protests and appeals have died down to almost nothing. The Nazis realizing that the world would grow indifferent, have simply gone on persecuting in the belief (shown to have been correct) that they would soon be able to persecute with great impunity. And this is what they are now doing. (*Jewish Chronicle*, quoted in News sheet).[13]

As noted in *So It Was True: The American Protestant Press and the Nazi Persecution of the Jews*, *The Friend of Zion* had one of the more extensive articles on the resignation of James G. McDonald as High Commissioner of Refugees (Jewish and Others) from Germany, of the League of Nations' Council, a resignation widely published in the secular and in the religious press worldwide.[14] Also, using information obtained from the news wire service known as JTA, the Jewish Telegraph Agency, *The Friend of Zion,* in its issues of April, May, and June, 1936, reported on a number of serious "pogroms" and anti-Jewish riots in a number of towns and cities in Poland.

The Friend of Zion maintained a steady record of recording the deteriorating situation in Germany, then from 1938 in Austria and as the Nazi regime enforced anti-Jewish legislation by decree, and in the wake of "Krystalnacht," the November 9-13, 1938, nation-wide attack on Jews and Jewish property throughout Germany. After the invasion of Poland and the beginning of World War II, *The Friend of Zion* became even more blunt and direct. In the March issue of 1940, Reverend Elias Newman, Director of the Zion Society for Israel, wrote an article, "A Piteous Cry for Help." It focused on Jews in Poland, but also Jews in all of Europe. The article concluded with, "After the Last World War, 3,000,000 Jews became beggars. Before this War ends 7,000,000 will be corpses. We must *not hesitate or linger. We must help!*" (Emphasis theirs.) What is so frightening is that his projection of Jewish dead was so close to accurate.[15]

Such reports of the projected death of millions of Jews continued to be made in the pages of this missionary magazine. The figure of projected dead, 6,000,000 appeared in an article, "Plight of Jews in Reich Told" quoting an address before the Minneapolis Jewish Federation by a Rabbi Morton M. Berman.[16] Stephen S. Wise and Nahum Goldmann were referred to in June, 1940, relative to conditions in Poland.[17] In 1941, the reports published in *The Friend of Zion* exactly paralleled the deteriorating conditions for Jews in the occupied countries. The early reports focus on starvation, disease, lack of available food, restrictions on travel, access to stores and those killed during the invasion of Poland by the Nazis.

By the spring of 1941, reports of forced labor began to appear, and by summer, mass expulsions of Jews in Poland, France, Holland, Bulgaria, and Norway are reported, but with no known destination given. By December, specific reference is being made to excessive death rates in the ghettos of Poland, with the Warsaw ghetto as the example. Sources cited for the information are the *National Jewish Monthly, JTA* (The Jewish Telegraph Agency) and the Polish Ministry of Information (London).[18]

Such reports continued to appear in *The Friend of Zion* until the War with Germany ended. It was, literally, more of the same: mass extermination, starvation, the elimination of the ghettos, the finding of the death camp at Majdanek (Lublin); in other words, the seemingly endless story of the Jewish tragedy being carried out right up to the end of the War. The major interest of *The Friend of Zion* continued to be successful missionary work among Jews, and the effort to combat anti-Semitism and Jew hatred among Christians. In both of these concerns *The Friend of Zion* is representative of those intradenominational magazines, in this case, an amalgam of five Lutheran bodies, cocerned about the Jews, and in their concern bearing a strong, consistent witness to the Nazi persecution of the Jews, and the terrors and tragedies of the Holocaust years.

Another source of information similar to, yet different from the denominationally sponsored mission programs for Jews, or the intradenominational cooperative missionary efforts such as that of the Lutherans, were the independent, self-supporting missionary organizations whose sole purpose was Jewish missionary work. They had a variety of names, and were located in several different cities in the United States, but they had a single task, missionary work among Jews. Also, several of these independent missionary organizations had as their leaders. or general secretaries, converted Jews or Jewish-Christians. The effort, then, is headed up by a Jew, converted to Christianity, who then turns to Jewish missionary work as a profession.

One such mission was called The American Board of Missions to the Jews, Inc., and was located in New York City (Brooklyn). Another, the International Hebrew Christian Alliance, was located in Chicago, Illinois. The Reverend Jacob Peltz was General Secretary and a former field worker in Europe for five years. The Friends of Israel Missionary and Relief Society, Inc. was located in Philadelphia. The Chicago Hebrew Mission was located on the south side of Chicago and The Million Testaments Campaigns had its headquarters in Philadelphia, while the Bethel Mission of Eastern Europe, Inc. was located in Los Angeles. On the opposite coast The New York Jewish Evangelization Society, Inc. carried on its work on the Lower East Side on Second Avenue.

What these independent missionary organizations have in common is that they all advertised their work in the Protestant religious press through purchasing paid advertising space. These ads, beginning in 1934, begin to tell in explicit language what is happening to Jews in Germany. The ads run in size from one column inch to full page, but all convey the message of concern for the plight of the Jews under the Nazis. The headline of a full page ad, published on the inside back cover of the *Moody Bible Institute Monthly* for February, 1934, reads "Shout It from the Housetops, It's Time to Help the Jews."[19] One of the last such paid ads, published in December, 1945, has the following headline, "Six out of Eight Million Jews in Europe Have Perished from Persecution."[20]

The significance of the ads cannot be overemphasized. As noted in *So It Was True: The American Protestant Press and the Nazi Persecution of the Jews,* these ads often appeared in religious periodicals that almost never mentioned the plight of the Jews in any other part of the publication.[21] The judgment may seem harsh, but one is left with the feeling that the business of the magazine, i.e., paying bills, dictated that such ads be accepted, but that the editorial side of the magazine chose virtual silence as its moral statement regarding the Jews under Nazi control. Since the paid ads appear over a period of *at least* eleven years, the omission of information elsewhere in the publication over this same span of years must be considered as something more than mere oversight.

Also, the paid ads are important because, from the very first ones published, the information provided about what was happening to Jews under the Nazis, was accurate and it was given uncompromisingly. In these ads, there is no equivocation. Where eye-witnesses could be cited, they were. Sources for the information were within the operational networks of these missionary organizations, was considered trustworthy and therefore the information was included in the ads. Furthermore, not only were the ads accurate, but they were timely.

The information conveyed was within the time context of the event reported. A careful scrutiny of these paid ads, widely published over the period, 1934-1946, could be the basis for such a bold statement as that the entire context of events detailing the Nazi persecution of the Jews and the Holocaust is contained in these ads. Were no other evidence or record available, the story could be reconstructed from the content of these ads.

A quick summary of key events reported in these ads will illustrate the above point, Suicide of Jews, and difficulty in leaving Germany, including Jews who are Christian converts; Jewish refugees at the borders as they were sent out of Germany under the citizenship decrees; the silence of the churches; the plight of the Austrian Jews and the suicides (1938); Krystalnacht; the Nazi concentration camps; ghettos; the Nuremberg laws being enforced in occupied countries; starvation in Poland; firing squads (1941); forced labor (1941); cholera and typhoid epidemics in the ghettos (1941); the extermination camps (October 10, 1942); "gas chambers" as a term (1943); the "official" starvation diet for Jews of "less than 300 calories;" "mass murder" of Jews; "human alaughterhouses" (1943); "4,000,000" Jews already dead (1943); death on the trains transporting Jews and use of "quicklime" (1943); the transport of Hungarian Jews (1944); "5,000,000" (1945). And all of this is a random selection taken from copies of these paid ads in hand. Not infrequently, the source for the information given is "our missionaries in Europe."[23]

Yet another form of missionary witness to the Nazi persecution of the Jews and the Holocaust existed in the period, 1933-1945. These were publications put out by missionary organizations doing missionary work among Jews. One such organization was the Hebrew Christian Alliance of America, which published a quarterly titled *The Hebrew Christian Alliance Quarterly*. What is confusing is that a very similarly named missionary organization, *The International Hebrew Christian Alliance* was also located in Chicago. They are not the same. In fact the latter organization whose paid advertising has been noted, was begun by the former General Secretary of the Hebrew Christian Alliance, who apparently, upon resigning, started a similar organization adding on the word *international* to his organization's name.[24] Jacob Peltz, in starting the new mission, turned to paid advertising as one means of publicizing his work. The Hebrew Christian Alliance of America preferred to publish its own quarterly.

This periodical, beginning with the issue dated June, 1933, began to give extensive coverage to the plight of the Jews in Germany under the Nazis. It did so in a section called The Jewish World, in which reprints of articles and news items were given as well as direct news from the wire services, including the Jewish Telegraph Agency.[25] In addition, Editoral Notes and articles were frequently devoted to information or comment on the plight of the Jews. The July-September issue for 1933 contained an extensive article on the "Aryan paragraph" of April 7, 1933, and the April 1, 1933, boycott, under the heading, "Hitler's Prosecution of the Jews."[26] A direct appeal from a missionary organization working among Jews in Germany was published, "Hebrew Christians in Germany," Taken from *Zion's Freund,* the translated article notes "Hebrew Christians of the various professions were dismissed and find themselves in dire circumstances."[27] This refers to the effect of the "Aryan paragraph" in the Reich law for the Reorganization of the Civil Service, April 7, 1933, paragraph 3, whereby Jews, even Jews of professed Christian faith, were dismissed from their jobs.

In an article, "Hebrew Christians in Germany Are Suffering," the point is made. "The Christian Jew is considered by the German people as a Jew still. . . ."[28] This theme of concern for Hebrew Christians continued, and in 1937, the need for relief for such Hebrew Christians, now refugees, was paramount. The work of the Swedish Mission for Israel through its agency in Vienna was highlighted in the fall, 1937, issue.[29] In 1938, refugee concerns continue to dominate, but by 1939 more specific references to situations in occupied Europe appear. In a reprinted article from England, mention was made of destruction of synagogues in Slovakia, application of the Nuremberg laws in Bohemia and Moravia, expulsion of Polish Jews from Ruthenia (Hungary), and reprisals by Poland on Czech Jews. Bulgaria, Rumania, Danzig and Memel are noted, and the expulsion of 15,000 Polish Jews from Germany "without a moment's warning and with only the clothes in which they stood. Not permitted by the Polish government to go beyond the frontier, they still remain there under miserable conditions."[30] One of the families was the Grynspan's (not mentioned in the article) and, of course, this leads directly to Krystallnacht, November 9-13, 1938, the worst anti-Jewish action taken against Jews through 1938.

As with the other agencies involved in missionary work among Jews, as the Second World War became a reality, the plight of the Jews in occupied Europe was followed and recorded in news notes, editorials, and articles. At the same time, anti-Semitism in America and the continuing need to assist refugees were major, constant themes. But by 1943, the concentration of information focused on Europe's Jews. An editorial mentioned, "Hitler Plans to Destroy European Jewry," shooting of people in transport, gas vans, suffocation on overcrowded trains, starvation through reduced diet, suicides, mass deportation and the "slaughter-houses in Poland." Sources were official statements about reduced populations of Jews, counting by country released by the U. S. State Department, the Polish underground and the Jewish Telegraph Agency. In all, fifteen countries were mentioned in the editorial, noting the transport of most of the Jews. A specific mention was made of death by firing squad, the Ensatzgruppen.[31] In the summer, 1943, issues, the destruction of the Warsaw Ghetto is mentioned, as well as the suicide of Sygmont Zygielboim in London.[32]

The report of the Director for winter, 1945, contains a complete summary of the fate of Europe's Jews. Using material from the War Refugee Board, the report cites death by poisonous gas, bullets, bayonets, ". . . and many other pitiless methods too horrible for public recital."[33] Interestingly enough, the report contains the phrase, ". . . this holocaust of life. . . ," certainly the choice of words of Jacob Bernheim, the Director, but it is the earliest use of the term, even with a small "h," to come to my attention. The details in Bernheim's report were confirmed in another article in the same issue by John Stuart Conning, "Israel! What of Tomorrow?"[34] The continued problems for Jews after the war ended are noted in an article, "Germany: Jews Are Saddest People; among Displaced Persons; They Have No Place to Go."[35] For Displaced persons, the Holocaust's long shadow hung over them long after the war was over. For some, it would last for five years.

So, here is the record of a perverse witness to the destruction of Europe's Jews after years of persecution by the Nazis. Hitler said he would do this. He did. Perverse, as used here, is meant to convey the meaning of ". . . opposition to what is reasonable or normal." What is reasonable or normal is, that U. S. Government sources, or the Jewish agencies would be the source for such a detailed, consistent, long-term record of Nazi persecution and destruction. They were, but we may add to these, the witness to ". . . this holocaust of life . . ." given by Christian organizations who were particularly involved with Jews because of their missionary concerns.

Whether one approves of such missionary activity is beside the point. Such missionary work was being carried out with the sincerest of motives, therefore the tendency to stress working with refugees should not be surprising. What is surprising is the accuracy and detail reported by these agencies, by reports by their leaders, through paid advertisements, through news notes, articles and editorials, even book reviews. As described above, virtually every phase of the Nazi process of persecution and destruction of Jews from 1933 through 1945, and in reference to Displaced Persons, beyond 1945, can be found in what the agencies reported. Granted, they reached a relatively limited audience, but they reached a concerned audience and the story they told was based on sources that could not be questioned. Among these sources were the missionaries and mission contacts that, somehow, seem to have been maintained, even through the war years. Their's was a witness, opposite to what is reasonable and normal. Sadly, only now is there an understanding of the significance of what they reported.

NOTES

1. See Conrad Hoffman, Jr. *The Jews Today: A Call to Christian Action* (New York: Friendship Press, 1941), frontispiece. John S. Conning served the Board of Missions as Director of the Office of Jewish Evangelization from 1920 to 1936. Hoffman assumed his work in 1937. See: The Fifteenth Annual Report, Board of National Missions, "Jews in the City," Part II, The Reports of the Boards to the One Hundred and Fiftieth General Assembly, Philadelphia, May 26-June 1, 1983, Third Series, Volume XVII, 1938, 23-24

2. Conrad Hoffman, Jr., "To Be a Non-Aryan in Germany," *Women and Missions* (January, 1938), reprinted by the Advisory Committee on the Christian Approach to the Jews of the Board of National Missions of the Presbyterian Church of the U.S.A., p. 2

3. Conrad Hoffman, Jr. *The Jews Today: A Call to Christian Action* (New York: Friendship Press, 1941), p. 4.

4. *Ibid.*, p. 5.

5. *Ibid.*

6. *Ibid.*, p. 6

7. *Ibid.*, p. 7.

8. *Ibid.*, pp. 61-62.

9. "Special Resolution on Anti-Semitism," *The Friend of Zion* (December, 1934), p. 39, refers to five Lutheran Church bodies who support the Zion Society for Israel.

10. "The Jewish World," *The Friend of Zion* (October, 1934), p. 31.

11. "Anti-Semitism — The Most Serious Obstacle to Jewish Evangelization: A Voice from Sweden," *The Friend of Zion* (September, 1935), p. 44.

12. *Loc cit.*, p. 48.

13. "Germany," *The Friend of Zion* (December, 1935), p. 71.

14. "I Cannot Remain Silent: The High Commissioner Voices the Wrongs of German Jewry," *The Friend of Zion* (March, 1936), pp. 18-19; and Robert W. Ross, *So It Was True: The American Protestant Press and the Nazi Persecution of the Jews* (Minneapolis, Minnesota: The University of Minnesota Press, 1980).

15. Rev. Elias Newman, "A Piteous Cry for Help," *The Friend of Zion* (March, 1940), 17-18.

16. "Plight of the Jews Told" (excerpt), *The Friend of Zion* (April, 1940), p. 27.

17. *Loc. cit.* (June, 1940), Various.

18. *Ibid.,* (1941), Various.

19. "Shout It From the Housetops. It's Time to Help the Jews," *The Moody Bible Institute Monthly* (February, 1934), cover 3.

20. "Six out of Eight Million Jews in Europe Have Perished from Persecution," *The Sunday School Times* (January 13, 1946), (17) 1069, the New York Jewish Evangelization Society.

21. Robert W. Ross, *So It Was True: The American Protestant Press and the Nazi Persecution of Jews* (Minneapolis: University of Minnesota Press, 1980), pp. 273-274.

22. See "Hebrew Christians Report from Europe," a paid ad placed by the International Hebrew Christian Alliance, in *The Sunday School Times* (January 20, 1943), p. 58 (118).

23. See "Resignation of General Secretary," *The Hebrew Christian Alliance Quarterly* (October-December, 1933), pp. 11-13.

24. See for example "The Jewish World," *The Hebrew Christian Alliance Quarterly* (June, 1933), pp. 38-40.
25. *Loc. cit.* (July-September, 1933), p. 28.
26. *Ibid.* (October-December, 1933), 19-20.
27. *Ibid.* (January, 1934), p. 3.
28. "German Refugees Relief," *loc. cit.* (Fall, 1937), pp. 25-27.
29. Captain R. M. Stephens, "Europe's Darkest Cloud," *loc. cit.* (Fall, 1939), pp. 26-27.
30. "Hitler Plans to Destroy European Jewry," *loc. cit.* (Winter, 1943), pp. 24-26.
31. "The Jewish Tragedy," *loc cit.* (Summer, 1943), p. 17.
32. "Report and Greetings from the Rev. Jacob Bernheim," *loc. cit.* (Winter, 1945), 18-19.
33. *Ibid.,* pp. 28-30.
34. John Stuart Conning, "Israel! What of Tomorrow?" *loc. cit.* (Winter, 1945), 28-30.
35. "Germany: Jews Are the Saddest People among Displaced Persons: They Have No Place to Go," *loc. cit.* (Summer, 1945), p. 26.

*The North American Mennonites Response to
Hitler's Persecution of the Jews*

Jack R. Fischel

The performance of American Christian Churches in protesting against Nazi Germany's persecution of the Jews in the 1930s and 40s is not a distinguished one. When church activity did take place it generally occurred in behalf of German Christian refugees. With the notable exception of the Quakers, it would appear that most clergymen (again with notable exceptions such as Harry Emerson Fosdick), and church institutions missed the opportunity to bring its great moral and material resources to bear in behalf of a small persecuted minority.

It is not as though American churches did not have ample precedents to justify mobilizing their membership against the oppression of Nazi Germany. American Catholics attempted to mobilize support for Catholics being persecuted by the Mexican government in the 1920s. Near East Relief was created in 1915 to meet the relief needs of persecuted Armenians and by 1930 it had raised some $91,000.000.[1] Similarly, in the 1920s against the background of Soviet persecution, North American Mennonites pooled their resources to help their brethren escape from the Soviet Union. The presence of Russian Mennonites in Canada and Mennonite colonies in Paraguay and Brazil are testimony to the successful relief operations of the Mennonites in behalf of their persecuted brethren.

Because of its own recent history, few American Christian groups were in a better position to empathize with the plight of European Jews than the North American Mennonites in the years between 1933-1945. Like the Jews, the descendants of the 16th century Anabaptists found themselves victims of religious intolerance and were persecuted for their beliefs. Because of their refusal to bear arms and to swear oaths the Mennonites, who originated in the Netherlands, Switzerland

and the Palatinate, were forced to migrate in order to maintain their religious practices. In the 18th century, many came to British North America and settled in Pennsylvania, Ohio, and many other parts of North America. Still other Mennonites were invited to settle in Russia by Catherine the Great, were given religious freedom, and were exempt from military service. Regardless of the new location, however, Mennonites brought with them their devotion to Scripture and their love of German culture. In fact for some Mennonites, the German language and the practice of religious devotional were seen as inseparable.

In Southern Russia, where most Mennonites lived, they mainttained a status of "a state within a state"whereby the German language and German culture flourished.[2] When, in the 19th century, the Czarist governments began their program of Russification, Mennonites were forced to leave. Towards the end of the 19th century, thousands of these Russian Mennonites left the Ukraine and came to North America. A great many of these Mennonites settled in Canada and from there attempted to retain their identity with German culture. In the 1920s, Mennonites found themselves victims of a severe famine as well as persecution from the Soviet government. In this moment of crisis for the Mennonites of Russia, their brethren in North American came to their aid. In 1920 the Mennonite Central Committee was formed to help the Mennonites in Russia from the severe famine that had begun in that year. Mobilizing the resources of the main Mennonite Conferences in North America, the M.C.C. was able to implement an effective relief program for Mennonites in the Soviet Union. Thus, like the organizational structure of their Jewish counterparts, Mennonites were able to create through the M.C.C. an organ of mutual aid which linked Mennonites throughout the world.

In 1929-1930, the Soviet government began their persecution of minorities and the Mennonites were among their victims. North American Mennonites rallied their resources and attempted to help these Russian Mennonites find a haven, and when both the United States and Canada refused to bend their immigration laws to allow these refugees entry, the situation looked hopeless. But it was the Weimar government that offered temporary sanctuary to the Russian Mennonites. For this aid, the Russian Mennonites, who would shortly find their way to South American countries as well as into Canada, would be grateful to the government of President von Hindenburg.

The advent of Hitler to power in January, 1933, brought mixed reactions from Mennonites in North America. Although Mennonites eschewed political involvement of any kind — even to the point that many Mennonites did not vote — nevertheless some Mennonites instinctively reacted to the excess of the Nazis. The influential *Chritian Monitor,* an organ of the (Old) Mennonite Church, in its world news column warned "that Germany is riding to her possible judgment and misery."[3] With regard to the Jews, . . .

> As I'm writing, the Jews of Germany are facing one of their sad days when Germany under Hitler [sic] boycott the Jews . . . What the future holds in store for the Jews of Germany, we do not know. But this we know, the days of the Jews will be days of sorrow and travail, until he will say from the heart, 'Blessed is He that cometh in the name of the Lord' . . . A word as to Germany. It has never paid any nation to misuse the Jews. Nations that kick this ancient and beloved people usually suffer seriously from stubbed toes. Hatred works like a boomerang. Germany beware."[4]

The *Christian Monitor* editorial illustrates a theme that is often found in the Mennonite press in the period, 1933-1945, amongst those who were sympathetic to the plight of the Jews in Europe. Concern for the Jews would go hand-in-hand with advice that only through conversion to Christianity could the travails of the Jews be ended. Thus in 1940 the *Christian Monitor* notes the following with regard to the plight of the Jews: In an article entitled "The Jews Awakening From their Age-Long Sleep," the writer states that Jews have begun to realize that they are not wanted in most nations and were only tolerated in others.

> These evil days have made him think. He is asking questions he never has been asking to large extent . . . this is the hour for the Christian Church! The Jew is cuddling closer

> to the Christian Church than any other group of people
> . . . Most evangelical Christians who are interested in the
> prophetic content of the Bible have a place in their hearts
> for Jews . . . There is more stir among the Jews concerning
> Christ than there has been for centuries."[5]

A Mennonite missionary, Kathe Weaver, reporting on "The Suffering Jew" for the (Old) Mennonite publication *Gospel Herald* tells her readers

> The Polish Mininstry of Information has recently reported
> that more than 500,000 persons, mostly Jews, have been
> put to death in a concentration camp at Oswiecim, south-
> west of Krakow. In a long report on Nazi atrocities the
> Ministries declared three crematories had been erected
> inside the camp to dispose of 10,000 bodies a day. Gas
> chambers were said to have been attached to the crema-
> tories . . . men, women, and children arrived by truckloads
> and were removed to the gas chambers where from ten to
> twenty-five minutes were required for execution. . . .

The above reference to the implementation of the Final Solution is one of the very few reports or notices of what was happening to European Jews to be found in the Mennonite press in the period, 1941-1945. In fact, in six important English-language Mennonite publications — *Missionary Messenger, Gospel Herald, Mennonites Weekly Review, The Mennonites, Sword and Trumpet,* and *Christian Monitor* — in the years, 1941-1945, this writer found only nine articles dealing with the plight of Jews in Europe and only two dealing with reports such as the one described above.[6]

Kathe Weaver's account of what was happening to Jews in Poland would have been a service to the Mennonite Community in alerting them to the stark realities of the Holocaust had the article not also included the following:

This is but a part of the price the Jew must pay for saying, when the Lord of glory was crucified "His blood be on us, and on our children." In Moses' farewell address to Israel he told them that continued disobedience to Jehovah would result in their world-wide dispersion . . . Our Lord Himself . . . gives an outline of events in Jewish history following His rejection until His return . . . 'Then shall they deliver you up unto tribulation and shall kill you: and ye shall be hated of all the nations for my names sake.' (Matthew 24:9)

For Kathe Weaver, even the Jewish return to Palestine is no solution, "for there is abounding evidence that the Jew is returning to Palestine in unbelief — Zionism is political, not religious."[7] It is true that a few quotations from selected publications do not necessarily lead to the conclusion that Jewish suffering was seen as an opportunity to convert Jews. But the evidence is there, that the plight of European Jewry as described, at least, in the English-language Mennonite press is, more often than not, followed by the Evangelical solution to the problem of European Jewry.

On the whole it can be argued that, as evidenced by its periodicals and weekly's, Mennoites were anti-Hitler. One could also make the case that the evangelical interest in the Jews was well meaning in the sense that Mennonites were sincerely motivated to save Jewish souls. But from the viewpoint of Jews, this misguided "philo-Semitism" didn't help them in their hour of peril, and, in fact, the evangelical solution represented an additional problem for Jews. Mennonites were not the only Christian denomination viewing the persecution of Jews in Europe as an opportunity to convert them. What is often overlooked in the sad history of the Holocaust is the fact that although milder in form and certainly not life-threatening, the missionary activity of Christian groups, both in America and in Europe, was an additional threat to Jewish existence.

Not all Mennonites concerned about the Jews of Europe were, however, offering the solution of conversion. In the pages of *The Mennonite,* a publication of the General Conference Mennonites, one can find articles on United States Immigration laws, the falsity of the *Protocols of the Elders of Zion* and in the late thirties, a series on the origins, causes and persistence of anti-Semitism.[8] A letter from a pro-Nazi Mennonite in Germany to Mennonite historian John Horsch, vehemently attacked an article in the *Christian Monitor* which exposed the anti-Jewish slanders of the Hitler regime. And, in perhaps the most pro-Jewish article found in the Mennonite press in the period, 1933-1945, the World News Editor of the *Christian Monitor* refuted, point by point, the attempt of the Nazi propaganda machine to link the Jews in Germany with Communism.[9] After "*Kristallnacht,* the *Mennonite* published vigorous denunciations of Hitler's policies towards the Jews. In May of 1939, the *Mennonite* urged that the immigration laws be amended to allow for more Jewish refugees to enter the United States and to perhaps allow them to enter without restrictions on number."[10]

Mennonites in the thirties and forties were primarily a rural people and probably had few contacts with Jews. What they knew of Jews may have come from their idealization of Jews as they emerged out of the pages of the Old Testament. Especially in the Eastern part of the United States, Mennonites were not only a deeply pious people but also, in different locations, attuned to the Fundamentalist challenge to modernism that swept eastward from places like Kansas and the South. The fundamentalism that made inroads amongst Mennonites was accompanied by the doctrine of pre-Millenialism. The pre-Millenial belief that God's plan unfolded in stages or dispensations led many Mennonites to view the persecution of Jews as part of God's plan. Perhaps the persecution of the Jews was God's way of moving the Jew to accept Christ, thus anticipating the "end of days." Mennoites of this kind were not callous to Jewish suffering but rather saw divine purpose behind what was happening. A decade later, this same type of pre-Millenialist would become one of the staunchest supporters of the newly-created state of Israel.

Stereotypes, however, work both ways. If some Mennonites connected the Jews with the Hebrews of the Old Testament, others tended to accept cultural negative stereotypes of the Jew and connected the Jews with the worst excesses of materialism and modernity. The thirties produced its share of anti-Semitic clergymen, ranging from Father Coughlin to Gerald L. K. Smith. Among Mennonites, Gerald B. Winrod, with his mixture of religious fundamentalism and anti-Semitic rhetoric, made significant inroads among Mennonites in the Middle-West as well as in the East. Winrod was a gifted orator, and Mennonites in Kansas came to know him by attending his prayer meetings as well as by reading his *Defender* — a militantly anti-Semitic, anti-New Deal and pro-Hitler publication. Reprints of *Defender* articles found their way into publications such as the *Mennonite* and the ultra-conservative Mennonite publication *Sword and Trumpet*. Although one Mennonite historian has argued that Mennonites were attracted more to Winrod's fundamentalist message than to his anti-semitism,[11] it should be pointed out that often they went together.

Among Mennonites, the fundamenalist attack on Modernism started out as an argument over the theory of evolution, the literalness of the Bible and the supernatural presence of Jesus.[12] The Modernist Controversy, as it came to be known in Mennonite circles, was linked with the triumph of atheism in the Soviet Union. Furthermore, among a small but influential number of Mennonites, there was a belief that behind the Communist Revolution in Russia was the Jew. This type of Mennonite, fundamentalist in outlook, anti-Communist and opposed to those aspects of modernity that threatened his religious "Weltanschauung," found in Adolf Hitler someone, who, he believed, was an ally against the forces of atheism and Bolshevism. The following examples illustrate how this type of Mennonite was able to combine support for Hitler with a callous disregard for what was happening to the Jews of Germany. The extracts are taken from the fundamentalist Mennonite publication *Sword and Trumpet* and are illustrative of the influence of Gerald B. Winrod among certain Mennonites.

> The Mennonites never persecute their enemies neither do they approve others doing so, but we do . . . wonder why the American press kept up such an editorial storm . . . against the heavy hand of Hitler while they can be as quiet as a dove . . . while the Communist of Russia, the promoters

of which are said to be mostly Jews, for fifteen years have kept up a campaign of oppression, enslavement . . . and extermination against the lovers of religion.

July, 1933, p. 23

Some say that the Protocols of the Elders of Zion are a forgery but it is amazing how world events seem to be shaping themselves to the pattern therein set forth.

January, 1934, p. 16

It is true that Red Communism is of Jewish origin and that its engineers and financiers are mainly Jews. Marx and Engels, the founders of the movement were Jews. It was a Jewish banking concern, Kuhn, Loeb and Co. of New York, that financed the Jews, Lenin and Trotsky, in precipitating the Russian Revolution. And 454 of the original 545 Communist offices of the Moscow dictatorship were filled by Jews. But these have been renegade Atheistic Jews, uncircumcized in heart, and he is not a Jew who is one outwardly only . . . there are only orthodox Jews who are reputable and useful citizens and we should be careful not to speak distastefully of Jews as Jews — the promise of Abraham has not run out yet.

October, 1934

It is interesting, to say the least, that at least 265 of the 454 Jews in Russia's governing circle came from the East side of N.Y. according to U.S. Senate records.

January, 1935, p. 36

Finally

The Pathfinder of Oct. 1937 records that an honor society of Jewish students has named 120 persons to a Jewish hall of fame in Chicago and gives leading names as follows: Felix Frankfurter, Albert Einstein, Leon Blum, Sigmund Freud, Paul Muni, Louis Brandeis, Benjamin Cardozo, Henry Morgenthau Jr., Maxim Litvinoff. If this list really expresses the true sentiment of the Jewish people they should not complain when they are charged with being friends, supporters, and promoters of the Communist revolutionary activities of the nation and the world.

January, 1938, p. 5

To the credit of mainstream Mennonite publications, many of these falsehoods were attacked, especially in the columns of C. F. Derstine in the *Christian Monitor*. But for those who saw the Bolsehvik Revolution as the triumph of modernism and materialism, Hitler was seen as a savior. John R. Thierstein, at one short interval, the editor of the *Mennonite* extolled Hitler's regime. According to Thierstein, the treatment of the Jews was justified because of the inordinate amount of influence they exercised in Germany. Writing in the *Bethel College Monthly* in 1934, Thierstein stated "harm done to the Jews was insignificant by comparison with the great service Hitler had performed in saving Germany from Communism and its Jewish adherents."[13]

In the years between 1933 and 1939, one could argue that whereas most Mennonites were probably anti-Hitler or indifferent to what was going on in Europe, this certainly was not true with regard to some Mennonite leaders and intellectuals. There were Mennonites such as Thierstein who suspected that what was reported with regard to the persecution of the Jews was in fact an exaggeration or a lie perpetrated by American Jews. Similarly, the influential Mennonite historian and immigrant from Germany John Horsch took a decidedly pro-Hitler position during the thirties. In response to his father-in-law, the Mennonite historian, Harold Bender challenged Horsch to prove that "wealthy Jews have worked America by propaganda" against Hitler. Bender, at the time Dean of Goshen College, and future author of the *Anabaptist Vision* further adds

> Winrod is known to be a great propagandist and has published a great deal of trash and propaganda himself. For instance he has all along upheld the truth of the ... "Jewish Protocols," and apparently, in spite of overwhelming evi-

> dence to the contrary . . . believes them to be true . . . In conclusion, my interest in Hitler and Germany . . . concerns the Christian church . . . and I feel that the situation has gotten worse. Then too, we must all feel that anti-Semitism in any respect is wrong and should not be tolerated. Hitler's official program includes this, so it can not be merely propaganda when Jews talk about. . . .[14]

Horsch, the author of books attacking modernism and Communism remained unconvinced, until the German invasion of the Netherlands, that anti-Hitler feeling in this country was not a result of Jewish propaganda. Although it would appear that Horsch's views, with regard to Jews, Communism and Hitler, were a minority voice in the Mennonite Community, his ideas would have found fertile soil among the Russian Mennonites in Canada.

The Russian Mennonite gratitude to the Weimar government for providing sanctuary in 1929-1930 was transferred to the Hitler regime. It is also not surprising that amongst the colony of Russian Mennonites in Canada, there was not only a hatred for the Soviet Union and Communism but also an admiration for Hitler who was perceived as standing up to Bolshevism.

In the pages of *Der Bote,* the leading Russian immigrant and Mennonite paper in Canada, Jews were credited with having founded Communism. The *Protocols of the Elders of Zion* were seriously discussed and the writings of Gerald B. Winrod were recommended to the paper's readership. In addition, writers from within Germany who were published in *Der Bote* assured the readership that "the maltreatment of Jews in Germany was highly exaggerated by the foreign Jewish-dominated press."[15]

How representative *Der Bote* and the immigrant Russian Mennonite press was of Russian Mennonites in Canada is difficult to determine but one historian of the period, Frank Epp, has written:

> the immigrant newspaper was a fairly representative reflection of the Mennonite immigrant mind, which in the 1930's was very strong on nurturing and preserving cultural German-

ism, as essential to the Mennonite way of life, strong also in its identification with racial Germanism, and though ambivalent on the question by and large also sympathetic to the political Germanism of the Third Reich.[16]

Epp further argues:

> The pro-German attitude of *many* Mennonites during the 1930's was common knowledge . . . The close ties with German sources in Germany and Canada, the circulation of National Socialist literature and Adolf Hitler photos, the participation in brownshirt organization and demonstrations . . . in Winnipeg there was an actual clash between Communists and brownshirts in which Mennonite blood was spilled — the actual enlistment of a few young men in the National Socialist cause and their return to Germany, the purchase of short wave radios in order to tune in Hitler's speeches and the supporting of a pro-Nazi paper could not be and were not kept a secret.[17]

But if many of the spokesmen for the Russian Mennonites in Canada were unsympathetic to the plight of European Jews, what of the overall Mennonite population in the United States? It would be exceedingly difficult ot make any general statement about Mennonite attitudes outside of what their periodicals wrote and their spokesmen said about the problem. But even if we could show conclusively that most Mennonites were concerned about the plight of the Jews in Europe, this concern would not have translated into action. Because of their belief in non-resistance and their tradition of non-involvement in politics, most Mennonites would have refrained from pressuring Congress to modify the immigration laws nor would they have joined in a boycott of Nazi Germany in behalf of German Jewry. (In Germany, some Mennonites helped Jews, others did nothing and most supported the Hitler regime going as far as serving in the German Army — in the Netherlands, Mennonites sheltered Jews).

But North American Mennonites did have a tradition of relief work.

In fact, throughout the thirties and forties, the Mennonite Central Committee was involved in relief work in many parts of Europe. M.C.C. workers aided refugees from Spain to Poland but although its charter called for the M.C.C. "to function as a charitable organization in the relief of human suffering and distress and in aiding . . . Mennonites and other refugees . . ." [18] its record is striking by its almost total absence of any relief work among Jews.

The reports and letters of M. C. Lehman, sent to Poland by the M.C.C. in 1939, for the purpose of organizing refugee relief, are notable for their lack of mention of Jews or awareness of a specific Jewish problem in Europe.[19] The official history of the M.C.C., which deals primarily with Mennonite relief work in Europe during the thirties and where possible, the forties, almost entirely ignores the plight of the Jews.[20]

Although it is true that the M.C.C. in the thirties and forties was not the well-organized and experienced relief organization it would become in the sixties, nevertheless this fact alone does not explain the omission of any reference to Jews in the official correspondence that reached the United States from Europe. Perhaps it was not simply indifference to the plight of the Jews but rather some practical dilemmas which Mennonite relief workers faced in their primary task of relieving the suffering of their Mennonite brethren. Was it possible, therefore, that the M.C.C. was afraid to rupture its good reputation with the German government and perhaps compromise the position of Mennonites in Germany by becoming advocates for the Jews? Or more to the point, was it possible that pro-Nazi Mennonites were in charge of relief on the other side of the Atlantic and thus affected the relief priorities of North American Mennonites?[21] Certainly Mennonite relief workers in Europe were in a unique position to witness the immense suffering of the Jews in Europe. Having offered possible explanations, the fact remains that this silence on the plight of the Jews remains one of the more perplexing unresolved questions in understanding Mennonite reactions to the suffering of the Jews in Europe.

The response of North American Mennonites to Jewish suffering was a complex one. If allowances are made to discount the influence of that small number of Mennonites who held anti-Semitic attitudes in the United States and a larger number in Canada, then the conclusion is reached that, as gleaned from Mennonite spokesmen and the press, most Mennonites were anti-Nazi Germany and probably concerned about the plight of the Jews. But if there was sympathy, it was not translated into action. Rather, many Mennonites believed — despite evidence to the contrary vis-à-vis Nazi racial laws — that Jewish suffering would be alleviated by accepting Christ. On an organizational level, the failure of the Mennonite relief organization even to approximate the efforts of the Quakers with regard to Jewish refugees is an unresolved question in evaluating Mennonite attitudes towards Jews. Finally, Mennonite theology simply did not allow for effective coalition politics in tandem with Jewish groups in order to bend the rigidly enforced immigration laws. Mennonites had little history in "working" Congress although there were examples of Mennonites petitioning government in behalf of their own. This last point may be a clue to the failure of not only Mennonites but most Protestant groups in bringing their resources to the aid of persecuted Jews. One can't help concluding that Protestant groups in America did not see themselves as Protestants but rather as Baptists, Methodists, Presyterians, etc.[22] It would appear, especially from the history of the M.C.C., that for the most part Mennonites thought of themselves first. What was happening to the Jews of Europe was only tangentially a Mennonite issue. That it concerned itself primarily with Mennonites caught in the European upheaval and not with refugees in general was not just a failure of the Mennonites but rather symptomatic of the overall failure of much of American Protestant denominations to transcend their sectarian loyalties in behalf of European Jewry.

NOTES

1. Nawyn, William, *American Protestantism's Response to Germany's Jews and Refugees, 1933-41,* UMI Research Press (Ann Arbor, 1980), p. 7.
2. Actually, the Russian Mennonites were Germanized Dutch, living in Russia as colonists.

3. *Christian Monitor,* March, 1933, p. 4.
4. *Ibid.,* May, 1933, p. 19.
5. *Ibid.,* July, 1940, p. 223.
6. There does exist a body of North-American German-language newspapers which the author did peruse. A sampling of these papers shows that for the most part they were concerned primarily with religious issues rather than current affairs. This does not mean that the issue of the Nazi treatment of the Jews was not addressed in these papers. Rather, this writer found nothing to substantially alter the conclusions gleaned from the English-language papers.
7. Weaver, Kathe, "The Suffering Jew," *Gospel Herald,* May 12, 1944, p. 114.
8. E. L. Horshberger, "History Views the Jewish Persecutions," *Mennonite,* February through April, 1939.
9. "Clearing the Atmosphere of Anti-Jewish Slander," *Christian Monitor,* April 13, 1936, p. 120.
10. *Mennonite,* May, 1939, p. 3.
11. Juhnke, James, *A People of Two Kingdoms: The Political Acculturation of the Kansas Mennonites* (Newton, Kansas: Faith and Life Press, 1975), pp. 132-134.
12. Horsch, John, *The Mennonite Church and Modernism* (Scottdale, Pennsylvania: Mennonite Publishing House, 1924), pp. 7-8.
13. Nawyn, *Ibid.,* p. 99.
14. See Harold Bender to John Horsch, March 9, 1935, Hist. MSS 1-8-1, John Horsch Letters, 1934-1940, Box 6.
15. Epp, Frank, Henry, "An Analysis of Germanism and National Socialism in the Immigrant Newspaper of a Canadian Minority Group, the Mennonites, in the 1930's" (unpublished Ph.D. dissertation, University of Minnesota, 1965), pp. 120-123.
16. *Ibid.,* p. 220.
17. *Ibid.,* p. 243.
18. Unruh, John, *In the Name of Christ* (Scottdale, Pennsylvania: Herald Press, 1952), p. 35.
19. See M. C. Lehman papers which are found in the archives of Goshen College.
20. Unruh, *op. cit.*
21. Epp, *op. cit.,* p. 224. Frank Epp shows the apparent pro-Nazi sympathies of Benjamin Unruh in his brief biographical sketch of the Mennonite Commissioner in Germany.
22. Nawyn, *op. cit.,* see Introduction and Conclusions.

The Death's Head and the Watchtower: Jehovah's Witnesses in the Holocuast Kingdom

Brian R. Dunn

In the years since World War II there has been tremendous and continuing interest in the Third Reich and the Holocaust. Thousands of books and articles, by both scholars and laymen, have been published. Yet, in this flood of literature, the experiences of one victim group have not been fully explored. They are the Jehovah's Witnesses. Though not a large group, their suffering was profound; and their resistance to the Nazi regime was unflinching. In 1933, when Hitler came to power there were 19,268 memebers of the sect in Germany, and while figures vary, there is no doubt that most of the Witnesses in Germany suffered in one form or another for their faith.[1] The literature describing the Jehovah's Witnesses in Germany is limited, but there are occasional, tantalizing, references in standard and less well known works.[2] William Ebenstein, writing in 1942, described a sect in which "each member seems to be a fortress which can be destroyed but never taken".[3] Bruno Bettelheim refers to a group who "showed unusual heights of human dignity and moral behavior," while Eugene Kogan says that "One cannot escape the impression that, psychologically speaking, the SS was never quite equal to the challenge offered them by Jehovah's Witnesses".[4] The Swiss Pastor Bruppacher observed in 1939 that "While men who call themselves Christians have failed in the decisive tests, these unknown witnesses of Jehovah, as Christian martyrs, are maintaining unshakable opposition against coercion of conscience and heathen idolatry . . . They suffer and bleed because, as Jehovah's witnesses and candidates for the Kingdom of Christ, they refuse the worship of Hitler and the Swastika."[5]

The Watchtower Society or Jehovah's Witnesses trace their beginnings to the ideas and activities of Charles Taze Russell.[6] He founded the group in Pittsburgh in 1870, and that city remained their international headquarters until 1908 when the offices moved to Brooklyn. The Witnesses are a millenarian sect. By a series of complex mathematical calculations based on clues gleaned from scripture, Russell predicted that Christ would become the ruler of heaven in 1914.[7] Christ's ascension to the heavenly throne would occasion upheaval in the temporal world. Many Witnesses misconstrued Russell's meaning and expected a more orthodox, protestant second-coming with a physical and visible presence.[8] When that did not occur, there was, predictably, a crisis. The organization was saved by Russell's successor as head of the movement. Joseph Franklin Rutherford took over control of the Watchtower Society in 1916 and was its leader until his death in 1942. Rutherford reinterpreted the scriptural clues and provided the Witnesses with major doctrinal innovations which not only permitted them to continue, but which stimulated great international growth. Rutherford's influence on the Jehovah's Witnesses in, what for this study are, the critical years of the 1920s and 1930s is incalculable. The Witnesses had no single official statement of their faith. Instead, the seminal concepts in the Witness ideology must be culled from the writings of Russell and Rutherford.[9] Incredibly prolific, Rutherford wrote most of the books which together with the Witness magazines made up the bulk of the material which poured from the society's presses during the 20s and 30s. The importance of the writings is twofold. First, the Jehovah's Witnesses primary method of proselytizing is through the spread of literature. Secondly, it is through the literature that we can most easily see the tenets of faith that made the society a hated minority destined for persecution in the Third Reich.

By the time that Hitler was appointed Chancellor in January, 1933, there was a large organization of German Witnesses. It was reported that during the week of April 8-16, 1933, approximately 19,000 workers had distributed more than 2.25 million pieces of literature (cf. US 20,000 workers distributed 877,000 pieces of literature).[10] The early 1930s was a litigious time for the Witnesses. Their vitriolic attacks on Roman Catholics and Catholicism and their distribution of literature on Sunday had brought them into court in this country and Germany to face charges of libel *vis-à-vis* their Catholic targets and the breaking of a myriad of local nuisance laws. In fact, during the years, 1931, and 1932, there were over 2,000 legal actions taken against the Witnesses in Germany alone.[11] The clash between Hitler and the Jehovah's Witnesses began within two months of the passage of the Enabling Act in March, 1933, and soon escalated.

In April, 1933, the Witness press at Magdeburg was temporarily seized and $25,000 worth of literature was destroyed. Rutherford responded by traveling to Germany in June to denounce Hitler at a rally. Hitler's answer was a second seizure of the Magdeburg facility, at which time he dissolved the Jehovah's Witnesses in Germany and confiscated all their property.[12] Legislation aimed at destroying the sect was initiated in 1934. The first laws prohibited meetings and distribution of literature.[13] Later laws eroded the rights of German Witnesses to work or claim any kind of state social or unemployment benefits.[14] The Witnesses were cited in the Malicious Gossip Law (*Heimtückegesetz*) of 1934 which defined their activities as foul play but not high treason.[15] Men and women indicted for violations of the Malice Law were brought before an SS *Sondergericht* (Special Court). These courts were presided over by "politically correct" judges and acquittals were rare. The sentences handed down in the *Sondergerichte* were generally fines or prison terms ranging from one month to five years.[16] In a feat of extraordinary organization and co-ordination, on October 7, 1934, Jehovah's Witnesses' meetings world-wide focused on the plight of the German Witnesses. On that night, congregations all over the world (including the underground congregations of Germany) met to pray about the problems of their German brethren. The following day, telegrams poured into the office of Wilhelm Frick, Minister of the Interior. They all bore the same message: "Your illtreatment of Jehovah's witnesses shocks all good people of earth and dishonors God's name. Refrain from further persecuting Jehovah's witnesses; otherwise God will destroy you and your national party."[17] Upon being informed about the flood of telegrams, Hitler became enraged and said that he was prepared to use the strongest measures to end the criticism of his government by the Witnesses.[18] Sentences became harsher and indictments more frequent after conscription went into effect.[19] By 1938, Custody Courts (*Vormundschaftsgerichte*) were confiscating Witnesses' children arguing that members of the sect were not fit parents of German children.[20] After the invasion of Poland, Witnesses indicted for their activities came before the *Reichskriegsgericht* (Imperial War Court) which had the power to hand down death sentences.[21]

The Jehovah's Witnesses were incompatible with Nazism for three basic reasons. First, the movement is international in scope. Second, the Witnesses are opposed to racism in any form. Finally, the winnesses believe that all earthly governments are evil and corrupt. Rejection of internationalism characterized Fascist/Nazi states. Organizations which imply international equality or those with international headquarters or leadership outside the state seemed especially threatening.[22] For this reason, the Witnesses, with their American headquarters and American leader, were unacceptable. Secondly, the Witnesses' interpretation of one verse of scripture, Acts, 17:26 "And he hath made of one blood all the nations of men for to dwell on the face of the Earth" eliminated, for them, racial or ethnic discrimination.[23] They could not accept the *übermensch/untermensch* concept. In regard to the Jews, Rutherford had strongly supported the creation of a Jewish state in Palestine. Furthermore, he opposed the conversion of Jews believing it to be contrary to scripture and he spoke out against the persecution of Jews in Nazi Germany.[24] Most important of the Nazi objections to the sect was the Witnesses attitude toward the state and their political neutrality.

One of Judge Rutherford's books, *Government* (1928), makes the official church position toward all Earthly states clear. Since the fall of man, all governments have been corrupt and all political leaders have been minions or dupes of Satan. Hitler became, for Rutherford, the quintessential example of the anti-Christ in power.[25] The attacks on Hitler began soon after his appointment to the Chancellorship, and many of the society's anti-government polemics that poured from the Witness presses were denunciation of his regime. The role of a Witness in such a society was complex. He should conscientiously and honestly obey the laws of the corrupt government under which he lived unless they directly conflicted with Jehovah's work. At the same time, he must in no way support the state. This meant that no believer could bear arms, vote, hold office, take part in public festivals, or make any sign of allegiance.[26]

After 1935, the refusal of Witnesses to serve in the armed forces, join the party, or give the Nazi salute resulted in a complete ban and long terms of imprisonment for recalcitrant Witnesses.[27] Despite these deterrents, the Witnesses could still mount an impressive "letter-box" campaign as late as December, 1936, even though by that time many of their number were already in concentration camps.[28] The major sources of information concerning the Witnesses in the camps come from their own literature. In the years since the Second World War, they have published interviews with camp survivors and eye-witness accounts of camp life in their magazines, *Consolation* (renamed *Awake* in 1946) and *The Watchtower*, and in their official history, *Jehovah's Witnesses in the Divine Purpose*. Admittedly, the sources are biased since the magazines are proselytizing tools, but the accounts are so frequently corroborated by survivors with no apparent debt to the Jehovah's Witnesses nor any attachment to the organization that it is not reasonable to reject these materials as propaganda without careful analysis and evaluation.

Jehovah's Witnesses were to be found in most of the major camps in the Holocaust Kingdom. After reading accounts by and about the Witnesses in the camps, one is struck by a commonality of experiences through which one can see the outlines of the SS policy toward the sect. The goal of the SS in dealing with the Witnesses was not to kill them, but to break their spirit and commitment. In the implementation of this policy many Witnesses would die, but there is no evidence to support the belief that there was an intention to apply the concept of the "final solution" to the sect. Himmler's attitudes toward the Witnesses provide the key to understanding SS policy. Himmler thought of the Jehovah's Witnesses as a racial tragedy because their imprisonment represented the loss to the Reich of valuable human material.[29] Racially acceptable, the Witnesses were sober and industrious; the membership was largely made up of uneducated working class men and women with few professionals or aristocrats among their numbers. The practice of the Witness faith requires many hours of voluntary service to the church each week.[30] The fact that these people were willing to work for an idea with such dedication and without thought for material compensation appealed to the *Reichsführer*. Such people, he believed, could be useful to the state in the "Germanization" of conquered territory. Once won to the service of the Reich, their families would be the nucleus of German farm communities to be established in the east.[31] Thus, with the goal of extending the *Gleichschaltung* to the Witnesses, Himmler employed three major stratagems, all of which failed. These stratagems may be called abuse, isolation, and incentives. While this essay deals with them individually, they were not enacted consecutively, but simultaneously.

From the moment of their arrival in camp the Witnesses were subjected to harsh treatment. The so-called "welcoming ceremonies" embodied perverse parodies of religious activities. Referred to as Bifos, Bible-Bees or Bible-worms, the new arrivals were frequently forced to do callisthenics until they were sick. The favored exercise was the deep knee bend with its obvious connection to the posture for prayer. At Sachsenhausen the "reception was connected with several hours of knee-crooking with the Saxon greeting (hands folded at the back of the neck).... Three SS men commanded: 'Up! Down! Roll!' till we had to vomit, and all this on ground that consisted of dusty, black coalcinder."[32] Witnesses also describe showers or drenchings with buckets of water in which the water temperature alternated between scalding and freezing, a mockery of the group's belief in adult baptism by immersion.[33] Once in the camp, the prisoners were issued uniforms bearing a purple triangle and assigned to work details. The work assignments were of the utmost importance to the Witnesses. Typically, Witnesses were set to hard labor on construction sites, in quarries or at crematoria. They were invariably forced to work a seven day week in order to insure that neither Sunday nor any other day was set aside for worship.[34] If assigned duties which they believed to be non-contributory to the war effort, their work was characterized by diligence and honesty. For example, SS officers employed them as domestic servants because there was no fear that the Witnesses would employ violence against children or spouses in the household. They acted as barbers because they could be trusted not to use a razor as a murder weapon. They acted as guards over valuables and foodstuffs because there was no fear of pilferage.[35] Additionally, Witnesses could work without guards because they would not attempt to escape. Indeed, rejection of escape as a tactic is best illustrated by the example of one camp inmate. In February, 1943, a group of prisoners was being transferred by train from one camp to another. During the course of the journey the train stopped to take on supplies which were loaded by a work party made up of prisoners. Among the prisoners was a group of Witnesses one of whom had been ordered to retrieve an item some distance from the train. While making his way back, he was horrified to see the train pull away. He immediately reported to a lineman's hut and persuaded the workman to drive him to the next stop where he boarded the train again. The SS guards were unaware of his absence until he reported back.[36] As Professor Pawelczynska noted in *Values and Violence in Auschwitz*, a Witness would perform every job, "even the most obnoxious, to the best of his ability, if it was morally neutral for him". On the other hand, "Everyone knew that no Jehovah's Witness would perform a command contrary to his religious belief and convictions or any action directed against another person, even if that person was a murderer and an SS officer".[37]

If Witnesses willingly shouldered the burdens of acceptable work, they were inflexible in the rejection of war-related activities. Stories of their intransigence in this matter are numerous. Some Witnesses refused to care for angora rabbits because the combings were believed to be used in the making of uniforms. Others refused work in vegetable gardens when it was learned that the produce went to military hospitals.[38] Perhaps the most spectacular refusal of work was in Ravensbruck in December, 1939. In that month, 500 Witness women working in a sewing block refused to sew ammunition pockets on military uniforms. Their punishment was severe. Coats and blankets were confiscated, rations were cut and all medical aid was denied. The offenders were then locked in dark, cold cells for three weeks. Ultimately, not one woman obeyed the exhortations and demands to return to the sewing block, and all were reassigned to pick and shovel details on farms, roads, and construction sites. Frequently, during their ordeal their guards would tell them: "If you don't agree to support the war effort, you won't get out of here except through the chimney!"[39]

If certain labor demands caused problems for the Witnesses, so too did the demands for military service. In 1939 when the war broke out, Witnesses were invited to volunteer for the armed forces. In Sachsenhausen, each refusal was followed by the killing of ten men. After forty men had been shot, the SS desisted. In Buchenwald, Witnesses were lined up and told that anyone refusing to fight against France and England would die. Although two companies of fully equipped SS guards were drawn up in front of them, the officer's appeal to fight for Germany went unanswered. In this case, the men were not killed; but they were assaulted, assigned to quarry duty and barred from hospital treatment.[40] These incidents are large scale versions of a drama that was played out time and time again in many of the camps. The scenario hardly varied. Witnesses were lined up, and a man or woman chosen at random was ordered to give the Hitler salute, deny Jehovah, denounce Judge Rutherford or do some war-related task. The invariable refusal was followed by physical abuse or execution. There are numerous examples. At Neuengamme, near Hamburg, seven Witnesses were asked, in front of other prisoners, the question: "How long will you remain a Bible Student?" Upon receiving the answer "Till my death," the interrogator adminstered twenty-five lashes with a steel rod sewn into leather. The officer desisted after all seven Witnesses had answered the question three times and received seventy-five lashes each.[41] At another camp, one Witness was handed a microphone and ordered to renounce the sect on pain of death. He took the opportunity "to witness about the kingdom of heaven" and was shot.[42] As a tactic, intimidation and abuse proved itself bankrupt time and time again.

The concept of isolation as it relates to the Witness prisoners can be seen from two perspectives. First, they were isolated from other prisoners in the camp. The tendency was to house the Witnesses together in blocks. While this did inhibit proselytizing in the camps, it also provided the environment in which the Witnesses could continue to affirm their faith together.[43] Although contact with other prisoners was rare, Witnesses did seek to bring new members to the faith. While numbers were small, there were some successes. Secret baptisms were carried out in the camps themselves.[44] An example of continued work within the camp is the attempt to convert Princess Mafalda of Hesse, daughter of the King and Queen of Italy. Maria Ruhnar, a Witness, had been assigned to the Princess as a servant in the isolation block of Buchenwald. When the Princess was killed in an air raid in August, 1944, Maria reported that she had been witnessing to the Princess.[45] Additionally, housing Witnesses together permitted newly arrived inmates to share, from memory, the most recent literature with those who had been incarcerated for long periods.[46] The housing arrangements allowed for the creation of an intense peer pressure to remain faithful. A group cohesiveness developed that while frequently assailed was never broken.

The attempt to isolate the Witnesses from outside contacts failed in a spectacular way. One goal of the isolation policy was to keep the Witnesses from obtaining Bibles or spiritual literature. While the Witness accounts do include isolated instances of Bibles being pushed into their hands and through the bars of their cells, they were most creative in smuggling *The Watchtower* into the camps. Although the German presses were closed, French Witnesses translated and duplicated literature as it came into their hands.[47] Standard mechanisms of getting the material into the camps usually hinged on the fact that Witnesses worked without guards. Contacts would pass the material to workers outside the camps and away from the guards. The papers would then be secreted on the body and taken back to the barracks. Detection meant death. One group of prisoners regarded themselves as peculiarly fortunate since one of their number had a hollow wooden leg which he would fill with literature obtained through an outside contact.[48] During times in which food parcels were permitted, *Watchtower*s were baked into breads and cakes and thus delivered.[49] The SS also saw mail restriction as a way to isolate the Witnesses and weaken their resolve. Incoming mail was rigorously censored and outgoing mail was strictly limited. The mail was closed to Witnesses altogether after 1939, and then a Witness could send one twenty-five word letter per month to his or her family.[50] Ironically, while they were not permitted to mention religion, each letter bore a stamp which read: "The prisoner is now as ever an obstinate Bible Student and refuses to renounce the heresy of the Bible Students. For this reason he had merely been deprived of the facility of the otherwise permitted exchange of letters."[51] The stamp was evidence of continued fidelity, and families at home were frequently less interested in the contents of the letter, "for what could one say in five lines", than the continued appearance of the stamp.[52] Whatever hopes Himmler may have cherished about isolation contributing to a weakening of resolve, they were dashed by the Witnesses' response.

Beginning as early as September, 1938, Witnesses in the camps could ransom themselves by signing a declaration abjuring their faith. The declaration consisted of six brief paragraphs which bound the signator to six agreements. The signator had to admit that the sect was evil, divorce himself from it, and promise to remain detached from the group. Further, he had to promise to turn over to the police any spiritual literature which should subsequently come into his hands, and reveal the names of the people who distributed the material. Finally, the signator had to agree to become a fully integrated member of the community of the state and expect arrest if any of these terms were broken.[53] The Witnesses are proud of the fact that so few signed the declaration. Even when the offer included, as it frequently did, guarantees of employment, Witnesses did not sign. Margaret Buber, while a block senior at Ravensbruck, persuaded a sick woman to sign the declaration to save her life. Other Witnesses were outraged and believed the signator's soul to be lost.[54] In the end it was apparent that Witnesses could neither be threatened nor cajoled into giving up their faith. Tactics of abuse, violence and deprivation had failed. Bribery had been contemptuously ignored. Himmler had failed to break the spirit of this small group.

In *The Informed Heart,* Bruno Bettelheim says that according to psychoanalytic theory, the Jehovah's Witnesses "would have had to be viewed as extremely neurotic or plainly delusional, and therefore apt to fall apart, as persons, under stress." But in fact they "seemed protected against the same camp experience that soon destroyed persons considered very well integrated by my psychoanalytic friends and myself."[55] There are three major reasons that explain why the Witnesses were able to meet the SS's challenge. First, Witness literature reveals a sense of predisposition toward martyrdom. Secondly, the Witnesses' beliefs were as fanatical and dogmatic as those of the Nazis. Thirdly, the Witnesses did not see their plight as the result of a conflict between themselves and Nazis, but as part of the cosmic struggle between Christ and anti-Christ.

In reading through accounts and interviews published by the Jehovah's Witnesses, it is impressive to notice how many times words like "suffering," "hunger," "pain, "danger" and "privilege" appear in the same sentence. The typical Witness attitude is eloquently expressed by a young woman at Mauthausen who says "I kept my eyes fixed on my parents' example of integrity. Often mother's words came back to me: 'The testing of our faith is a privilege and good training.' . . . I remembered that persecuted Christians are a spectacle to outsiders."[56] A woman risking her life to smuggle literature to her co-religionists says "It was a privilege to take over the sending of food parcels containing excerpts from *The Watchtower* into Dachau."[57] On the night before his execution a young Witness wrote to his father, "Now I, too, have been given an opportunity to prove my faithfulness to the Lord unto death, yes, in faithfulness not only up unto death, but even into death."[58] The union of suffering and privilege is not merely a sentiment seen over and over in the documents relating to the Witness camp experience. This attitude is clearly evident in the official literature of the Witnesses. In his book *Enemies* (1937), Rutherford has this to say about persecution: "It is certain, therefore, that all the true followers of Christ Jesus, who constitute his church, must suffer more or less at the hands of the Devil, and which suffering and punishment is inflicted upon them by the religious agents of the Devil on earth, just as they afflicted the Lord Jesus Christ. For this reason some of the sufferings of Christ was [sic] left over for the body's sake. . . ."[59] If one asks why the faithful must suffer, and why they are not safeguarded from pain, the answer is "that if God should do so, then the Devil would not have a free hand in his effort to prove his wicked challenge; and, furthermore, those who have agreed to serve God could prove their integrity and faithfulness to God only by resisting the assaults of the Devil, and under all conditions of persecution continuing to maintain their integrity toward God."[60] This attitude, so prevalent among the Witnesses, laid the foundation for an acceptance of — if indeed not a quest for — suffering and pain. Many of the accounts written by Witness survivors end on a note of thanksgiving. The Witnesses were grateful for the opportunity to prove themselves under duress: ". . . we have experienced the truthfulness of the words at [sic] Malachi 3:10: 'Test me out, please, in this respect'."[61]

In *Enemies,* Rutherford says that Germany is "outwardly ruled by the fanatic Hitler," but secretly ruled by the Roman Catholic Church and the Devil.[62] "Fanatic" is a word hedged round with dark, unkind — even sinister connotations. On the other hand, the *Oxford English Dictionary* defines the word as "a person possessed by a deity or a demon." In that sense, perhaps, Witnesses will not be offended at the suggestion that their attachment to their religious beliefs was at least as fanatical as the attachment of the Nazis to their political creed. The dogmatic nature of the Witness faith did not allow for compromise. It is well known, for example, that the Witnesses' interpretation of Leviticus 17:14, ". . . I said unto the children of Israel, Ye shall eat the blood of no manner of flesh. . ." is the basis of their refusal to eat a portion of their already insufficient food rations. "And as they served a slice of blood sausage several times a week, which we refused, we were given nothing at all. Did not Jesus say: 'It is written, 'Man must live, not on bread alone, but on every utterance coming forth through Jehovah's mouth? I came to deeply appreciate those words, for it was in truth the spiritual food that could keep us alive."[63] There was no room for rationalization, flexibility or compromise. To employ a somewhat worn analogy, faith to the Witnesses, was like virginity to a chaste woman. It was not possible to give up part of it without losing it all. On the occasions at which a confrontation between the Witnesses and the SS was a test of wills, the SS invariably lost. There are even indications that some SS guards developed a grudging sense of admiration for their victims. As one officer noted, "Look at these people! One can imprison them, take everything away from them and even kill them, but they do not give up their belief in Jehovah. They do their work well and are honest people, but for war they are no good."[64] Gerhard Oltmanns, a Witness prisoner, relates that he once commented to an SS overseer, "'Sir, you are a soldier. I also am a soldier.' I had in mind 2 *Timothy* 2:2-4,"[65] For the most part, the army of the *Watchtower* instilled a greater sense of discipline and dedication than the army of the Reich.

Finally, the Witnesses clearly viewed the clash between themselves and Hitler's government as a battle in the war between Christ and anti-Christ. In 1939 Himmler himself addressed a group of Witness prisoners at the Lichtenberg concentration camp. When none of the Witnesses would abandon their faith he flew into a rage and cried: "If you like, your Jehovah may reign in heaven, but here upon earth it is we who rule! We'll show you who will endure longer, you or we!" One survivor who heard Himmler that day spent the following six years in Ravensbruck enduring "the most horrible conditions imaginable. Yet, we Witnesses survived, although Himmler, Hitler and their crowd are gone!"[66] Himmler stood against Jehovah, and the devil was seeking to destroy the fidelity of God's people through suffering. Because the camp experiences were seen as an episode of Holy War, it was important for the Witnesses to work for group survival. One woman who had been among the resisters at the Ravensbruck sewing block reported: "We should have died off like flies. But Jehovah God, who had been directly challenged by Himmler, showed that He can sustain His people under the worst circumstances. Not one of our 500 sisters fell seriously ill, nor did any die. Even a few SS people said: 'That's because your Jehovah has helped you.' And, more importantly, not one sister had given up; all remained loyal. It was a real triumph of integrity to Jehovah!"[67] Witness testimonials are filled with accounts of actions beneficial to the group. For example, if a Witness began to lose weight dramatically and show signs of becoming a "Moslem," that is a prisoner whose will to live had dissolved, the community mobilized to share their meager rations in order to restore the brother. One young Witness who lost weight dramatically in the camp environment reported that he was given food overtly, and on one occasion he reports "Finally we went back to the barracks, and I felt a piece of bread being put into my hand by a Witness from another section of the camp. I was the only one with a little food."[68] In April, 1945, prisoners were evacuated from Sachsenhausen. The intention was to march them to Lubeck, but in fact the march ended in Schwerin. Although prisoners were organized by nationality, the Witnesses, representing six nations, were kept together. The SS had put the Witnesses in charge of a cart containing valuables taken from the prisoners. They knew that the Witnesses would not steal from the treasure. While at first pulling the heavy cart seemed an additional burden on an already difficult march, it was quickly interpreted as a blessing from God. SS guards were dispatching anyone who could not keep up. Of the 26,000 who began the march, more than 10,000 were shot on the road. None of the 230 Witnesses died. As one would begin to falter, he would be hoisted on to the cart until his strength had sufficiently recovered. The Sachsenhausen death march is described as a victory of Jehovah over the SS.[69] Survival as a group, so important in the Holy War, had been achieved.

The persecution of Jehovah Witnesses in the Holocaust Kingdom has taken its place among other times of trial in their history and mythology. Historical analysis suggests that the treatment and options of the sect in the camps were unique. As dedicated to their own convictions as the Nazis, the Witnesses could not be moved by derision, abuse, exhortation, isolation, or incentives. Every SS stratagem foundered on the Witnesses' interpretation of their experiences under the Nazi regime as a confirmation of God's plan and their place in it. Less than two months before World War II began, the *Daily News* of Natal, South Africa, carried a story that included these lines: "It is not generally known that the 'Bibelforschers' constitute the sole obstacle within the old Reich which Hitler has not been able to sweep from his path . . . But, like a light that never flickers, this little body of Christian men and women stand steadfast in their faith, a thorn in the side of the Monarch of Munich and a living testimony to his mortality."[70] Now that report seems like observation turned prophesy. Six years after it was published, Hitler's mortality had been definitively demonstrated and the little sect was still an unflickering light. The Jehovah's Witnesses not only survived Nazi persecution, but in an extraordinary fashion it strengthened their devotion. They were among the triumphant survivors.

NOTES

1. For membership, see *Jehovah's Witnesses in the Divine Purpose* (Brooklyn, 1959), p. 129. Estimates of the numbers of Witnesses arrested, imprisoned, executed or died whilst in prison vary. The most conservative estimates come from the Witnesses themselves. Their calculations indicate that "6,019 were arrested, several of them, two, three or more times. Two thousand suffered in concentration camps. A total of 635 Witnesses died in prison, 203 being executed." See *The Watchtower,* July 1, 1979, p. 8. The figures of 4,000-5,000 lost lives in Michael Kater, "Die Ernsten Bibelforscher im Dritten Reich," *Vierteljahrshefte fur Zeitgeschichte,* 17 (1969), 181, is based on new sources and represents the highest estimate. In Friedrich Zipfel, *Kirchenkampf in Deutschland, 1933-1945* (Berlin, 1965), p. 176, and Gunther Weisenborn, *Der Lautlose Aufstand. Bericht uber die Widerstandsbewegung des deutschen Volkes 1933-1945* (Hamburg, 1953), pp. 77-78, the estimates fall between the high and low figures.

2. In addition to the works cited in this paper, the following may be profitably examined: Ernst Christian Helmreich, *The German Churches under Hitler* (Detroit, 1979), and J. S. Conway, *The Nazi Persecution of the Churches, 1933-1945* (New York, 1968).

3. William Ebenstein, *The Nazi State* (New York, 1943), p. 215.

4. Bruno Bettelheim, *The Informed Heart* (United States, 1960), p. 20, and Eugene Kogon, *The Theory and Practice of Hell* (New York, 1979), p. 43.

5. Quoted in *Witnesses in Divine Purpose,* p. 173.

6. For an excellent brief history of the Witnesses see Anthony A. Hoekema, *The Four Major Cults* (Grand Rapids, 1963).

7. *Ibid.* For an explanation of these extraordinary calculations see pp. 252=254.

8. There are still misunderstandings as to what was to happen in 1914. Two recent issues of *The Watchtower* (April 1, 1984, pp. 5-8, and April 15, 1984, pp. 3-6) have included articles dealing with the meaning of 1914. Even scholars are occasionally confused, see David R. Manwaring, *Render unto Caesar* (Chicago, 1962),, p. 19, for an example of inaccuracy.

9. Rutherford's writings are no longer as central to Witness doctrine.

For example, the anti-Catholic sentiment, so prominent in Rutherford, is somewhat less evident. Although it is by no means complete, there is a list of Rutherford's major works in Hoekema, p. 432, see also *The National Union Catalog* (London, 1977), vol. 512, pp. 102-110.

10. *Witnesses in Divine Purpose*, p. 129.

11. See *The Watchtower*, January 1, 1968, p. 35, and *The Watchtower*, August 1, 1955, p. 461.

12. *Witnesses in Divine Purpose*, pp. 129-130, and *The Watchtower*, August 1, 1955, pp. 461-462.

13. Kater, pp. 192-193.

14. *Ibid.*, pp. 195-196.

15. *Ibid.*, p. 197.

16. *Idem.*

17. *Witnesses in Divine Purpose*, p. 142.

18. *Ibid.*, p. 142.

19. Kater, p. 198.

20. *Ibid.*, p. 200.

21. *Ibid.*, pp. 198-199.

22. William Ebenstein, *Today's Isms* (United States, 1954), pp. 102-103.

23. J. F. Rutherford, *Government* (Brooklyn, 1928), pp. 27 and 53-54.

24. See J. F. Rutherford, *Comfort for the Jews* (Brooklyn, 1925), *passim,* and J. F. Rutherford, *Fascism or Freedom* (Brooklyn, 1939), p. 11.

25. See *Fascism or Freedom,* pp. 11-14 *passim,* J. F. Rutherford, *Enemies* (Brooklyn, 1937), p. 323, and J. F. Rutherford, *Theocracy* (Brooklyn, 1940), frontispiece is a drawing of Satan, Hitler and the Pope presiding over the world.

26. *Government,* p. 27 *passim.* See also *Theocracy, passim.* In a recent article, a French writer has suggested that German and English Witnesses did take an active role in World War I, and that French Witnesses worked in non-combat positions for the French underground during the Nazi occupation of France. See Regis Dericquebourg, "Note sur l'attitude des temoin de jehovah et des Baptistes face a l'occupant pendant la seconde guerre mondiale," *Revue du Nord,* 60 (1978), 439-443.

27. Kater, p. 181.

28. On December 12, 1936, 15,000 Witnesses distributed 300,000 copies of *The Watchtower* (20 each) by putting them in mailboxes between the hours of 5:00 and 7:00 in the evening. They were not to communicate with anyone, but merely to distribute the magazine. See *Witnesses in Divine Purpose,* p. 164.

29. Kater, pp. 190-191, and Christine E. King, "Strategies for Survival: An Examination of the History of Five Christian Sects in Germany, 1933-1945," *Journal of Contemporary History,* 14 (1979), p. 220.

30. Kogon, p. 273. To be an active participant in the Witness faith requires an extraordinary investment of time spent in distributing the literature and witnessing to those who are not members of the sect.
31. Kater, p. 191, and King, p. 220.
32. *Witnesses in Divine Purpose*, p. 167.
33. *Ibid.*, p. 267.
34. Kater, p. 209, and *The Watchtower*, November 1, 1979, p. 11.
35. Franz Zürcher, *Kreuzzug gegen das Christentum* (Zurich, 1938), p. 105.
36. *Witnesses in Divine Purpose*, pp. 169-170.
37. Anna Pawelczynska, *Values and Violence in Auschwitz* (Berkeley, 1979), p. 89.
38. King, p. 219.
39. *The Watchtower*, November 1, 1979, p. 11.
40. Kogon, p. 42.
41. *Witnesses in Divine Purpose*, p. 167.
42. *Ibid.*, 172.
43. In Neuengamme, when it was discovered that housing Witnesses together facilitated worship, they were dispersed throughout the camp. "But instead of being a hindrance to the work, possibilities for coming into contact with the other prisoners increased. In this way each block was thoroughly worked...," *Witnesses in Divine Purpose*, p. 171.
44. *Witnesses in Divine Purpose*, pp. 170 and 172.
45. *Ibid.*, p. 107, and Kogon, p. 50.
46. *Witnesses in Divine Purpose*, p. 170.
47. Deriquebourg, p. 441.
48. *Witnesses in Divine Purpose*, p. 170.
49. *The Watchtower*, October 1, 1978, p. 22.
50. Kogon, p. 123.
51. *Witnesses in Divine Purpose*, p. 168.
52. *Ibid.*, p. 168.
53. *Ibid.*, p. 166.
54. Quoted in King, p. 218.
55. Bettelheim, pp. 21-22.
56. *The Watchtower*, October 1, 1978, p. 23.
56. *Ibid.*, p. 23.
58. *The Watchtower* November 1, 1979, p. 4.
59. *Enemies*, p. 137.
60. *Ibid.*, p. 88.
61. *The Watchtower*, November 1, 1979, p. 14.
62. *Enemies*, p. 323.
63. *Witnesses in Divine Purpose*, p. 161.

64. *The Watchtower*, March 15, 1968, p. 190.
65. *The Watchtower*, October 1, 1968, p. 600, "and what you have heard from me before many witnesses entrust to faithful who will be able to teach others also. Share in suffering as a good soldier of Christ Jesus. No soldier on service gets entangled in civilian pursuits, since his aim is to satisfy the one who enlisted him." 2 *Tim.* 2-4, *Revised Standard Version*.
66. *The Watchtower*, November 1, 1978, p. 8.
67. *Ibid.*, p. 11.
68. *Awake*, October 8, 1978, p. 22.
69. *The Watchtower*, August 15, 1980, pp. 7-10.
70. Quoted in *Witnesses in Divine Purpose*, p. 173.

ACKNOWLEDGMENTS

Even in the writing of a small article one incurs debts. I benefitted from the skills of Erika Klusener and Don and Christine Totten in the translation of some very difficult German. Suzanne Van Meter and George Barber made valuable stylistic suggestions during the writing of the piece. Most importantly, Bryce Gray put his own library of Witness literature at my disposal and spent many hours locating the long out-of-print and difficult-to-find works of Joseph Rutherford.

The Churches' Response to the Holocaust:
A Selected Bibliography

BOOKS

Bauer, Yehuda. *American Jewry and the Holocaust.* Detroit: Wayne State University Press, 1981.

Cardinale, Igino. *Le Saint-Siege et la Diplomatie: Apercu Historique, Juridique et Pratique de la Diplomatic Pontificale.* (*The Holy See and Diplomacy: a Historical, Juridical, and Practical Survey of Pontifical Diplomacy.*) Paris: Desclee et Cie, Editeurs, 1962.

———. *The Holy See and International Order.* Gerards Cross: Colin Smythe, 1976

Cochrane, Arthur C. *The Church's Confession under Hitler.* Philadelphia: Westminster Press, 1962.

Conway, John S. *The Nazi Persecution of the Churches, 1933-1945* New York: Basic Books, 1968.

Deschner, Karlheinz. *Mitt Gott und den Faschisten: der Vatikan im Bunde mit Mussolini, Franco, Hitler und Pavelic.* (*With God and the Fascists: the Vatican in League with Mussolini, Franco, Hitler, and Pavelic.*) Stuttgart: Hans E. Gunther Verlag, 1965.

Donohue, James. *Hitler's Conservative Opponents in Bavaria 1930-1945: a Study of Catholic, Monarchist and Separatist Anti-Nazi Activities.* Leiden, 1962.

Duclos, Paul. *Le Vatican et la Seconde Guerra Mondiale: Action Doctrinal et Diplomatique en faveur de la Paiz.* (*The Vatican and the Second World War: Doctrinal and Diplomatic Action in Favor of Peace.*) Paris: Editions A. Dedone, 1955.

Falconi, Carlo. *The Silence of Pius XII.* Translated by Bernard Wall. Boston: Little, Brown, & Co., 1970.

Fireside, Henry. *Icon and Swastika: the Russian Orthodox Church under Nazi and Soviet Control* Cambridge, Massachusetts: Harvard University Press, 1971.

Friedlander, Saul. *Pius XII and the Third Reich: a Documentation.* Translated by Charles Fullman. New York: A. A. Knopf, 1966.

Gallin, Mary Alice. *German Resistance to Hitler: Ethical and Religious Factors.* Washington: 1961.

Giordani, Igino. *Vita Contra Morte: la Santa Sede per le Vittime della Seconda Guerra Mondiale. (Life Against Death: the Holy See on Behalf of Victims of the Second World War.)* Rome: Arnolde Mondadori, 1956.

Glenthø, Jørgen. "The Little Dunkerque: the Danish Rescue of Jews in October 1943," in Michael D. Ryan, ed., *Human Responses to the Holocaust: Perpetrators and Victims, Bystanders and Resisters.* New York: Edwin Mellen, Publishers, 1981.

Graham, Robert A. *Vatican Diplomacy: a Study of Church and State on the International Plane.* Princeton: Princeton University Press, 1959.

Gutteridge, Richard. *The German Evangelical Church and the Jews, 1879-1950.* New York: 1976.

Helmreich, Ernst Christian. *The German Churches under Hitler: Background, Struggle, Epilogue.* Detroit: Wayne State University Press, 1979.

Jardini, Domenico, Cardinal. *Memories of Pius XII.* Translated by Rosemary Goldie. Westminister: Newman Press, 1961.

Jelinek, Yeshayahu. "The Vatican, the Catholic Church, the Catholics, and the Persecution of the Jews during World War II: the Case of Slovakia," in Bela Vago and George L. Mosse, eds., *Jews and Non-Jews in Eastern Europe, 1918-1945.* New York: John Wiley & Sons, 1974.

Lewy, Guenther. *The Catholic Church and Nazi Germany.* New York: McGraw-Hill Book Co., 1964.

Lichten, Joseph L. *A Question of Judgment. Pius XII and the Jews.* Washington: 1963.

Littell, H. Franklin. *The German Phoenix. Men and Movements in the Church in Germany.* New York, 1966.

———. "Protestant Churches and Totalitarianism (Germany 1933-1945) in Carl J. Friedrich, ed., *Totalitarianism.* Cambridge: Harvard University Press, 1954.

———, and Hubert G. Locke, eds. *The German Church Struggle and the Holocaust*. Detroit: Wayne State University Press, 1974.

Macfarland, Charles S. *The New Church and the New Germany: a Study of Church and State*. New York, 1934.

Mason, John Brown. *Hitler's First Foes: a Study of Religion and Politics*. Minneapolis, 1936.

Micklen, Nathaniel. *National Socialism and the Roman Catholic Church, Being an Account of the Conflict between National Socialist Government of Germany and the Roman Catholic Church, 1933-1938*. London: Oxford University Press, 1939.

Morley, John F. *Vatican Diplomacy and the Jews During the Holocaust, 1939-1945*. New York: KTAV Publishing House, 1980.

Mother Mary Alice Gallin. *German Resistance to Hitler: Ethical and Religious Factors*. Washington, D.C.: The Catholic University of America Press, 1961.

Nawyn, William, *American Protestantism's Response to Germany's Jews and Refugees, 1933-14*. Ann Arbor: UMI Reserach Press, 1980.

Neusner, Jacob. *Stranger at Home: "The Holocuast," Zionism, and American Judaism*. Chicago: University of Chicago Press, 1981.

Nichols, Peter. *The Politics of the Vatican*. London, 1968.

The Persecution of the Catholic Church in Germany: Facts and Documents translated from the German. Assembled by Walter Mariaux, S.J. London.

Rhodes, Anthony. *The Vatican in the Age of the Dictators, 1922-1945*. New York, 1974.

Robertson, Edwin H. *Christians Against Hitler*. London, 1962.

Ross, Robert W. *So it Was True: the American Protestant Press and the Nazi Persecution of the Jews*. Minneapolis: University of Minnesota Press, 1980.

Shuster, George N. *Like a Mighty Army: Hitler versus Established Religion*. New York: D. Appleton-Century Co., 1935.

Snoek, Johan M. *The Grey Book: a Collection of Protests against the Anti-Semitism and the Persecution of the Jews Issued by Non-Roman Catholic Churches and Church Leaders during Hitler's Rule*. Assen, The Netherlands: Van Gorcum, 1969.

Spotts, Frederic. *The Churches and Politics in Germany*. Middletown, Connecticut: Wesleyan University Press, 1973.

von Oppen, Beate Ruhm. *Religion and Resistance to Nazism*. Princeton: Princeton University Press, 1971.

Walker, Lawrence D. *Hitler Youth and Catholic Youth 1933-1936.* Washington, D.C., 1970.
Zabel, James A. *Nazism and the Pastors. A Study of the Ideas of Three Deutsche Christian Groups.* Missoula, Montana, 1976.
Zahn, Gordon C. *German Catholics and Hitler's Wars.* New York: Sheed and Ward, 1962.

ARTICLES

Berman, Aaron. "American Zionism and the Rescue of European Jewry: an Ideological Perspective," *AJHQ*, 70 (March, 1981), 310-330.

Cavalli, Fiorello. "La Santa Sede contro le Deportazion degli Ebrei dalla Slovacchiadurante la Seconda Guerra Mondiale," (The Holy See against the Deportation of the Jews from Slovakia during the Second World War), *LCC*, 112, no. 3 (1961), 3-18.

Chadwick, Owen. "Weizsacker, the Vatican and the Jews of Rome," *JEH*, 28, no. 2 (April, 1977), 179-199.

Conway, John S. "The Silence of Pope Pius XII," *RP*, 27 (1965), 105-131.

———. "Pius XII and Nazi Germany in Historical Perspective, *HS*, VII (1969).

———. "The Vatical, Great Britain, and Relations with Germany, 1938-1940," *JH*, 16 (1973), 147-167.

Dahm, Karl-Wilhelm. "German Protestantism and Politics, 1918-1939," *JCH*, 3 (1968), 29-49.

Davidowicz, Lucy S. "American Jews and the Holocaust," NYTM, (April 18, 1982), 46-48.

———. "Indicting American Jews," *C*, (June, 1983), 36-44.

Delpech, Francois. "Pie XII et al Persecution Nazie," (Pope Pius XII and Nazi Persecution), *H*, 32 (1981), 25-36.

Gallin, Mary Alice. "The Cardinal and the State: Faulhaber and the Third Reich," *JCS*, 12 (1970), 385-404.

Graham, Robert A. "The 'Right to Kill' in the Third Reich: Prelude to Genocide," *CHR*, 62 (1976), 56-76.

——. "La Strana Condotta di E. von Weizsacker, Ambasciatore del Reich in Vaticano," (The Strange Behavior of E. von Weizsacker, Ambassador of the Reich at the Vatican), *LCC*, 121, no. 2 (1970), 455-471.

Graubart, Judah L. "The Vatican, and the Jews: Cynicism and Indifference," *J*, 24, no. 2 (Spring, 1975), 53-64.

Grobman, Alex. "What Did They Know? The American Jewish Press and the Holocaust, 1 September 1939-17 December 1942," *AJHQ*, 68 (March, 1979), 327-352.

Harrigan, William M. "Nazi Germany and the Holy See, 1933-1936: The Historical Background of 'Mit breunender sorge,'" *CHR*, 47 (1961), 164-198.

——. "Pius XII's Efforts to Effect a *Detente* in German-Vatican Relations, 1939-1940," *CHR*, 49, no. 2 (July, 1963), 173-191.

Helmreich, Ernst C. "The Arrest and Freeing of the Protestant Bishops of Wurtemberg and Bavaria, September-October 1934," *CEH*, II (1960), 159-169.

——. "The Nature and Structure of the Confessing Church in Germany under Hitler," *JCS*, 12 (1970), 405-419.

Helmreich, W. B. "Making the Awful Meaningful: American Orthodox Jews and the Holocaust," *S*, 19 (September-October, 1982), 62-66.

Hill, Leonidas E. "The Vatican Embassy of Ernst von Weizsacker, 1943-1945," *JMH*, 39 (1967), 138-159.

Hughes, John Jay. "The Pope's 'Pact with Hitler': Betrayal or Self-Defense?," *JCS*, 17 (1975), 63-80.

Kent, George O. "Pope Pius XII and Germany: Some Aspects of German-Vatican Relations, 1933-1943." *AHR*, 70, no. 1 (October, 1964), 59-78.

Lazin, Frederick. "The Response of the American Jewish Committee to the Crisis of German Jewry, 1933-1939," *AJHQ*, 68 (March, 1979), 283-304.

Leiber, Robert. "Pio XII gli Ebrei di Roman, 1943-1944," (Pius XII and the Jews of Rome 1943-1944), *LCC*, 112, no. 1 (1961).

Lewin, Isaak. "The Hour of the Holocaust," *PP*, 21, nos. 7-8 (1978), 16-24.

Lewy, Guenther, and John M. Snoek. "The Holocaust and the Christian Churches: Roman Catholics, Protestant, Eastern Orthodox," *EJ*, 8 (1971), 910-916.

Lichten, Joseph L. "Pius XII and the Jews," *CM*, 57 (March-April, 1959), 159-162.

Ludlow, Peter W. "The International Protestant in the Second World War," *JEH*, 29, no. 3 (1978), 311-362.

Martini, Angelo. "La Santa Sede egli Ebrei della Romania durante la Seconda Guerra Mondiale," (The Holy See and the Jews of Romania during the Second World War), *LCC*, 112, no. 3 (1961), 449-463.

——. "Silenzi e Parole di Pio XII per la Polonia durante la Seconda Guerra Mondiale," (Silences and Words of Pius XII for Poland during the Second World War), *LCC*, 113, no. 2 (1962), 237-249.

Mayeur, Jean-Marie. "Les Eglises et la Vie Religieuse Pendant la Deuxieme Guerre Mondiale: Introduction," (Churches and Religious Life during World War II), *RHDG*, 32, 128 (1982), 3-5.

Papeloux, L. "La Diplomatie Vaticane et la Belgique (Juin 1949-Octbre 1942)," (Vatican Diplomacy and Belgium (June 1940-October 1942), *LVW*, 47, no. 344 (Fall 1973), 215-224.

——. "Le Vatican et le Probleme Juif, 1941-1942," (The Vatican and the Jewish Problem, 1941-1942), *RHDG*, 27, no. 107 (1977), 75-84.

Penkower, Monty Noam. "The World Jewish Congress Confronts the International Red Cross during the Holocaust," *JJSS*, 41, no. 334 (1979), 229-256.

Poliakov, Leon. "The Vatican and the 'Jewish Question': the Record of the Hitler Period — and After," *C*, 10, no. 5 (November, 1950), 439-499.

Rausch, David A. "Our Hope: an American Fundamentalist Journal and the Holocaust, 1937-1945," *FH*, 12 (Spring, 1980), 89-103.

Rotkirchen, Livia. "Vatican Policy and the 'Jewish Problem' in 'Independent' Slovakia (1939-1945)," *YVS*, VI (1967), 27-53.

Subczak, Janusz. "Watykan a Sprawy Polskie w Czasie II Wojny Swiatowej w Swietle Dokumentow Owczesnej Ambasady RP Przy Stolicy Apostolskieji, (Vatican and Polish Affairs during World War II as documented by the Polish Embassy to the Apostalic See), *PZ*, 36, no. 2 (1980), 108-139.

Syrkin, Marie. "What American Jews Did During the Holocaust," *M*, XXVIII (October, 1980), 6-12.

Trefel, Hans. "The German Lutheran Church and the Rise of National Socialism," *CH*, 41 (1972), 326-336.

Vischer, Lukas. The Holy See, the Vatican State, and the Churches' Common Witness: a Neglected Ecumenical Problem," *JES*, 11 no. 4 (Fall, 1974), 617-636.

Volk, Ludwig. Episkopat und Kirchen Kampf im Zweiten Weltkrieg: II. Judenverfolgung und zusammenbruch des NS-STAATS," (Episcopacy and chruch conflict in World War II: II: The persecution of Jews and the collapse of the Nazi State), *SZ*, 198, no. 10 (1980), 687-702.

von Oppen, Beate Ruhm. "Nazis and Christians," *WP*, XXI (1969), 392-424.

Wall, Donald D. "The Reports of the Sicherheitsdienst on the Church and Religious Affairs in Germany, 1933-1944," *CH*, 40 (1971), 437-456.

Zahn, Gordon C. "Catholic Responses to the Holocaust," *T*, 56, no 221 (1981), 153-162.

DOCUMENTS

Blet, Pierre, and Robert A. Graham, Angelo Martini, and Burkhart Schneider, eds. *Actes et Documents du Saint Siege relatifs a la Second Guerra Mondiale. (Records and Documents of the Holy See Relating to the Second World War)*. 9 volumes. Vatican City: Libraria Editrice Vaticana, 1965-1975.

DISSERTATIONS

Camp, William D. "Religion and Horror: the American Religious Press Views Nazi Death Camps and Holocaust Survivors." Unpublished Ph.D. dissertation, Pittsburgh, Pennsylvania: Carnegie-Mellon University, 1981.

Lookstein, Haskel. "American Jewry's Public Response to the Holocaust, 1938-1944." Unpublished Ph.D. dissertation, New York: Yeshiva University, 1975.

Peter, Richard A. "Nazi Germany and the Vatican, July 1933-January 1938." Unpublished Ph.D. dissertation. Norman, Oklahoma: the University of Oklahoma, 1971.

Riede, David C. "The Official Attitude of the Roman Catholic Hierarchy toward National Socialism, 1933-1945." Unpublished Ph.D. dissertation. Iowa City, Iowa: University of Iowa, 1957.

Svensbye, Lloyd. "The History of Developing Social Responsibility among Lutherans in America from 1930-1960, with reference to the Evangelical Lutheran Church, and the United Lutheran Church in America." Unpublished Ph.D. dissertation, Union Theological Seminary, New York, 1966.

Wentz, Frederick K. "The Reaction of the Religious Press in America to the Emergence of Nazism (1933-1937)." Unpublished Ph.D. dissertation: New Haven, Connecticut: Yale University, 1954.

Journal Abbreviations

American Historical Review	*AHR*
American Jewish History Quarterly	*AJHQ*
Catholic Historical Review	*CHR*
Catholic Mind	*CM*
Central European History	*CEH*
Church History	*CH*
Commentary	*C*
Encyclopedia Judaica	*EJ*
Fedes et History	*FH*
Histoire	*H*
Journal of Church and State	*JCS*
Journal of Contemporary History	*JCH*
Journal of Ecclesiastical History	*JEH*
Journal of Ecumenical Studies	*JES*
Journal of History	*JH*
Journal of Jewish Social Studies	*JJSS*
Journal of Modern History	*JMH*
Judaism	*J*
La Civilta Cattolica	*LCC*
La Vie Wallonne	*LVW*
Midstream	*M*
New York Times Magazine	*NYTM*
Polish Perspectives	*PP*
Przeglad Zachodni	*PZ*
Rev. d'Hist. de la Deuxieme Guerre Mondiale et des Conflits Contemporains	*RHDG*
Review of Politics	*RP*
Society	*S*
Stimmen der Zeit	*SZ*
Thought	*T*
World Politics	*WP*
Yad Vashem Studies	*YVS*

Index

Abrahamsen, Samuel, "The Relationship of Church and State during the German Occupation of Norway, 1940-1945, 1-26, 54
Adam, Karl, 111
American Jewish Committee, 177
"Anschluss", 59, 75
Anti-Leftism, 28-43
Anti-Semitic Clergy, 147
Anti-Semitism, 28-43, 49-51, 89-118
Auschwitz, 14, 161, 171
Baranowski, Shelley, "From Rivalry to Repression: The German Protestant Leadership, Anti-Leftism and Anti-Semitism, 1933", 28-43
Berggrav, Bishop Eivind Josef, 4, 5, 7, 11, 12, 21, 47, 49
Berning, Wilhelm, 67, 68, 81, 92
Bertram, Adolf Cardinal, 55, 58, 59-62, 66, 67, 68, 70, 74-76, 78-83, 92-94, 96, 100
Bettelheim, Bruno, 155, 164, 171
Bender, Harold, 149-150, 154
Between the Fronts, by Arvid Brodersen, 12
Bolshevism, 34, 38, 39, 58, 59, 72, 114, 139
Bonhoeffer, Dietrich, 39
British Jews, 77
Brown Shirts, 30, 36, 40
Buber, Margaret, 164
Buchenwald, 162, 163
"Casti Connubi" (On Christian Marriage), 1930, 90, 91, 94, 119
"Catholic Action", 64, 70
Catholic Jews, 56, 57, 61, 62, 67, 72, 73, 76-78
"A Challenge to God: Jehovah's Witnesses in the Holocaust Kingdom", by Brian Dunn, 155-172
Christian Joint Council for the Norwegian Church, 47
Christian Monitor, 143, 146, 149, 154
Christian Social Party, 33, 41
Communism, 146-150
Confessing Church, 32, 38, 39, 46, 177
Crystal Night, 56, 57, 64, 65, 75, 114, 131, 134, 136, 146
Dachau, 30, 40, 107, 165

Danish Jewry, 50, 166
"The Death's Head and the Watchtower: Jehovah's Witnesses in the Holocaust Kingdom", 155-172
Decalogue Letter, 62, 63, 73, 74
Defender, p. 147
Der Bote, 150-151
Derstine, C. F., 149
Dibelius, Oho, 38
Dietrich, Donald, "Racial Eugenics in the Third Reich: The Catholic Response, 87-126
Dietz, Johannes, 55, 61, 74
Displaced Persons, 136-138
Dunn, Brian, "The Death's Head and the Watchtower: Jehovah's Witnesses in the Holocaust Kingdom", 155-172
Enemies, by Joseph F. Rutherford, 165, 166
Epp, Frank, 150-151, 154
Eugenics, 87-126
Euthanasia, 72, 88-90, 95, 96, 98, 99, 100, 101, 104, 106, 108, 116-122
Faulhaber, Michael Cardinal, 55, 58, 59, 60, 63, 64-66, 68-70, 74, 79-84, 93, 99, 100, 109
Final Solution, The, 28, 110, 116-118, 144
Fischel, Jack, "The North American Mennonites' Response to Hitler's Persecution of the Jews", 141-154
Fjellbu, Dean, 9, 10
Frank, Karl, 94, 95
The Friend of Zion, 129-132, 138
Frings, Joseph, 56, 61, 74
"From Rivalry to Repression: The German Protestant Leadership, Anti-Leftism and Anti-Semitism, 1933", by Shelley Baranowski, 28-43
Fulda Conference, 55, 59, 60, 61, 67, 79, 84, 91, 99, 101, 104, 107
von Galen, Clemens August, Count, 55, 59, 61, 70, 71, 83, 93, 101-104
"The German Catholic Bishops and the Jewish Question: Explanation and Judgment", by Ethel Mary Tinneman, 51-85
German Catholic Church, 34, 45-97, 100, 105-124, 156-157, 166, 175
German Christian Movement, 36-39, 46
German Communist Party, 28, 35, 38, 72
German Jews, 55-78, 127-131, 134
German Luthern Church, 51, 53, 179
German Protestant Church, 28-43, 45-54, 87
German Witnesses, 156-169, 170
Gestapo, 58, 59, 67
Grober, Conrad, 55, 60, 61, 72, 83, 84, 92
Hartl, Albert, 105, 106
Hebrew Christian Alliance of America, 134, 135
Hebrew Christians, 134, 135, 138
Hefelmann, Hans, 105, 106

Hilfrich, Antonius, 73, 103
Himmler, Heinrich, 13, 49, 159, 164, 167
von Hindenburg, Paul, 37
Hitler, Adolf, 3, 21, 30, 31, 35, 37, 40, 47, 49, 50, 53-60, 64-71, 81, 88, 89, 91, 95-98, 103-107, 110, 115-118, 135-139, 143-147, 150, 155-158, 162, 167, 168, 175, 176-178
Hoffman, Conrad, Jr., "To be a Non-Aryan in Germany", 127
Holy Roman Empire, 52
Horsch, John, 149-150, 154
Hurth, Franz, 90-93
Jehovah's Witnesses, 155-172
"Jewish Question", 110, 113, 114, 115, 116, 117
Jewish Telegraph Agency, 131, 132, 135, 136
Joint Christian Council, 5, 21
Klausener, Erich, 64, 70, 85
"Kulturkampf", 64, 67, 109
"Law Preventing the Transmission of Hereditary Disease", 1933, 91
"Lebensraum", 89, 117
Legal Sterilization of the Mentally Ill, by Josef Mayer, 90
Lehman, M. C., 152, 154
Leiber, Robert, S.J., 92, 93
Lichtenberg Concentration Camp, 167
Lichtenberg, Bernhard, 75
Lubeck, 168
"Lutheran Conscience and the Holocaust: The German and Norwegian Cases", by Stephen C. MacDonald, 45-54
Luther, Martin, 1, 11, 17, 48, 49, 52, 54
MacDonald, Stephen C., "Lutheran Conscience and the Holocaust: The German and Norwegian Cases", 45-54
Marxism, 31, 109
Mauthausen, 165
Mayer, Josef, 90-93, 104, 105, 107-109
Mayer, Josef, *Legal Sterilization of the Mentally Ill,* 90
Mein Kampf, by Adolph Hitler, 109
Mennonite Central Committee, 142, 152
Mennonites, 141-154
"Mischehen", 56, 61, 76
"Mischlinge", 56, 61, 76
National Socialist Party, 28-32, 35, 38, 39, 42, 45, 46, 51, 54, 58, 59, 60, 64, 67, 68, 69, 72, 77, 78, 87, 89, 102, 107, 113, 154
National Socialist Ideology, 87-89, 103, 116
Nazism, 3, 4, 10, 14, 17, 18, 28, 30, 31, 32, 36, 38-43, 46-49, 51-54, 55-95, 110, 113, 114, 127-130, 133, 138, 141, 153, 155-158, 165, 167, 173, 176-180

Near East Relief, 141
Niemoller, Martin, 3, 4, 35, 42, 46
"The North American Mennonites' Response to Hitler's Persecution of the Jews", by Jack Fischel, 141-154
Norwegian Catholic Church, 16, 25
Norwegian Jews, 14-19, 48-51
Norwegian Lutheran Church, 1-8, 10, 12-17, 19-22, 47-54
Norwegian Nazi Party, 3, 5, 12, 13, 14
Norwegian Resistance Movement, 4
Nuremberg Laws, 55, 56, 98
Memoirs from the War Years, by Dean Fjellbu, 9
"On the Church in Germany", papal encyclical, 58
Peltz, Jacob, 132, 135
"Perverse Witness to the Holocaust: Christian Missions and Missionaries", by Robert W. Ross, 127-139
Polish Jews, 131-135
Pope Pius XI, 90
Pope Pius XII, 60, 77, 99-102, 166, 173, 176-178
Protocols of the Elders of Zion, 146, 148, 150
von Preysing, Konrad Count, 55, 56, 58, 59-61, 64, 65, 66, 69-71, 74-78, 80, 82, 84, 85, 101, 103, 107
Quakers, 141, 149
Quisling, Vidkin, 3, 5, 7, 8, 12-15, 18-21, 24, 26, 47, 49, 50, 51, 53
"Racial Eugenics in the Third Reich: The Catholic Response", by Donald Dietrich, 87-126
Ravensbruck, 161, 164, 167
Reich Citizenship Law of 1935, 56
Reich Law for the Reorganization of the Civil Service (1933), 135
Reichstag, 30
"The Relationship of Church and State during the German Occupation of Norway, 1940-1945, by Samuel Abrahamsen, 1-26
Roman Catholic Church, 45, 52, 173-179
Ross, Robert W., "Perverse Witness to the Holocaust: Christian Missions and Millionaires", 136-143; "So It Was True. The American Protestant Press and the Nazi Persecution of Jews", 133, 138, 175
Russell, Charles Taze, 155
Rutherford, Joseph Franklin, 156-158, 162, 165, 166, 169, 170
Sachsenhausen, 160, 162, 168
Schilling, Otto, 94
Schulte, Joseph Cardinal, 55, 56, 74
Skancke, Ragnar, 6, 7
Schwerin, 168
Social Darwinism, 88, 89, 118

Sommer, Margarete, 65, 76, 84
Soviet Union, 142, 148, 173, 174
Sproll, Johannes, B., 59, 60
Sterilization, 72, 88, 89, 90-99, 117-120
"Summi Pontificus", 1939, 99
Sword and Trumpet, 144, 147-149
Terboven, Josef, 5, 8, 12
Thierstein, John R., 149
Third Reich, The, 30, 32, 35, 40, 43, 46, 58, 68, 71, 80, 87-125, 131, 151, 155, 159, 174, 176, 179
Tinneman, Ethel Mary, "The German Catholic Bishops and the Jewish Question: Explanation and Judgment", 55-85
Unruh, Benjamin, 154
Versailles Treaty, 31, 32, 64
Warsaw Ghetto, 131
The Watchtower, 159, 163, 165, 167, 169-172
Watchtower Society, 155
Weaver, Kathe, 144, 145, 154
Wehrmacht, 15
Weimar Republic, 30, 35, 41, 42, 47, 63, 64, 69, 71, 81, 82, 108, 109, 142
Wienken, Heinrich, 106, 108
Winrod, Gerald B., 147, 150
World Jewish Congress, 178
Wurm, Theophil, 36, 46, 99, 101